Indigenous Journeys, Transatlantic Perspectives

Indigenous Journeys, Transatlantic Perspectives

Relational Worlds in Contemporary Native American Literature

Edited by Anna M. Brígido-Corachán

MICHIGAN STATE UNIVERSITY PRESS | *East Lansing*

Michigan State University Press
East Lansing, Michigan 48823-5245

LIBRARY OF CONGRESS CATALOGING-IN-PUBLICATION DATA
Names: Brígido-Corachán, Anna M., editor.
Title: Indigenous journeys, transatlantic perspectives :
relational worlds in contemporary Native American literature /
edited by Anna M. Brígido-Corachán.
Other titles: American Indian studies series.
Description: East Lansing : Michigan State University Press, [2023]. |
Series: American Indian studies series | Includes bibliographical references.
Identifiers: LCCN 2023001809 | ISBN 9781611864694 (paperback) |
ISBN 9781609177461 | ISBN 9781628955118
Subjects: LCSH: American literature—Indian authors—History and criticism. |
Literature and transnationalism. | Indians of North America—Intellectual life.
Classification: LCC PS153.I52 I55 2023 | DDC 810.9/897—dc23/eng/20230418
LC record available at https://lccn.loc.gov/2023001809

Cover design by Erin Kirk
Cover art: *On the Grave of the Giant*, by Jonathan Thunder.

Visit Michigan State University Press at *www.msupress.org*

CONTENTS

ACKNOWLEDGMENTS

Books rest on the shoulders of many, and this one is no exception. Its long journey began in Valencia, Spain, in 2018, with a wide array of inspiring papers and the exciting conversations that followed them over coffee breaks, walks, and communal dinners during the celebration of the international symposium "Teaching and Theorizing Native American Literature as World Literature." The brilliant constellation of international scholars who participated in the event provided the warmest food for thought, and among them I would like to thank Gordon Henry Jr., Silvia Martínez-Falquina, Ewelina Bańka, David Moore, Kathryn Shanley, A. Robert Lee, Aitor Ibarrola, Phillip Round, Chris LaLonde, and Ingrid Wendt for their incredible encouragement and support through the editing of two interrelated volumes of transatlantic scholarship over the last four years. Collaborating with the symposium in various ways and sustaining me with their wisdom, academic expertise, and friendship, I would like to express my deepest gratitude to Gloria Chacón, Carme Manuel, Elena Ortells, and Joanna Ziarkowska. Exchanging stories, critical insights, and pedagogical experiences through the years with all of these and many other wonderful colleagues in the field of Native American and Indigenous studies—in a variety of place-worlds on both sides of the Atlantic—is one of the most precious gifts that I owe my profession. My warmest note of appreciation goes to Gordon Henry Jr. for his great generosity and advice and for inviting us to send a proposal to Michigan State University Press.

This is the second volume to emerge from our 2018 symposium. The first volume, *Indigenizing the Classroom: Engaging Native American/First Nations Literature and Culture in Non-Native Settings* (2021), focuses on critical pedagogies and strategies when teaching Native American Literature in a global/transatlantic/non-Native context, taking into account questions of cultural distance, tribal context, respect, and responsibility. Warmest thanks are also due to all of the contributors to this companion publication, who became a central part of our ongoing conversation.

Many of the ideas in this volume came out of stimulating transatlantic meetings in the United Kingdom, Spain, and the United States. I had the privilege of listening to and learning from many gifted participants in the American Indian Workshop, the Small/Minor Literatures Network, the Spanish Association for American Studies, and the international conference "Indigenous Writers and Their Critics," organized by Gloria Chacón at the University of California, San Diego. Among them, I would like to particularly thank Arturo Arias, Susana Bautista, Jorge Cocom Pech, César Domínguez, Sue P. Haglund, Inés Hernández-Ávila, Victor Masayesa Jr., and Rebecca Tillett for the generous exchange of ideas. Huge thanks are also due to Catherine Cocks, former interim director at Michigan State University Press, for her invaluable advice and help with the manuscript, to the two anonymous reviewers from MSUP for their encouraging words, sensible critique, and suggestions for revision, as well as to my colleagues John Howard, Belén Vidal, and Maria del Pilar Blanco, for their hospitality, academic advice, and support during two research stays at the University of Oxford and King's College London, while I read and wrote parts of the introduction and of my own chapter in this volume.

I would also like to gratefully acknowledge the Conselleria d'Innovació, Universitats, Ciència I Societat Digital of the Valencian Government for financing two research projects that provided a broader intellectual framework for this volume, as it slowly took final shape during the pandemic years: "Las literaturas (trans)étnicas en un context global: Representaciones, transformaciones y resistencias" (Ref. GV/2019/114) and "Reconfiguraciones de género, raza y clase social en la literatura étnica norteamericana de la era Obama/Trump" (Ref. GV/AICO/2021/249).

Infinite gratitude beyond words goes to my partner, Alex, and to my kids, Cora and Beren, for their endless patience, creativity, and love.

Introduction

Place-Worlds in Contemporary Native American Literature

Anna M. Brígido-Corachán

n the last decades, Native American novels, stories, poems, plays, and essays
have reached a wide variety of readers beyond North America, journeying
through translation into major and minoritized languages, and establishing
creative, educational, and intellectual networks with other literary communities around the world. A quick search in the global library catalogue Worldcat.
org shows that the novels of 2021 Pulitzer Prize winner Louise Erdrich have been
translated into a wide array of languages including Spanish, German, French,
Chinese, Russian, Japanese, Dutch, or Catalan, while Tommy Orange's novel *There,
There* was translated into over a dozen languages right after its publication in 2018.[1]
During this period Native American and Indigenous authors have continued to
expand their themes and interests in engaging transnational contexts and foreign
realities, and have intervened in a variety of trans-Indigenous and global debates.[2]
These transnational networks are the natural continuance of much older journeys,
interconnections, transatlantic encounters, and intertribal alliances that have been
examined by Jodi Byrd in *The Transit of Empire: Indigenous Critiques of Colonialism*,
by James Cox in *The Red Land to the South: American Indian Writers and Indigenous
Mexico*, by Jace Weaver in *The Red Atlantic: American Indigenes and the Making of
the Modern World*, and by Scott Richard Lyons in the collected volume *The World,*

the Text, and the Indian, to name a few. In fact, as Craig Womack or Scott Richard Lyons have poignantly argued, Native American literature, like Native American and Indigenous cultures, has been global and relational from its very start.[3]

This book was born in an intercultural academic context, most precisely in the city of Valencia, Spain—in a region with a dreadful colonialist history (being part of the Crown of Aragon, which expanded through the Mediterranean coasts during the sixteenth and seventeenth centuries, and of the brutal Spanish Empire). Valencia has also been a site of cultural conflict and exchange for over two thousand years, as it was invaded, colonized, and transformed by the Phoenicians, Romans, Visigoths, Arabs, and Catalan-Aragonese. Today, its cultural history and traditions center around a minoritized romance language, Valencian (a dialectal variant of Catalan), which was banned by the Castilian-leaning authorities at different points in the eighteenth to twentieth centuries. Sensitive to the plight of communities, cultures, and languages that were persecuted and minoritized through extreme forms of violence, and aware of the role our ancestors played as both perpetrators and victims of such violence, Native American literatures have been continuously taught at the University of Valencia (and at many other universities in Spain and in Europe) as an effort to decolonize the American and European studies curriculum since at least the 1990s. In 2018, I was fortunate to host an international symposium titled "Teaching and Theorizing Native American Literature as World Literature" at this site. Scholars participating in the event were European, Asian, and North American, including Native American authors and intellectuals Gordon Henry Jr. and Kathryn Shanley. The chapters that compose this book, have been mostly penned by non-Native and largely European academics, and as such, we would like to acknowledge our role as outsiders to tribal lived experience and the challenges posed by our geographical and cultural distance. We all openly and critically question the colonial past and its intricate legacies in our nations today. It is undeniable that deep colonial and imperialist traces can still be found in a significant percentage of Western scholarship, language, and storying engaging Native American and Indigenous communities (especially in popular media and the press), and the complications of intercultural translation, mediation, and interpretation have to be noted.[4] In this volume we have faced such challenges and difficulties as responsibly and ethically as possible through collaboration, conversation, and deep immersion in tribal contexts and sources. Our humble aim is to contribute to ongoing debates around Eurocentrism in academia both in the Americas and in Europe through a decolonizing lens that interrogates imperialist and racist legacies while highlighting the central role of Indigenous cultures and stories in the literary world and in all the other fields and worlds they continue to engage today. As Elvira Pulitano expressed in the introduction to the multiauthored collection of essays *Transatlantic Voices*: engaging, enlightening, and respectful interpretations of Native American works fill European conferences hosted by organizations such as the American Indian Workshop, the Society for Multi-Ethnic Studies: Europe and the Americas (MESEA), or the European Association of American Studies, and can also be found in many European university presses, journals, and classrooms.

The methodologies and theories deployed in the chapters that follow nicely complement one another. Their variations and specificities will be delved into by each of their authors, but they have one general aim in common: they all take tribal-centered approaches and contexts strongly into account while being relational, intercultural, and/or comparative in a decolonizing manner. As Diné poet Luci Tapahonso points out, "We must remember the worlds our ancestors traveled. Always wear the songs they gave us."[5] We believe that Indigenous journeying practices, whether physical, metaphysical, historical, or existential, are a key component of Native American cultures past and present. Our chapters aim to humbly engage some of these traveling practices and words in motion, which are also forms of journeying toward the self and toward the other.

In his study *Wisdom Sits in Places*, Keith Basso describes Western Apache storytellers as "place-makers," creators of "place-worlds" through their imagining of alternative possibilities that are given "expressive shape."[6] According to Basso, "every developed place-world manifests itself as a possible state of affairs" and therefore, "building and sharing place-worlds, in other words, is not only a means of reviving former times but also of *revising* them, a means of exploring not merely how things might have been but also how just possibly they might have been different from what others have supposed."[7] Contemporary Native American writers have continued to build "place-worlds" in a relational manner that revises not just Indigenous localities past and present, but other realities, regions, nations, and communities of beings as well. These relational place-worlds are connective, speculative, and critical—and, through comparison, they amplify, reconsider, and reinforce alternative possibilities and *expressive shapes*. As LeAnne Howe points out in an interview regarding her writing, Choctaw stories are "the base, the core narrative from which to reach out to other parts of the world," while talking to others is "Tribalism 101."[8] Nonetheless, in her essay collection *Choctalking on Other Realities* she also warns us that transnational encounters and intercultural conversations are too often complicated by translation and by the unwillingness of foreign institutions, intermediaries, and audiences to fully understand and acknowledge Indigenous narratives and political needs.

Since the Indigenous rise in consciousness that took place globally between the 1960s and the early 1990s we have seen a heightened awareness of shared histories of colonial oppression, environmental racism, and genocide connecting many communities around the world, from the Native and Indigenous Americas to Africa or China. As Glen Coulthard points out, decolonization for Indigenous communities has been strongly shaped by the intimate relationships that are established between the people and the land but also informed by global developments and their effects at the local level.[9] For example, the #NoDAPL movement proved that environmental racism could be more effectively answered through collective, transnational, or trans-Indigenous political efforts that respect local specificities while necessarily seeking common ground to stir the conversation toward concrete material, sociopolitical, and legal change.[10]

At the turn of the twenty-first century Arnold Krupat referred to this transnational lens or context as a "cosmopolitan" approach that was practiced by many Native American authors whose "cosmopolitan perspectives in Native American literatures read them in relation to other minority or subaltern literatures elsewhere in the late-colonial or postcolonial world."[11] Although cosmopolitanism, with its urban "expat" associations, has been often considered a Eurocentric term, Indigenous planetary frameworks that consider universality and the human soul *in relation* to the cosmos are an intrinsic part of many Native authors' creative place-worlds, as we can see in the poetry of Simon Ortiz, where humanity and its various cultural manifestations is not the limit but rather "the vastness [of the universe] we do not enter."[12] Moreover, Native American literary works such as James Welch's *The Heartsong of Charging Elk*, Gerald Vizenor's *Blue Ravens*, Leslie Marmon Silko's *Gardens in the Dunes*, or some of the poems by Ofelia Zepeda and Gordon Henry Jr. feature Indigenous journeys that can be considered cosmo-*politan* in the post/modernist, urban, or transatlantic sense as well. Tohono O'odham writers like Ofelia Zepeda are also intrinsically transborder, crossing and traveling through the artificially imposed borders that came along with the constitution of modern nations as a matter of natural practice.

Native American tribal literatures in the United States do not exist in a vacuum but constantly have to position or reestablish themselves in relation to and in connection with other literatures in the Americas and across the Atlantic as they secure their place within publishing spaces, reading publics, educational curriculums, and even academic departments. These literary exchanges have drawn from the traditions of settler communities and from the much older oral, scriptural, and pictoideographic traditions established by many Indigenous cultures throughout the continent. These Indigenous traditions have been tackled in comparative volumes such as Gordon Brotherston's *Book of the Fourth World: Reading the Native Americas through Their Literature*, which encompasses Indigenous stories and textualities that are located south of the U.S. border and where we find other Indigenous and European languages in conflict.

According to David L. Moore and A. Robert Lee in two of the chapters that comprise this volume, writers Louis Owens and James Welch understood transnationality as a system of relations between a wide diversity of Native nations and the colonial settler nation that imposed its brutal authority over them. Moore specifically argues that the "transnational dynamics" developed by Owens are not articulated through binaries but are, in fact, multidirectional and complex, for they engage the "porous boundaries between human and more-than-human 'nations' or 'peoples'" as well.

In fact, replacing cosmopolitanism in the twenty-first century, we find a traditional Indigenous concept, relationality, at the center of theoretical and epistemological frameworks that transcend not just tribal borders but also the limits of our human worlds. Native American philosophies and traditional practices are relational because they actively engage the land and all the beings that inhabit it, who are seen as interdependent. And such connectedness actively interrogates the individualism, binary logic, and epistemological compartmentalization common in Western philosophical thought.

As Silvia Martínez-Falquina explains in this volume, Anishinaabe conceptions of "being as being-in-relation" understand relationality as a "field of relationships" that are land-based. Pueblo philosopher Gregory Cajete has also described the strong relational sensibilities that can be perceived in Indigenous art as the product of Native people's grounded connection to place—and this connection includes sacred orientation and a deep relationship with more-than-human beings.[13] In a similar manner, Acoma poet Simon Ortiz has often argued that "being and place are conceptually linked," and this "Indigenous principle . . . is maintained as such within Indigenous cultural philosophy and expressed in the most common or ordinary way."[14]

Native American literature is grounded in specific cultural landscapes but it is also *worldly* and *worlding*, as pointed out by Scott Richard Lyons in *The World, the*

Text, and the Indian.[15] It is *worldly* because, as the late Edward Said often argued, literary texts are "situated in the world, and about that world";[16] they are "events, and, even when they appear to deny it, they are nevertheless a part of the social world, human life, and of course the historical moments in which they are located and interpreted."[17] It is such relationality and sociopolitical commitment that makes Native American texts *worldly* but, as Lyons points out, the worlds they record, narrate, and mobilize have to be attentively listened to and appropriately historicized.[18] Native American narratives can build place-worlds with the power to mobilize local and also regional, national, and transnational imaginaries and agents as we saw in the case of the #NoDAPL movement in 2016 and its large international coverage and support.[19]

Following cutting-edge critical anthologies that have recently engaged Native American literature within such a global context,[20] this collection of essays explores the distinctive place-worlds that have been poetically crafted by well-known Native American and Indigenous authors who set them in conversation with related realities, literary, social, and political debates in North America, Africa, and Europe. It provides a compelling set of relational case studies, transborder strategies, and Native-centered methodologies and reflections that can help us to think through a variety of trans/national matters, drawing from specific Indigenous localities and considering the complex legacy of other imperial, colonialist languages in the Americas such as Spanish.

In the first chapter, "Grounded Relationality: A Reading of Contemporary Anishinaabe Literature (Gordon Henry, Leanne Simpson, Louise Erdrich)," Silvia Martínez-Falquina provides a review of the concepts of relationality and interdependence in Native and non-Native philosophies and scholarship. She examines some recent terms that have adopted the relational turn in contemporary academia (transmodernity, cosmodernism, or planetarity) and identifies some commonalities but also key differences between these global frameworks. She specifically considers Anishinaabe conceptions of relationality and then proceeds to analyze three texts penned by writers Gordon Henry Jr., Leanne Simpson, and Louise Erdrich using Anishinaabe relational thought as her research paradigm—one that is "grounded on the understanding of the land as both essential for survival and the source of American Indian identity, spirituality, history, sovereignty." In her chapter we can see how "the Anishinaabe articulation of being as being-in-relation in theory and writing provides a particularly interesting example of how the local can exemplify and illuminate the worldly," and how these relational identities and place-worlds necessarily refer to the more-than-human worlds as well.

In the second chapter, titled "Spider's Embrace: Louis Owens's Web of Identities in *Dark River*," David L. Moore warns us that in this "web of relations" that lies at the heart of Native and mixedblood identities, as described by Louise Erdrich and Louis Owens, "interdependence and relationality may give life, but they also make it vulnerable." Through poetic and insightful close-reading, Moore delves into Owens's novel *Dark River* aiming to further understand the concept of "frailty" as a form of uncertainty and vulnerability in Owens's web of relational identities. He describes uncertainty as a trickster approach that actively questions fixed Native stereotypes such as that of the tragic and vanishing "Chief Doom," described by Owens in *Mixedblood Messages*.[21] Within such a trickster approach, frailty as uncertainty can indeed become a source of power. Additionally, Moore also explores discursive forms of relationality such as ironic juxtaposition, which is strategically used by Owens to develop his sociopolitical and historical criticism. Owens's place-worlds also engage other languages, narratives, and territories (such as those of the spider and the river) and considers their roles in shaping human lives.

Both Moore and Martínez-Falquina warn us that interdependence—the relational web connecting humans and more-than-human beings—is empowering but can also be hindered by the vulnerability and frailty that come from dependence. We are not self-sufficient beings but are born into "a condition of radical dependency" on each other and also on the environment.[22] The most intricate challenge then is precisely how to carve a "sense of place" that takes into account such multiple and overlapping worlds, including the more-than-human worlds.

In his essay "Cross-Worlds: The Sight and Sound of James Welch," A. Robert Lee introduces the concept of "cross-worlds" to describe such multiplicities as presented in the novels of the pioneering Blackfeet/Gros Ventre author. "Cross-worlds" is used by Lee in the "sense of worlds colliding, or at the very least overlapping," and these include various worlds inside and outside the reservation—place-worlds built out of casinos, federal prisons, state courthouses, or basketball courts. Through a poetic analysis of the sensorial elements that articulate Welch's five novels, Lee guides us through the diverse spaces and places that shape Welch's historical fiction and that include traditional and modern worlds, gendered worlds, and even "tribal worlds within tribal worlds." Welch's literary imagination, woven through an insightful "eye and ear," reminds us that Native place-worlds have also changed over time and space and can simultaneously interact within Native identities as intersecting territories and languages of the mind.

In her chapter, "Slender Vial of DNA / For Sale: Dismantling Genomic Articulations of Indigeneity in the Poetry of Heid E. Erdrich," Joanna Ziarkowska discusses Western scientific discourse and global conceptions of Native identity through genomic research projects carried out among Indigenous communities in the United States and Brazil. Heid Erdrich's poetry openly criticizes these genomic projects as yet another embodied form of colonization, which she names biocolonialism. For Ziarkowska, Erdrich's activist poetry denounces the ethical problems caused by scientific research carried out without consent, the "commodification of Indigenous bodies" it engenders, as well as its "potential threat to Indigenous people's cultural and political sovereignty." Genomic conceptions of identity displace land-based connections, tribal-specific kinship structures, or relationality as the central ontological element grounding cultural belonging. Erdrich's poems clearly emphasize land ethics, trans-Indigenous solidarity, and relational thought while considering the impact of Western science on Indigenous cultural world views and sovereign struggles at a planetary scale. According to Ziarkowska, "Erdrich adopts a global perspective to draw attention to how the problem affects Indigenous peoples around the world and constitutes a basis for transnational coalitions."

Further exploring such transnational coalitions and parallelisms, Kathryn W. Shanley's chapter, "A Futurism that Sees No Future: Recognition in Ayi Kwei Armah, James Welch, and Corwin Clairmont," compares anticolonial movements of resistance in the Native Americas and in Ghana in the late 1960s and the early 1970s through kindred novels whose authors may have never read or known about each other: Ayi Kwei Armah's *The Beautyful Ones Are Not Yet Born* and James Welch's *Winter in the Blood* and *The Death of Jim Loney*. She explores several instances of global Indigenous echoes between the novels and examines these authors' views of a world at the edge of destruction. The second part of the chapter establishes an insightful contrast between these anticolonial visions and those of contemporary Salish artist Corwin Clairmont, whose environmental, critical questions in the exhibit *Two-Headed Arrow / The Tar Sands Project* force viewers to imagine a future that is necessarily informed by human/nonhuman interconnectedness, recognition, responsibility, and hope (grim as it may be).

Aitor Ibarrola-Armendariz's chapter, "Atonement and Forgiveness as Reparatory Justice in Louise Erdrich's *LaRose* and Fernando Aramburu's *Homeland*," also applies a transatlantic perspective in comparing two highly awarded novels in the United

States and in Spain, taking into account their representation of community-based justice. After defining the concept of reparatory justice in volatile contexts of colonialist oppression, political coercion, or cultural genocide, Ibarrola-Armendariz analyzes the traumatic realities undergone by Anishinaabe and Basque families in the twentieth century, as described by Erdrich and Aramburu in their multilayered texts. Ibarrola-Armendariz examines the distinct ways in which key concepts such as retaliation, atonement, and reparation are articulated through specific character relations in the community. He also considers commonalities and contextual differences in the strategies of resilience, reconciliation, and healing presented by both authors, bearing in mind the limitations of these alternative judicial systems. Although the novels take place in specific territories and complex historical moments shaping divided communities at the turn of the twenty-first century, they also refer to much vaster worlds and realities and point to the difficulties in tracing clear "boundaries between saints and sinners, progressivists and fundamentalists, civilized and savages." In fact, the limits between these sets of fixed identities or binary pairs are "constantly scrutinized and problematized" in dynamic contexts of mediation and restorative community action.

Anna M. Brígido-Corachán's chapter, titled "Relational Bodies in Motion: A Trans-Indigenous Reading of Ofelia Zepeda and Irma Pineda's Place-Based Poetry," brings further attention to the comparative paradigm of trans-Indigeneity in a multilingual setting. Coined by Chadwick Allen, trans-Indigenous methodologies place Indigenous literatures and arts across national borders in a mutually enriching conversation with the potential to circumvent and challenge hegemonic assumptions and interpretations.[23] Through a place-based, trans-Indigenous comparison of the books *Xilase qui rié di' sicasi rié nisa guiigu' / La nostalgia no se marcha como el agua de los ríos* and *Where Clouds Are Formed*, Brígido-Corachán considers the poems of Zapotec writer Irma Pineda (Mexico) and Tohono O'odham poet Ofelia Zepeda (United States) as decolonizing actions or movements that question settler colonial borders and reinscribe alternative languages and experiences of place in the Americas.

Historically grounded and community-bound, Pineda's and Zepeda's poetic works engage a multiplicity of Native experiences on the move and contribute to reverse the colonial "cognitive mapping of Native lands and bodies,"[24] while establishing new relational maps that underline the complexity of Indigenous place-based experiences in the U.S./Mexico border areas today. Giving creative shape to these dynamic worlds in Tohono O'odham and Diidxazá, English and

Spanish, Ofelia Zepeda and Irma Pineda also listen to the more-than-human languages that can be heard in these borderlands as they walk with the land, so that their overlapping territories, multilingual experiences, and needs are also acknowledged and respected.

Focusing on Simon Ortiz's book *After and Before the Lightning*, Ewelina Bańka's closing chapter, "A Prayer from the Galaxy of the Soul: Simon J. Ortiz's Poetry of Continuance," explores his poetic "galaxies of human nature" as they connect to a wider community and universe beyond his Native Pueblo. According to Bańka, "the inclusive and outward-oriented view of the world that informs Ortiz's work is based on the principle of interrelatedness, compassionate love, and purposeful living that is found at the heart of Indigenous systems of knowledge." Ortiz's poetry engages and strengthens the "continuance of the Indigenous world" where Indigenous communities are seen as an intrinsic part of "an interdependent body of creation" that is "universal in scope." For Simon Ortiz, we are all part of a bigger and all-encompassing creative energy, and in many ways, the human fight against forces of destruction such as colonial exploitation, cruelty, or hatred is common to us all, despite the specific shape these fights may take in each cultural and historical context. Our place and circumstances will determine the particular strategies, methodologies, and community tools to be chosen when we engage these conflicts and struggles.

As both Martínez-Falquina and Bańka argue in the opening and closing chapters (drawing from Erdrich's and Ortiz's literary and philosophical works), a simple stone, found or given as a gift, can become a symbol of relationality and care binding the self to a community that extends to the more-than-human world. The stone becomes the ultimate embodiment of the land and humbly emerges as a reminder of the relational systems of reciprocity, responsibility, and care we are all a part of. Bańka's words perfectly capture this key idea: "taking care of the land—the provider and sustainer of life—becomes people's moral obligation. What traditional knowledge teaches is therefore that through responsible relationships with the land and others one forms cultural self-consciousness and expresses one's full-fledged humanity."

Transnational conversations can shed further light on political conflicts and on human/more-than-human encounters and relations that are becoming further interconnected in the global age. However, as Birgit Däwes reminds us, this "politically local and translocally informed perspective" must be Indigenized when applied to Native texts.[25]

Largely penned by European and non-Native authors, the chapters that follow aim to "decolonize comparison" and to enrich perspective while keeping Native methodologies and local/tribal world views at the center of the discussion.[26] They examine theories, literary practices, and methods that are deployed when Native American literature is engaged in a world/global context or from a *worldly* vantage point that respects tribal specificities, demands, and interests while focusing on authors and texts that are grounded on the land while in motion.

NOTES

1. The multiauthored volume *Indigenizing the Classroom*, edited by Anna María Brígido-Corachán, specifically considers the impact of Native American/First Nations literature and critical theory in educational contexts outside the United States and Canada.

2. See, for example, Robert Warrior's account of the 1990 intercontinental, intertribal meeting that took place in Quito, Ecuador, to address the quincentenary celebrations of the European invasion of the Americas. This hemispheric, trans-Indigenous encounter is examined in Warrior's essay "The Sweetgrass Meaning of Solidarity: 500 Years of Resistance" and is also mentioned by Joy Harjo in her memoir *Crazy Brave*. A more comical and poignant review of trans-Indigenous encounters, complicated by colonialist mediation and intercultural translation, is provided by LeAnne Howe in her essay collection *Choctalking on Other Realities*, where she discusses her participation in several international meetings in the Middle East or Japan. The anthology *The World Is One Place: Native American Poets Visit the Middle East*, edited by Diane Glancy and Linda Rodríguez, provides a more literary approach to the political realities of the Middle East through poetic interventions by Jim Barnes, Kimberly Blaeser, Natalie Diaz, Joy Harjo, Linda Hogan, Craig Santos Perez, or James Thomas Stevens, among others.

3. See Womack, "A Single Decade," or Lyons's "Globalizing the Word," which served as an introduction to the volume *The World, The Text, and the Indian*.

4. As a case in point which clearly evinces colonialist language in the press, I can mention the recent uproar in Spanish newspapers (and among transatlantic historians) when Mexican president Andrés Manuel López Obrador asked the Spanish king to apologize for the colonization of Mexico and the genocide of Indigenous peoples. See, for example, David Marcial Pérez, "Las polémicas de López Obrador con España: Del 'pida perdón' al Rey al'a mí no me paga Repsol,'" *El País*, February 9, 2022, https://elpais.com/mexico/2022-02-09/las-polemicas-de-lopez-obrador-con-espana-del-pida-perdon-al-rey-al-a-mi-no-me-paga-repsol.html.

5. Tapahonso, *A Radiant Curve*, 89.
6. On Indigenous storytellers as place-makers, see specifically Basso, *Wisdom Sits in Places*, 32.
7. Ibid., 6.
8. In Kirwan, "Choctaw Tales," 269–270.
9. See Coulthard, "Once We Were Maoists." In his lecture, Coulthard drew from the work of Leanne Simpson when he made this remark. See for example Simpson, *Dancing on Our Turtle's Back*.
10. Brígido-Corachán, "Material Nature, Visual Sovereignty, and Water Rights," 84.
11. Krupat, *Red Matters*, 19.
12. See Ortiz's poem "Culture and the Universe," in *Out There Somewhere*.
13. Cajete, "'Look to the Mountain.'"
14. Ortiz, "Indigenous Language Consciousness," 135.
15. Lyons, *The World, the Text, and the Indian*, 14.
16. Said, *Reflections on Exile*, 375.
17. Said, *The World, the Text, and the Critic*, 4.
18. Lyons, *The World, the Text, and the Indian*, 15.
19. International pressure made several European banks review their investment policies in companies such as Energy Transfer Partners. This transnational impact is discussed by Brígido-Corachán in "Material Nature," 73–74.
20. See for example Cox, *The Red Land to the South*; Lyons, *The World, the Text, and the Indian*; or Ghanayem and Macklin, "Native American Narratives."
21. Owens, *Mixedblood Messages*, 85.
22. Judith Butler, "Ethics and Politics of Non-Violence," Centre de Cultura Contemporània de Barcelona, April 17, 2018, http://www.cccb.org/es/multimedia/videos/la-etica-y-la-politica-de-la-no-violencia/228942, qtd in Martínez-Falquina in this volume.
23. See Allen, *Trans-Indigenous Methodologies*.
24. Goeman, "Notes," 170.
25. See Däwes, "'The Past Was a White Man's Illusion,'" 203.
26. Allen, "Decolonizing Comparison."

BIBLIOGRAPHY

Allen, Chadwick. "Decolonizing Comparison: Toward a Trans-Indigenous Literary Studies." In *The Oxford Handbook of Indigenous American Literature*, edited by James J. Cox and Daniel Heath Justice, 377–394. Oxford: Oxford University Press, 2014.

————. *Trans-Indigenous: Methodologies for Global Native Literary Studies*. Minneapolis: University of Minnesota Press, 2012.

Basso, Keith H. *Wisdom Sits in Places: Landscape and Language among the Western Apache*. Albuquerque: University of New Mexico Press, 1996.

Brígido-Corachán, Anna María, ed. *Indigenizing the Classroom: Engaging Native American/ First Nations Literature and Culture in Non-Native Settings*. Valencia: Publicacions de la Universitat de València, 2021.

————. "Material Nature, Visual Sovereignty, and Water Rights: Unpacking the Standing Rock Movement." In "Studies in the Literary Imagination," special issue, *Twenty-First Century American Crises: Reflections, Representations, Transformations* 50, no. 1 (2017): 69–90.

Brotherston, Gordon. *Book of the Fourth World: Reading the Native Americas through Their Literature*. Cambridge: Cambridge University Press, 1995.

Byrd, Jodi A. *The Transit of Empire: Indigenous Critiques of Colonialism*. Minneapolis: University of Minnesota Press, 2011.

Cajete, Gregory. "'Look to the Mountain': Reflections on Indigenous Ecology." In *A People's Ecology: Explorations in Sustainable Living. Health, Environment, Agriculture, Native Traditions*, 3–20. Santa Fe, NM: Clear Lights Publishers, 1999.

Coulthard, Glen Sean. "Once We Were Maoists: Fourth World Anti-colonialism." Zoom lecture. University of Warwick. Decolonial/Postcolonial Working Group. December 15, 2021.

Cox, James H. *The Red Land to the South: American Indian Writers and Indigenous Mexico*. Minneapolis: University of Minnesota Press, 2012.

Däwes, Birgit. "'The Past Was a White Man's Illusion': The Temporal Continuum and Trans/ Nationalism in Louis Owens' *Nightland* and *Dark River*." In *Louis Owens: Writing Land and Legacy*, edited by Joe Lockard and A. Robert Lee, 201–219. Albuquerque: New Mexico University Press, 2019.

Ghanayem, Eman, and Rebecca Macklin, eds. "Native American Narratives in a Global Context." Special issue, *Transmotion* 5, no. 1 (2019), https://journals.kent.ac.uk/index.php/ transmotion/issue/view/37.

Glancy, Diane, and Linda Rodríguez, eds. *The World Is One Place: Native American Poets Visit the Middle East*. Kansas City: BkMk Press, University of Missouri-Kansas City, 2017.

Goeman, Mishuana. "Notes toward a Native Feminism's Spatial Practice." *Wicazo Sa Review* 24, no. 2 (Fall 2009): 169–187.

Harjo, Joy. *Crazy Brave: A Memoir*. New York: W. W. Norton and Co., 2012.

Howe, LeAnne. *Choctalking on Other Realities*. San Francisco: Aunt Lute Books, 2013.

Kirwan, Padraig. "Choctaw Tales: An Interview with LeAnne Howe." *Women: A Cultural Review* 27, no. 3 (2016): 265–279.

Krupat, Arnold. *Red Matters: Native American Studies*. Philadelphia: University of Pennsylvania Press, 2002.

Lyons, Scott Richard, ed. *The World, the Text, and the Indian: Global Dimensions of Native American Literature*. Albany: State University of New York Press, 2017.

Ortiz, Simon. "Indigenous Language Consciousness: Being, Place, and Sovereignty." In *Sovereign Bones: New Native American Writing*, edited by E. L. Gansworth, 135–148. New York: Nation Books, 2007.

———. *Out There Somewhere*. Tucson: University of Arizona Press, 2002.

Owens, Louis. *Mixedblood Messages: Literature, Film, Family, Place*. Norman: Oklahoma University Press, 1998.

Pulitano, Elvira, ed. *Transatlantic Voices: Interpretations of Native North American Literatures*. Lincoln: University of Nebraska Press, 2007.

Said, Edward. *Reflections on Exile and Other Essays*. Cambridge, MA: Harvard University Press, 2009.

———. *The World, the Text, and the Critic*. Cambridge, MA: Harvard University Press, 1983.

Simpson, Leanne Betasamosake. *Dancing on Our Turtle's Back: Stories of Nishnaabeg Re-Creation, Resurgence and a New Emergence*. Winnipeg: Arp Books, 2011.

TallBear, Kim. *Native American DNA: Tribal Belonging and the False Promise of Genetic Science*. Minneapolis: University of Minnesota Press, 2013.

Tapahonso, Luci. *A Radiant Curve. Poems and Stories*. Tucson: The University of Arizona Press, 2008.

Warrior, Robert. "The Sweet Grass Meaning of Solidarity: 500 Years of Resistance." *Border/lines* 23 (Winter 1991): 35–37.

Weaver, Jace. *The Red Atlantic: American Indigenes and the Making of the Modern World, 1000–1927*. Chapel Hill: University of North Carolina Press, 2014.

Womack, Craig. "A Single Decade: Book-Length Native Literary Criticism between 1986 and 1997." In *Reasoning Together: The Native Critics Collective*, edited by Janice Acoose et al., 3–104. Norman: University of Oklahoma Press, 2008.

Grounded Relationality

A Reading of Contemporary Anishinaabe Literature
(Gordon Henry, Leanne Simpson, Louise Erdrich)

Silvia Martínez-Falquina

I n recent times, relationality has become a keyword to define our lives and place in the world. Especially at the start of the 2020s, after the outbreak of Me Too, Black Lives Matter, or the COVID-19 pandemic, it seems that we are more aware than ever before of our inescapable connections with every other human on the planet, and of how this can make us stronger—when we enhance community and solidarity—but vulnerable as well, for our dependence on others, even those who are far from us, can also bring us harm. Moreover, we are making progress in our consciousness of our relations to the environment and of the devastating effects of the loss of balance caused by human action. To mention just some of the numerous examples of the current critical discussion about interrelation, Judith Butler argues that we are all born into "a condition of radical dependency" on social and material structures, but also on the environment, "all of which makes life possible."[1] Such interdependency evidences our equality and makes self-sufficiency a fiction. Virginia Held studies care as the clearest characteristic of ancestral human nature, and she defines humans as "relational, rather than as the self-sufficient independent individuals of the dominant moral theories."[2] Jeremy Rifkin argues that we are a fundamentally empathic species, and he optimistically observes that "the Age of Reason is being eclipsed by the Age of Empathy."[3] On her part, Naomi Klein remarks how the coronavirus epidemic "has forced us to think about interdependencies and relationships" in a way "that capitalism teaches us not to think about."[4] Clearly, the planet is far from an easy place to inhabit for those most affected by injustice, inequality, or climate change, and aggressive individualism is still too often associated with socioeconomic success and political power. However, it seems evident that calls for solidarity and community are being more manifestly heard and that the visibility and value of those who care for others are being increasingly vindicated, which urges us to examine relationality more closely.

The potential of relationality for cultural and literary criticism is undeniable. On the one hand, relationality has an ethical significance, for it posits the essential interconnection of the self with others, including place and other beings, in a way that allows for recognition of and openness to the not-me. On the other hand, it has an aesthetic value in its articulation of fluidity, transgression, and the revision of established and new creative forms. Hence, a general appreciation of relationality appears in the most significant efforts to define our current time and creativity. One example is the new sociocultural, political, and philosophical paradigm known as transmodernity, first conceptualized by Spanish philosopher Rosa María Rodríguez Magda.[5] Transmodernity incorporates and transcends modernity and postmodernity, and it has globalization as its main narrative. Its proponents insist that our time is characterized by a "new [*sic*] *relational* consciousness" that enhances our awareness of shared risks and interdependencies as it leads us to reengage with nature.[6] Another example is cosmodernism, Christian Moraru's account of the new cultural paradigm taking shape in the recent decades of accelerating globalization. As illustrated in a number of representative authors and critics, cosmodernism is based on relation, turning "on self and other's foundational co-relationality with respect to one another." Cosmodernism thus calls for a move from egology to ecology, assuming that culture's well-being needs to be conceived in terms of "an 'ecological' balance understood as co-presence, co-implication, and co-responsibility of self and his or her 'cultural other,' in short, as ethical relatedness."[7]

A related and promising attempt at redefining "artists' and critics' new speculations about our world" which also places a special importance on the relational is the planetary turn in contemporary criticism and theory. Moving away "from the totalizing paradigm of modern-age globalization,"[8] planetarity challenges what is perceived as "the homogenizing historical and discursive pressures and logics of globalization by centering instead on a methodology and ethic of relationality."[9] In fact, the most significant counter to the global of this transcultural phenomenon is precisely "its relationality model and return to ethics."[10] Inspired and informed by a concern with ecological crises, most notably rapid climate change and the Anthropocene,[11] planetarity reflects how thinking has become "thinking with the planet" lately, so that we are witnessing "an intellectual turn to the planet; the reciprocity of planetarization and thought."[12] Writers and artists perceive themselves and their aesthetic practices in relation to "the planet as a living organism, as a shared ecology, and as an incrementally integrated system" that encompasses human and nonhuman.[13] This leads Masao Miyoshi to posit that

> literature and literary studies have one basis and goal: to nurture our common bonds to the planet—to replace the imaginaries of exclusionary familialism, communitarianism, nationhood, ethnic culture, regionalism, "globalization," or even humanism, with the ideal of planetarianism.[14]

Critics of the planetary turn pronounce that the planetary is not "a one-world, genetically determinant, uniform and homogeneizing totality," and they warn against the "reglobalization" of planetarity.[15] In fact, they emphasize how in contrast to globalization's focus on circuits of capital and financial debt, "the planetary privileges a relational ethos of cultural debt." Its methodology, therefore, "both recognizes and hinges on principles of difference," considering worldly interconnections and interdependencies as well as the indebtedness to other peoples. This includes in particular "the worlds of often-neglected others."[16] Yet, part of the ambivalence of the planetary is the "uneasy conjunction between the planetary and the parochial,"[17] which is why we have to be open and attentive to different ways of perceiving the planet.

Moraru's call to scan "the micro for signs of the macro"[18] and to embrace the challenge of discerning the planet's inscription in the local and apparently humble is, I contend, the best way to approach relationality and avoid the risk of reglobalization.[19] No matter how well-intentioned and optimistic the attempts to focus on relationality may be, overgeneralizing will empty the idea of specific, solid content. Moreover, essentializing relationality would bring about an erasure of the differences and inequalities that it should contribute to visibilizing instead. This is why it is particularly relevant to note that the language of relationality is not necessarily the same everywhere or for everyone: we should carefully contextualize it in order for its representative and transformative potential to be fulfilled. Relationality is spoken, for instance, very differently by Indigenous and non-Indigenous peoples on the planet. In the aforementioned efforts to define the new cultural paradigm, we can see that Western critics treat relationality as something new, offering it as an alternative to the dominant narrative of individualism. On their part, and in spite of evident culture-specific articulations of this idea, Indigenous peoples have been speaking the language of relationality all along. For them, being has always meant being-with, and relations with the environment, including all its creatures—human or not, alive or not, visible or not—are inextricable from the conception of the self. In this context, relationality is something that persists—albeit hidden, as in the original layer of a palimpsest—in spite of the devastation brought on by colonization and patriarchy, which is why it is articulated as part of a narrative of return and continuity of ancient traditions in contemporary literature and criticism. With all this in mind, in this essay I will focus on a specific manifestation of relationality that can contribute to the current conversation about this concept and pave the way for promising transcultural and transethnic critical alliances. Set in the Native American context at large, the Anishinaabe articulation of being as being-in-relation in theory and writing provides a particularly interesting example of how the local can exemplify and illuminate the worldly, or how we can find the whole planet in one place.

Irrespective of their diversity, Native American literatures generally transmit a definite way of being open to otherness. This openness extends to all there is, animate or inanimate, present or past. In Winona LaDuke's words, "Native American teachings describe the relations all around—animals, fish, trees, and rocks—as our brothers, sisters, uncles, and grandpas. Our relations to each other, our prayers whispered across generations to our relatives, are what bind our cultures together."[20] Articulated in stories and reenacted through ceremonies, this emphasis on relations is grounded on the understanding of the land as both essential for survival and the source of American Indian identity, spirituality, history, sovereignty. Yet, more than a material object of profound importance to Indigenous cultures—which it also evidently is—the land is first and foremost articulated as a field of relationships.[21] In fact, the "ethics of reciprocity and sharing" that underlies Native American understandings of their relationship to the land is the most distinctive aspect that separates Indigenous and Western views on the world and the place of human beings in it.[22] However, in order to avoid romanticizing this Native American reciprocal relation to the land, we must understand that it involves much more than the stereotypical nature-loving image of the Indian that is broadly generalized in popular culture and parts of academia. Non-Native critics should be very aware of the risk of oversimplification and appropriation of Indigenous relationality and try to apprehend the diversity, dynamism, and complexity of tribal people's views on their own terms.

One way to start is by recognizing that Native Americans have their own interpretive models and how some authors like Opaskwayak Cree Shawn Wilson are using a creatively transformed academic language to vindicate them. Through theorization and storying, Wilson articulates a research paradigm that follows Indigenous codes of conduct and honors Indigenous systems of knowledge and world views.[23] Because a relational way of being—including relatives, land, spirits, cosmos—is "at the heart of what it means to be Indigenous," "an Indigenous research paradigm is relational and maintains relational accountability":

> An Indigenous paradigm comes from the foundational belief that knowledge is relational. Knowledge is shared with all of creation. It is not just interpersonal relationships, not just with the research subjects I may be working with, but it is a relationship with all of creation. It is with the cosmos, it is with the animals, with the plants, with the earth that we share this knowledge.[24]

This approach to knowledge assumes that life experience and relations, as well as culture, determine one's beliefs and also research, for "we cannot remove ourselves from our world in order to examine it."[25] Moreover, "it is imperative to relational accountability that as a researcher I form a respectful relationship with the ideas that I am studying."[26] Because "the purpose of all ceremony is to transform and restore wholeness to build stronger relationships or bridge the distance between our cosmos and us," then Indigenous research, which allows us "a raised level of consciousness and insight into our world," is "a life changing ceremony."[27] Wilson vindicates the fact that an Indigenous research paradigm has existed for millennia, but it is only in the past few years that it is speaking back to mainstream academia, a sign that Indigenous scholars are asserting their power and are "no longer allowing others to speak in [their] stead."[28] This is part of a broad movement of Native American scholars who "question the perceived ownership of theory,"[29] previously assumed to be beneficial for the colonizer only.

A good example of the turn to theory made by Native studies recently is Leanne Betasamosake Simpson's conceptualization of Indigenous resurgence, "a set of practices through which the regeneration and reestablishment of Indigenous nations could be achieved."[30] This Michi Saagiig Nishnaabeg scholar, writer, artist, and musician responds to the shame derived from cognitive imperialism—"an insidious mechanism to promote neo-assimilation and obfuscate the historic atrocities of colonialism"—by finding the stories of resistance that celebrate that, in her words, "after everything, we are still here."[31] She claims that "all Nishnaabeg people are theorists in the sense that they hold responsibilities to making meaning for their own creation and their own life. . . . Theory is collectivized through the telling of stories and the performance of our ceremonies."[32] The stories were part of the resistance of her ancestors, who survived occupation and subjugation by holding onto these seeds of their culture and political systems and putting them away until another generation might be able to plant them.[33] This act of regeneration and restoration takes place in stories—especially origin stories—and is inherently relational:

> The original knowledge, coded and transmitted through complex networks, says that everything we need to know about everything in the world is contained within Indigenous bodies, and that these same Indigenous bodies exist as networked vessels, or constellations across time and space intimately connected to a universe of nations and beings.[34]

Déné political theorist Glen Coulthard also notes how people are "an insepara-ble part of an expansive system of interdependent relations covering the land and animals, past and future generations, as well as other people and communities."[35] Coulthard theorizes such connection to the land as grounded normativity. This is an ethical framework provided by the land as a mode of reciprocal relationship, itself informed by "place-based practices and associated forms of knowledge [which] ought to teach us about living our lives in relation to one another and our surround-ings in a respectful, nondominating and nonexploitative way."[36] This place-based ethics stresses "the importance of sharing, egalitarianism, respecting the freedom and autonomy of both individuals and groups, and recognizing the obligations that one has not only to other people, but to the natural world as a whole."[37] Aware of the position that land occupies as "an ontological framework for understanding *relationships*,"[38] white supremacist and heteropatriarchal powers attacked and keep attacking the Indigenous peoples' relationship to the land as "a mechanism to submit Indigenous lands and labor to the demands of capitalist accumulation and state-formation."[39] Logically, then, the reconnection of Indigenous bodies to the land that resurgence is based on is an essential element of decolonialization.

Among the Anishinaabeg, a specific act of resurgence is that of the restoration of this tribe's basic ethical frame. According to White Earth Anishinaabe Adam Spry, mino bimaadiziwin—or simply bimaadiziwin—is "a complex moral philosophy by which traditional Anishinaabeg life was, and continues to be, largely defined."[40] The term—which can be roughly translated as "the good life" or "well-being"—refers to one's ability to exist without hardship, starvation, and disease, "but one could only achieve such a life through a complex relational process."[41] Maintaining relationships of interdependency formed a critical aspect of Anishinaabe philosophy and daily life, for "achieving mino bimaadizi relied on the individual's ability to open themselves as widely as possible to relationships of interdependency in order to secure well-being for both themselves and those with whom they maintained relations."[42] Insofar as this means "a radical openness to assistance from others," including human and other-than-human people,[43] it assumes a permeable view on the individual. Whereas the Eurocentric view emphasizes self-knowledge and personal virtue to master one's place in the world and happiness is an individual pursuit, mino bimaadiziwin focuses on the collective nature of well-being so that whenever balance is broken or circumstances are adverse, the responsibility is never simply the individual's. All in all, mino bimaadiziwin's "radically expansive idea of interdependency . . . stretches the value of social obligation beyond the mere humans to plants, animals, manidoog, and everything else that comprises the natural world."[44]

Evidently, mino bimaadiziwin is a very relevant part of the reconstruction of the Anishinaabe world view in response to the new reality after what Lawrence Gross has characterized as "the apocalypse of their worlds."[45] In his words,

> For the old Anishinaabeg, *bimaadiziwin* informed the myths, fasting, relations with animals, health and healing, the Midewiwin, and relations with the dead. In the modern age, *bimaadiziwin* is helping the Anishinaabeg to reconstruct their worlds in the postapocalyptic period.[46]

The basic teachings about how to live in this world are most present in stories, the preservation and restoration of which is an exercise in Anishinaabe resurgence. To Leanne Simpson, storytelling is decolonizing, for it creates a way out of cognitive imperialism and it remembers, visions, and creates "a just reality where Nishnaabeg live as both *Nishnaabeg* and *peoples*."[47] To illustrate and expand this theoretical and ethical frame of Anishinaabe relationality, in what follows, I will look into the articulation of Anishinaabe resurgence and recreation of mino bimaadiziwin in three recent texts by Gordon Henry, Leanne Simpson, and Louise Erdrich. Their focus on relationality emphasizes the ceremonial—transformative, activist—motivation of contemporary texts that, while specific to the Anishinaabe world view, reaches beyond national borders to speak about planetary concerns too.

Something Like Love: Gordon Henry's "Through the Refuge"

Gordon Henry's "Through the Refuge," published in *Iperstoria* in 2017—and later reprinted in his poem compilation *Spirit Matters* (2022)—places us in the realm of inbetweenness and relationality from the start. The poem thematizes a journey, its short, enjambed lines with no end punctuation—save for a pair of commas and the final full stop—moving fluidly toward its destination. Along the way, we find changing horizons, Catholic and Anishinaabe beliefs, lovers and fighting relatives, life and death, grief and love.[48]

The poem begins with an external speaker who bears witness to a land of roads and waterways. As if gifted with agency, roads hold "More than memory" (line 2) and take us places. At each turn, they offer a different horizon or meeting place of pines and clouds, lakes and rice crops. The waterways are "Signs of an ancient flood / Of tears" (lines 8–9), for this is a place that carries the pain of loss and dispossession. But the waterways are "Overseen by nesting / Eagles now" (lines 10–11), and the eagle—who can fly high and see from great distances, who is a loving parent and teacher of their offspring—is the representative of love and the carrier of knowledge. The traumatic past and its consequences are visible in the present, and memory is gushing, fluid—hence expressed in the water; but it can also be held at bay by love and Anishinaabe teachings. Then, in a somewhat abrupt change, we take a left turn and learn that our final destination is a funeral, and the natural landscape is transformed by a sequence of four sites—dance grounds, the tribal school, the cemetery, and the Catholic church (lines 22–25)—that signify the road of life and death, framed by two models of spiritual understandings, only to end with the Catholic symbol of colonial overwriting on land, bodies, spirits.

Upon arrival, the pace of the poem becomes slower to describe a common scene in the context of funerals: the community of the gathering relatives is disrupted by the materialistic interests of some people, fighting over possessions left by the deceased. Signaling memory again, the first of those things is a series of boxes filled with letters and photographs accumulated over the decades: their faces are the part for the whole "Absent bodies" (line 33), and they encompass both the living and the dead. There is also an address book, the names we imagine written on it another synecdoche for contacts and relations around the deceased. And because intentions need to be put down on paper—how different this world from that we saw from the road, where the language of nature was expressive enough—there are legal instructions on belongings for an executer to distribute them. Next, grieving more deeply, but not enough to forget about material possessions, we find the deceased half-sisters, focused on more coveted artifacts: a winnowing basket that is valuable both because it is unique and because it belonged to their common grandparents, thus another object of memory; and, less sentimentally, a set of jewels given by a man from the city. The dead person in line 29 is now specified as a woman, and one who had a suitor from the city, who married more than one man, a woman who loved.

While the poem accounts for these interests with no more criticism than that involved in the very mentioning of it—for the poetic speaker is merely observing, overseeing like the eagles, and not judging human nature—a clear reminder of rules being broken is introduced. The action has moved to the "survival school / gymnasium" (lines 56–57)—which seems like an appropriate place to gather to mourn and celebrate life—where

> Someone says
> We should not speak
> Her name now
> She's Traveling
> Traveling,
> She is Traveling
> on that big star
> road (lines 58–65)

In the midst of the previous focus on objects and legal documents, this Anishinaabe traditional belief of the four-day journey of the deceased is given a preeminent space, and its recovery is an act of resurgence. Evidently, the rules of proper behavior are not followed by all the mourners in the poem: fighting over possessions goes against traditional emphasis on sharing and giveaways, and someone must have mentioned the woman's name for such a reminder to be necessary. But the old ways have a continuity, they are still remembered, alive: the mourners believe that the dead woman could hear her name if pronounced, and they assign her a place on the spiritual star road of their tradition. Layer upon layer of missionary interventions may have been written upon these people and their ways. However, as with the original layer of a palimpsest, these old teachings persist; they demand respect and to be set in conversation with what has been written upon them.

The poem then takes another turn to include the poetic speaker—implicit until now—and an old Dakota man sitting by his side in the bleachers, another ex of the dead woman who carries an eagle staff. This man whispers, remembering the woman,

> "she spoke
> Used to speak, fluently
> At night
> In the language
> While dreaming
>
> I didn't understand
> But she was smiling
> In her sleep
> I thought maybe
> She was dreaming
> Of something like
> Love, something like
> That." (lines 73–85)

The abundance of verbs referring to speech acts in the final part of the poem underscores this relevant theme. We perceive the inability to fully apprehend or communicate: relations need to be reestablished, the old traditions of grieving are not naturally followed by all, some people are taking rather than giving, and the memory that the roads and rivers hold may not be for all humans to grasp. Nonetheless, the poem leaves us with a powerful and certain presence. The Dakota man may have not understood his wife's dreams in Anishinaabemowin, but he does understand what lies underneath her words: the fluency, the smile, the depth of what was being expressed, can be nothing but love, the ultimate and most universal language of connection.

Maintaining strong relationships with the dead is an important part of the ethical frame of mino bimaadiziwin. In spite of the idea found in much scholarship that the Anishinaabe honored their dead but also kept them at a safe distance, Lawrence Gross sustains that the dead are believed "to take an interest in what is going on in our lives and will, on occasion, visit us in order to provide their help, guidance, and support."[49] Their help centers on this world: "the dead are still with us, and they are doing their best to help us live the good life, to live by the dictates of bimaadiziwin."[50] As Henry's poem leaves us with the connections she fostered—the poetic speaker and the old Dakota man, the close and distant relatives and mourners, the two languages, the two spiritual traditions—the absent woman is made very present. Moreover, the emphasis on love at the end of the text gives us a new perspective on those horizons at the beginning as the actual destination of the poem beyond the funeral. Overseen by nesting eagles and expressed in the language of dreams, the end of the road is the meeting place of love, the deepest, truest, and most connective language of all, that comes to the surface in this act of poetic resurgence.

Small Things Are Actually Big, Important Things: Leanne Simpson's "All Our Relations"

Leanne Simpson's *The Gift Is in the Making: Anishinaabeg Stories*, published in 2013, is a compilation of traditional stories aimed at transmitting Anishinaabe values and teachings to a new generation. With the exception of "Good Neighbors," which Simpson composed for her kids, they are all retellings of previously published or orally told stories. As explained in her introduction, Simpson's intention was to liberate these stories "from the colonial contexts in which they are too often documented"—she uses, for example, interchangeable gender terminology—and to "connect our children to our land and waters, our language and oral literature":

> At the most basic level, the stories in this collection teach both individuals and collectives how to promote, nurture, and maintain good relationships, how to function within a community, how to relate to the land, how to make collective decisions, and how to be a good person—that is, by being true to our traditions.[51]

In order to adapt the texts for today's children, Simpson incorporates contemporary language and popular culture references, but she also intercalates words in Anishinaabemowin, for which she provides a translation in a note after each text. This and her constant focus on interconnection and interdependence is part of Simpson's project of regeneration of Anishinaabe—although she spells it "Nishnaabeg"—culture and nation. For this act of resurgence she gives a new life to the stories, which "pointed to invigorating a particular way of living. A way of living that was full of community. A way of living that was thoughtful and profoundly empathetic. A way of living that considered, in a deep profound way, relationality."[52]

"All Our Relations" is the third story in the book, and it starts with a direct reference to this basic relational frame: "The old people say that we are all related—not just to the people that live in our house, but to the plants, the animals, the air, the water, and the land." The moon, the earth, the sky, the sun, are all part of the Nishnaabeg family, "one big, beautiful family, with many different branches." This is something that the people have always known, "but sometimes, just sometimes, we get busy. We forget the small things, and, when we do, we learn that they are actually big, important things."[53] The story focuses on one such time when the people forgot to properly relate to an apparently minor being, the rose, and this brought on important consequences. The people were suffering because of the lack of food. There were no berries, many flowers and insects were missing, and bear meat was too sour to eat. Knowing that solutions had to be found communally, they first consulted with the Elders, the Grandmothers, the Grandfathers, and the Medicine People, who then sent them to Makwa, the bear, who suggested they ask Aamoo, the bee, who finally told them to talk to the flower. It was Waawaasgoneh, the flower, who told them the sad story of the rose, Ginii, who left because the people did not value or pay respect to it. As a result of the people's neglect of the roses, the whole balance of species was broken, bringing hunger and suffering. Accepting their responsibility and trying to find a solution for the disruption they had caused, the people asked for the help of Bineshiinyag, the birds, who went all over the world to look for the rose. Finally, Naanooshkeshiinh, the ruby-throated hummingbird, brought a wilted rose plant that the people took care of:

> They sang to her.
> They gave her nibiish.
> They made sure her leaves felt the morning sun. Most importantly, and in their quietest and most gentle voices, they talked to her. They told her how much they had missed her, how much they loved her.

They talked about the deep raspberry colour of her petals. They talked about how soft those petals were on their cheeks. They talked about the tea they loved to make out of her rose hips.[54]

Responding to this restoration of their relation, the rose got better, and after her came more roses, then the bees, who pollinated and made honey, then the bears, who got fat from eating all that honey. Henceforth, the people felt stronger and healthier, and they remembered that they should always consider the rose and all the flowers in their land. This is the message for today's readers and listeners, directly addressed in the text:

So, you see how important each one of those plants and animals are? We should never destroy anything.

That's what those old Elders always say.[55]

This apparently simple story incorporates the full depth of the Anishinaabe traditional ethics of mino bimaadiziwin. In correspondence to Coulthard's definition of Indigenous grounded normativity, the story makes clear that "we are as much a part of the land as any other element." This means that we hold certain obligations to the land, animals, plants, in the same way as we hold obligations to other people, and if these obligations are met, then those beings will "reciprocate and meet their obligations to humans, thus ensuring the survival and well-being of all over time."[56] As Simpson argues, the radical move, aimed at cultural survival and resurgence, is to go beyond land-based pedagogies to an understanding of the land as pedagogy.[57] "All Our Relations" shows this agency of the land and all its creatures, who teach and collaborate with humans but ask for something from them in return. In this ethics of reciprocity, it is the responsibility of all beings to show respect and nurture relationship. As is also made evident here, the land does not exist for the sake of humans, for "intelligence flows through relationships between living entities."[58] The way to live a good life is to open oneself to relations, and the participants in the story do so as a group. Well-being is collective, never individual, and so is the responsibility to make amends when the balance has been broken.

The land in this story is also articulated as process, showing dynamism and the possibility to make amends, two key elements of mino bimaadiziwin. As accounted for in the text, the fact that the old people knew about these things—how we are all related and part of one big family, and how we need to take care of all its members, or else life for all will be affected—does not mean that people always act accordingly. Humans can fail, and accepting this possibility with humility is also a way of respecting nature, for humans are part of and made of nature. Living in a good way is "an ongoing process,"[59] pointing to continuous rebirth. In Gross's words,

> the stories teach that we all make mistakes. The important thing is not to dwell on them, but learn from them and move on with one's life. This is a factor of *bimaadiziwin*, and the inclusion of self-forgiveness as an explicit aspect of the game points to the continued relevance of Anishinaabe values today.[60]

Clearly, the emphasis not on destination but on process qualifies relation just as it does everything else for the Anishinaabeg, whose language, Margaret Noodin reminds us, is focused on verbs and expresses an active and engaged thinking about being in the world.[61] Native stories like "All Our Relations" are not focused on reaching a sense of closure. Instead, by presenting a sequence of lost balance followed by a restoration of such balance through reconnection—a common pattern in many stories—they ponder on the dynamic, ongoing nature of learning and life, showing an acceptance of such sequence as a part of life. Relation is, thus, verb, action, process.

All in all, stories like "All Our Relations" take Indigenous bodies as the subjects of theory. When the story focuses on the participation of people, vegetation, and animals, it requires a similar engagement on the part of listeners or readers. Knowledge is relational because it requires from us an engagement with others. As a consequence, in this kind of story, readers have no choice but to participate in the intimate reciprocity that we are presented with.

A New Episode of Time: Louise Erdrich's "The Stone"

Delving into the relation of human and nonhuman worlds, "The Stone," an independent story published by Louise Erdrich in 2019, revolves around the stone that becomes a woman's companion from the time when she is a little girl until she dies. While playing in the woods on an island in Lake Superior, an unnamed girl finds a black and rounded basalt stone "half the size of a human skull and very smooth."[62]

Making her feel that someone is staring at her, the symmetrical hollows scoured by water give the stone "an owlish look, or a blind look, or, anyway, some quality that was oddly attractive." The girl takes the stone home, cherishes it, sleeps with it, puts it in a safe place, hides it from her parents and siblings. After an upsetting incident at school where a boy cuts a piece of her hair, the girl puts "the little clump of severed hair into one of the empty hollows in the face of the stone," thus starting a ritual that calms her. Subsequently, she finds solace in the stone during difficult times, and it even accompanies her in her exploration of sexuality. Excited by the interest she sees in the face looking at her while she bathes, the young woman holds the stone to her chest, presses it between her legs. The stone is satisfying and also a soothing companion that offers an alternative to invasive masculinity. When she goes out on a date with the boy who cut her hair years before, she "put[s] up with the kissing" although she finds his touch and breath unpleasant. But when she gets home, the stone reclaims her from the drawer where she kept it: "Everything [is] understood," and the girl chooses to sleep with the stone from then on.

Protective and somewhat possessive, the stone accompanies the young woman through college—where another girl, jealous of the protagonist's self-sufficiency, gets hurt by the stone falling on her head after stealing it—and in her successful musical career, where she plays the piano with the stone in a bag sitting next to her. Mirroring human romantic relationships, the girl and the stone quarrel after an incident in the bathroom when the girl gets hurt and the stone is smashed in two pieces on the bathroom floor, which destroys its beauty: "The spell was broken. It was like falling out of love." After this, the girl puts the two pieces into a drawer and starts seeing a man who will soon become her husband. The marriage slowly deteriorates because of the woman's "glassy distraction" and the "invisible distance" that it causes, and the husband ends it when he understands "that he didn't want to live with a simulacrum of intimacy." In order "to restore her balance" after the breakup, the woman recovers the two pieces of the stone and fits it back together with special glue. This is something that had never happened to the stone, which, in its 1.1 billion years of age,

> had been broken time and again. It had been rolled smooth by water and the action of sand. Because of its strange shape, it had been picked up by several human beings in the course of the past ten thousand years. It had been buried with one until a tree had devoured the bones and pulled the stone back out of the ground. It had

been kept by a woman who revered it as a household spirit and filled its eyes with sweetgrass. It had been shoved off a dock, lifted back up with a shovel, deposited in a heap. It had surfaced in a girl's left hand.

The intimacy of the woman and the stone is thus restored—she oils it when it looks dry, puts it out to watch the bird feeder when it looks bored, places it by her when she reads—and will remain so until the woman's death at a very old age. At this final mutation she has the stone by her and dreams that she enters "a new episode of time, in which she and the stone . . . would be joined with the stone's molecules, over and over in age after age."

Such final reference to circular time sets the story in the realm of myth. An early mention of the young girl having a digital clock on her nightstand might lead us to assume that the story starts sometime in the last quarter of the twentieth century and place it in a realistic frame. However, the woman's life span surpasses that chronology, for she becomes "very old in [her] comforting life," which points to the future and mythical time. After all, linear time is simply not enough to understand the nature of the stone, and being aware that the stone had been "thrown from a rift in the earth 1.1 billion years ago" in fact "says nothing." Stones have a history longer than we can apprehend or express with words, and the story offers an intriguing conversation of human time with stone time, which become fused over and over in age after age in the end.

As Erdrich declares when commenting on her short story, "a stone is alien, but deeply familiar. It is a heavy secret and a messenger from an epoch of time beyond comprehension."[63] Calling upon us to revise our expectations about strangeness and familiarity, the known and the unknown, this involves that a stone can tell us the secrets that we cannot apprehend through conventional, everyday language. In fact, the lack of a language to express the full dimension of the stone is a key theme of the story. The language of science is not valid to describe the stone: "Basalt is a volcanic rock composed of augite and sometimes plagioclase and magnetite, which says nothing." This stone "had been called *nimishoomis*, or 'my grandfather,' and other names, too. The woman had not named the stone. She had thought that naming the stone would be an insult to its ineffable gravity." The text thus posits that we need to be open to a different way of perception, to recall what we know intuitively, restoring the language of relation.

The unnamed woman listens to that language, and even if she does not—possibly could not—speak about it, she responds by relating to the stone, a referent from the natural world, through ritual. As Erdrich expressed in an interview, "We all enact odd little rituals we don't understand," and they can make us feel better.[64] Ritual is essential to knowledge, and it is here performed as small acts that connect us to the world. As seen in the last sentence of the story, relation becomes transcendence as the dying woman dreams of a mystical marriage of human and stone that will be the seed of a new future: "Flesh would become stone and stone become flesh, and someday they would meet in the mouth of a bird."

Yet the woman's choice to relate to and share her life with the stone through ritual is not enough for such a transcendental union to be possible, for the agency of the stone is also required. Consensual relations of all beings are emphasized in the Anishinaabe world view, and ritual is "a mechanism to set up a relationship . . . that is based on mutual respect, reciprocity, and caring."[65] Consent is also required for knowledge, for

> coming to know is an intimate, unfolding process of relationship with the spiritual world. Coming to know also requires complex, committed, *consensual* engagement. Relationships within Nishnaabewin are based upon the consent—the informed (honest) consent—of all beings involved.[66]

The consent of this particular stone is made evident in the story through the will ascribed to it: it projects some kind of abstract energy and calls the girl's attention to go with her, to be taken out of the drawer after her date, to move it from one place to another. It also punishes the jealous college girl who stole it by falling from the shelf and causing a fracture and concussion. The insistence on the stone's agency gives us a view on the Anishinaabe interest in animacy, defined by Lawrence Gross as "exercising a will or agency of its own," and that is reflected in "a verb-based language [that] places the spotlight on the processes and events that flow through the world."[67] In this view, "the world is one of processes, events, and change. It is dynamic and full of life and energy. Seeing the world in this way helps the Anishinaabeg tap into the healing powers of the universe."[68] "A stone," writes Erdrich in her story, "is a thought that the earth develops over inhuman time. It is a living thing to some cultures and a dead thing to others." But as she makes clear when commenting on her text, in Ojibwe, "the word for stone, *asin*, is animate."[69]

As Vanessa Watts claims, in the Euro-Western view, "agency has erroneously become exclusive to humans, thereby removing non-human agency from what constitutes a society." It is therefore essential to reaffirm the "sacred connection between place, non-human and human in an effort to access the 'pre-colonial mind'" and undo the attack on the relation of humans and the land launched by settler colonialism.[70] Watts refers to this Indigenous connection as "Place-Thought," which expresses the impossibility of separating those two elements and which is based "upon the premise that land is alive and thinking and that humans and non-humans derive agency through the extensions of these thoughts."[71] Agency in reference to Place-Thought can be found "in animals, in humans, in plants, in rocks, etc.," and it is tied to spirit, so that because "spirit exists in all things, then all things possess agency."[72] The result of such restoration of agency and the articulation of Indigenous connection as Place-Thought is a view of the world where

> habitats and ecosystems are better understood as societies from an indigenous point of view; meaning that they have ethical structures, inter-species treaties and agreements, and further their ability to interpret, understand and implement. Non-human beings are active members of society. Not only are they active, they also directly influence how humans organize themselves into that society.[73]

With "The Stone," Erdrich offers a creative representation of one such society where relationality is part of a political project. Colonization consciously attacked the Indigenous peoples' ability to communicate with place, and this resulted in a loss of agency. The vindication of Place-Thought and agency in this story undoes the violence done to the relation of humans and the land and renews the ability to communicate with the land that Indigenous peoples are vindicating in various ways.

Grounded Relationality: The Anishinaabe Contribution to the Planet

The ethic, aesthetic, and political value of relationality is made manifest in its growing presence in recent mainstream criticism. The most interesting articulations of the current paradigm change—most notably those characterized as transmodernity, cosmodernism, or planetarity—focus on relationality and a return to ethics. But the defining potential of these trends may be limited by their risk of homogenizing relationality, of making it a sort of centripetal force that absorbs all the different manifestations of relation that exist in the world. Focusing on the local and Indigenous and setting it in conversation with the global and planetary, then, is required for any representative paradigmatic discussion to occur. Since relationality is perceived as promising to account for and encourage sociopolitical transformation at the current time of crisis, engaging in such conversation is particularly urgent today.

Connected to Native American epistemologies and ontologies at large, but made manifest in a unique plethora of theoretical and creative manifestations, the case of Anishinaabe relationality is particularly illuminating. As I hope that the previous lines have made clear, the emphasis on relationality in both literary and theoretical texts proves that this is an essential value for the Anishinaabe, one that they deliberately and extensively define as inherent to their sense of individual and communal identity. Being is necessarily being-with, and it involves a broad understanding of family, community, place. This requires the acknowledgement and nourishing of values like reciprocity, accountability, or respect. Literary creation is particularly rich in the articulation of relationality, which in itself is an act of resurgence, or the recovery of traditional Anishinaabe ways in the context of settler colonial overwriting.

Gordon Henry's "Through the Refuge" acknowledges the barriers that separate beings, beliefs, norms. The old ways are at odds with the new, some things cannot be easily expressed, and this is the source of misunderstanding and disconnection. Cleverly avoiding a sentimental image of harmonious coexistence, the poem, however, holds onto the teachings of mino bimaadiziwin, the traditional ethical frame of the Anishinaabe, to set different elements—the natural and the human, the landscape and buildings, the living and the dead, the traditional and the Catholic—in relation. Difference does not have to be tragic, inbetweenness is an intrinsic quality of life, and they can both be approached through the language of love, which comes from both the depth of dreams and the elevation of flying eagles to remind us of its presence and connective power.

Leanne Simpson's "All Our Relations" is a good example of resurgence that connects today's young readers to valuable teachings from the past. The text compels us to look at ourselves as part of a large family where our actions will always have an impact on the whole. In this ethics of reciprocity, taking care of the other is a way of taking care of ourselves. No matter how unquestionable this knowledge—which comes from the land as pedagogy—may be, people can be expected to make mistakes and break the desirable balance. This is also part of life, and when it happens, it is accepted as a lesson: relation can always be restored, and it starts with an acknowledgement of the other as deserving respect and care. Relation is never static or fully accomplished; reflecting the way that Anishinaabemowin favors an active and engaged way of being in the world, it is process, connected to action, filled with possibility.

In her short story "The Stone," Louise Erdrich explores a captivating view on the world as a society where nonhumans and humans are all endowed with agency. In such society, place cannot be separated from thought, a relation that is the very source of life. Far from appropriative or dominating, relations here are consensual, for the agency of all there is is recognized and valued in correspondence with the Anishinaabe verb-based language. Erdrich participates in the necessary restoration of agency in the natural world by establishing a relation of mutual respect and reciprocity of different beings—the stone and the woman—that points to transcendence and creativity in an expanded cycle of life: an age after age fusion, the seed in the mouth of a bird. An exercise in humility, the story evidences human incapacity to apprehend or express the real nature of the world with the language of history or science. Yet, once the communication with place is properly restored, the language of relation speaks, companionship is made evident, and we can feel the ancestral familiarity with what previously seemed strange.

Bringing Anishinaabe ways of understanding relationality to the conversation on the nature of today's larger world is relevant in various ways. First, this is a vindication of unique cultural values that are restored from under the layers of settler colonialism. Essential to the emphasis on resurgence that moves much of contemporary Native American criticism and creative writing, relationality speaks of the beauty of the Anishinaabe, the validity and strength of their ways, and the possibilities they offer for a healthy, strong definition of contemporary identity. Very importantly, the lesson that relationality teaches us here is, to borrow Watts's words, "not simply a question of accessing something, which has already come and gone, but simply to listen. To act."[74] Relationality is thus a marker of Anishinaabe difference and resistance with respect to the settler colonizer, and is thus connected to nationalism and decoloniality.

Apart from preserving values associated with a specific tradition, a study of Anishinaabe relationality can also make an invaluable contribution to the reflection on the world we have today, and the world we want for the future. Fostering connection may well be the only way for the human race to survive on this planet, and any ideas about how to do that are welcome. A solid, well-defined, and illustrated account of relationality like that we find in Anishinaabe texts should be taken into serious consideration by Euro-Western critics interested in this concept. Like Spry, I also hold that we should preserve "those beliefs that might someday help us build a more inclusive, more balanced understanding of humanity and its place in the world."[75] As he offers,

> the Anishinaabe nation is worthy of sustaining not because of cultural tradition or an abstract sense of justice, but because the values held and defended by the Anishinaabeg for centuries—a faith in the interconnectedness of the natural world and a resolute love of living for its own sake—might help us to heal the damage wrought by racism, industrialism, and the unchecked expansion of capitalism.[76]

Vindicating the values of mino bimaadiziwin means looking for social and political change that may lead to a more inclusive, balanced world. Anishinaabe writers, activists of sorts, encourage us to reconsider our place in the world and our responsibility to it. It is worth listening to what they are struggling so hard to say.

NOTES

Research for this chapter was supported by the Spanish Ministry of Economy, Industry, and Competitiveness (MINECO) (PID2021–124841NB-I00) in collaboration with the European Regional Development Fund (DGI/ERDF) and the Government of Aragón (H03_20R).

1. Butler, "Ethics and Politics of Non-Violence."
2. Held, *The Ethics of Care*, 13.
3. Rifkin, *The Empathic Civilization*, 1.
4. Viner, "An Interview with Naomi Klein."
5. See Rodríguez Magda, *Transmodernidad* and "The Crossroads of Transmodernity."
6. Ateljevic, "Visions of Transmodernity," 213.
7. Moraru, *Cosmodernism*, 17, 50.
8. Elias and Moraru, "The Planetary Condition," xi.
9. Keith, "The Novel as Planetary Form," 271.
10. Elias and Moraru, "The Planetary Condition," xvii.
11. Keith, "The Novel as Planetary Form," 278.
12. Moraru, "Decompressing Culture," 215, 216.
13. Elias and Moraru, "The Planetary Condition," xii.
14. Miyoshi, "Turn to the Planet," 295.
15. Elias and Moraru, "The Planetary Condition," xxv, and Giles, "Writing for the Planet," 144, respectively.

16. Keith, "The Novel as Planetary Form," 271, 272, 274.

17. Giles, "Writing for the Planet," 144.

18. Moraru, "Decompressing Culture," 223

19. Ibid., 213.

20. LaDuke, *All Our Relations*, 2.

21. Coulthard, *Red Skins, White Masks*, 61.

22. Ibid., 62.

23. Wilson, *Research Is Ceremony*, 8.

24. Ibid., 80, 71, 73–74.

25. Ibid., 8, 14.

26. Ibid., 22.

27. Ibid., 137, 11, 60–61.

28. Ibid., 8.

29. Simpson and Smith, "Introduction," 7.

30. Simpson and Smith, "Introduction," 1; Simpson, *As We Have Always Done*, 16.

31. Simpson, *Dancing on Our Turtle's Back*, 32, 12.

32. Ibid., 43.

33. Ibid., 15.

34. Simpson, *As We Have Always Done*, 21.

35. Coulthard, *Red Skins, White Masks*, 63.

36. Ibid., 60.

37. Ibid., 63–64.

38. Ibid., 60.

39. Coulthard and Simpson, "Grounded Normativity / Place-Based Solidarity," 254.

40. Spry, *Our War Paint Is Writer's Ink*, 166.

41. Ibid.

42. Ibid.

43. Ibid., 167.

44. Ibid., 179.

45. Gross, *Anishinaabe Ways*, 46.

46. Ibid., 206.

47. Simpson, *Dancing on Our Turtle's Back*, 33.

48. Henry, "Through the Refuge." References to specific lines of the poem are included in parenthesesand they refer to the version published in *Iperstoria*.

49. Gross, *Anishinaabe Ways*, 211.

50. Ibid., 212.

51. Simpson, *The Gift Is in the Making*, 3, 2.

52. Simpson, *As We Have Always Done*, 22.

53. Simpson, *The Gift Is in the Making*, 19.

54. Ibid., 21.

55. Ibid., 22.

56. Coulthard, *Red Skins, White Masks*, 61.

57. Simpson, *As We Have Always Done*, 160.

58. Ibid., 155.

59. Simpson, *Dancing on Our Turtle's Back*, 27.

60. Gross, *Anishinaabe Ways*, 218–219.

61. In Carnes, "Margaret Noodin in Conversation," 17–18.

62. Erdrich, "The Stone." All subsequent references to Erdrich's story in this chapter are from this source.

63. In Treisman, "Louise Erdrich on the Power of Stones."

64. Ibid.

65. Simpson, *As We Have Always Done*, 157.

66. Ibid., 161.

67. Gross, *Anishinaabe Ways*, 90, 83.

68. Ibid., 109.

69. Treisman, "Louise Erdrich on the Power of Stones."

70. Watts, "Indigenous Place-Thought and Agency," 20.

71. Ibid., 21.

72. Ibid., 26, 30.

73. Ibid., 23.

74. Ibid., 32.

75. Spry, *Our War Paint Is Writer's Ink*, 185.

76. Ibid.

BIBLIOGRAPHY

Ateljevic, Irena. "Visions of Transmodernity: A New Renaissance of Our Human History?" *Integral Review* 9, no. 2 (2013): 200–219.

Butler, Judith. "Ethics and Politics of Non-Violence." Centre de Cultura Contemporània de Barcelona, April 17, 2018. http://www.cccb.org/es/multimedia/videos/la-etica-y-la-politica-de-la-no-violencia/228942.

Carnes, Jeremy. "Margaret Noodin in Conversation." *Wasafiri* 32, no. 2 (2017): 17–18.

Coulthard, Glen Sean. *Red Skins, White Masks: Rejecting the Colonial Politics of Recognition.* Minneapolis: University of Minnesota Press, 2014.

Coulthard, Glen, and Leanne Betasamosake Simpson. "Grounded Normativity / Place-Based Solidarity." *American Quarterly* 68, no. 2 (2016): 249–255.

Elias, Amy J., and Christian Moraru. "Introduction: The Planetary Condition." In *The Planetary Turn: Relationality and Geo-aesthetics in the Twenty-First Century*, edited by Amy J. Elias and Christian Moraru, xi–xxxvii. Evanston, IL: Northwestern University Press, 2015.

Erdrich, Louise. "The Stone." *The New Yorker*, September 2, 2019. https://www.newyorker.com/magazine/2019/09/09/the-stone.

Giles, Paul. "Writing for the Planet: Contemporary Australian Fiction." In *The Planetary Turn: Relationality and Geo-aesthetics in the Twenty-First Century*, edited by Amy J. Elias and Christian Moraru, 143–159. Evanston, IL: Northwestern University Press, 2015.

Gross, Lawrence W. *Anishinaabe Ways of Knowing and Being.* New York: Routledge, 2014.

Held, Virginia. *The Ethics of Care: Personal, Political, and Global.* Oxford: Oxford University Press, 2006.

Henry, Gordon. *Spirit Matters: White Clay, Red Exits, Distant Others.* Duluth: Holy Cow! Press, 2022.

———. "Through the Refuge." *Iperstoria: Testi Letterature Linguaggi* 9 (Spring 2017): 101–102.

Keith, Joseph. "The Novel as Planetary Form." In *The Cambridge Companion to the Novel*, edited by Erik Bulson, 268–283. Cambridge: Cambridge University Press, 2018.

LaDuke, Winona. *All Our Relations: Native Struggles for Land and Life.* Chicago: Haymarket Books, 2015.

Miyoshi, Masao. "Turn to the Planet: Literature, Diversity, and Totality." *Comparative Literature* 53, no. 4 (2001): 283–297.

Moraru, Christian. *Cosmodernism: American Narrative, Late Globalization, and the New Cultural Imaginary.* Ann Arbor: University of Michigan Press, 2011.

———. "Decompressing Culture: Three Steps toward a Geomethodology." In *The Planetary Turn: Relationality and Geo-aesthetics in the Twenty-First Century*, edited by Amy J. Elias and Christian Moraru, 211–244. Evanston, IL: Northwestern University Press, 2015.

Rifkin, Jeremy. *The Empathic Civilization: The Race to Global Consciousness in a World in Crisis.* New York: Jeremi P. Tarcher/Penguin, 2009.

Rodríguez Magda, Rosa María. "The Crossroads of Transmodernity," translated by Jessica Aliaga-Lavrijsen. In *Transmodern Perspectives on Contemporary Literatures in English*, edited by Jessica Aliaga-Lavrijsen and José María Yebra-Pertusa, 21–29. New York: Routledge, 2019.

———. *Transmodernidad.* Barcelona: Anthropos, 2004.

Simpson, Audra, and Andrea Smith. "Introduction." In *Theorizing Native Studies*, edited by Audra Simpson and Andrea Smith, 1–30. Durham, NC: Duke University Press, 2014.

Simpson, Leanne Betasamosake. *As We Have Always Done: Indigenous Freedom through Radical Resistance*. Minneapolis: University of Minnesota Press, 2017.

———. *Dancing on Our Turtle's Back: Stories of Nishnaabeg Re-Creation, Resurgence and a New Emergence*. Winnipeg: Arp Books, 2011.

———. *The Gift Is in the Making: Anishinaabeg Stories*. Winnipeg: Highwater Press, 2013.

Spry, Adam. *Our War Paint Is Writer's Ink: Anishinaabe Literary Transnationalism*. Albany: State University of New York Press, 2018.

Treisman, Deborah. "Louise Erdrich on the Power of Stones." *The New Yorker*, September 2, 2019.

Viner, Katharine. "'We Must Not Return to the Pre-Covid Status Quo, Only Worse': An Interview with Naomi Klein." *The Guardian*, July 13, 2020.

Watts, Vanessa. "Indigenous Place-Thought and Agency amongst Humans and Non-Humans (First Woman and Sky Woman Go on a European World Tour!)." *Decolonization: Indigeneity, Education & Society* 2, no. 1 (2013): 20–34.

Wilson, Shawn. *Research Is Ceremony: Indigenous Research Methods*. Halifax: Fernwood Publishing, 2008.

Spider's Embrace

Louis Owens's Web of Identities in *Dark River*

David L. Moore

The canoe didn't move, the waters didn't flow, the grass . . . didn't grow.

—Louis Owens, *Dark River*

C hoctaw-Cherokee scholar and novelist Louis Owens addressed his theoretical and fictional writings to America's transnational challenges of identity and diversity, even as he negotiated specific historical oppressions that deepen those challenges. Poverty and marginality weave with Native American mixedblood realities in his creative loom. The larger American problem—and perhaps its eventual strength—has always been transnational, because of hundreds of Indigenous nations that met a handful of colonial nations on the shores, along the rivers, across the deserts, the mountains, and the plains, "from sea to shining sea." To illuminate these transnational dynamics is to rewrite simple frontier binaries in a more vital complexity, and thus to elude reductive frontier oppressions through expressive resistance. Owens critiques those transnational relations, even as he illuminates their bones and blood.

Pointedly, Owens focused on "the problem of identity . . . for American Indians," as they face "centuries of colonial and postcolonial displacement, often brutally enforced peripherality, cultural denigration . . . and systematic oppression."[1] Exposing such brutal centuries, he also mapped the ground of literary resolve: "The recovering or rearticulation of an identity, a process dependent upon a rediscovered sense of place as well as community, becomes in the face of such obstacles a truly enormous undertaking. This attempt is at the center of American Indian fiction."[2] As we shall see, Owens's own fiction ultimately finds a literary trick, a surprising trickster energy to finesse the enormity of that "truly enormous undertaking." In a world of "colonial and postcolonial displacement," his five novels attempt an agile, narrative mutability to rediscover that "sense of place." We will see how his last novel, *Dark River*, is an essential example of that process of rearticulation.

Owens's clarification of this attempt to recover, to rediscover, and to rearticulate identity and community amounts to an Indigenous aesthetic. Because Indigeneity and Indigenous nations precede modern national boundaries, even as they often conceive porous boundaries between human and more-than-human "nations" or "peoples," what Owens offers here amounts to a transnational aesthetic as well. Where Birgit Däwes refers to "a politically local and translocally informed perspective, an Indigenous rewriting of transnationalism" in Owens's fiction,[3] she indeed points to the novelist's own prior theoretical concerns with such transnationalism within what he calls "a spiritual tradition that escapes historical fixation, that places humanity within a carefully, cyclically ordered cosmos and gives humankind irreducible responsibility for the maintenance of that delicate equilibrium."[4] Where "humankind" is irreducibly responsible, Owens allows a fictional spectrum from humor to terror, though he tends to tip the balance more toward the comic than the tragic. As we shall see in *Dark River*, he explicitly allows authorial manipulation, as narrative chance, to maintain "that delicate equilibrium" in a startling, lighthearted, freeing affirmation of such responsibility between death and life.

I will apply Gerald Vizenor's neologism "narrative chance" to Owens's strategic use of self-reflexive dialogue in (re)structuring the narrative in process. Vizenor's term illuminates precisely the adventurous spirit of agency in Owens's fictional characters who rewrite their own text in its unfolding. "The postmodern opened in tribal imagination; oral cultures have never been without a postmodern condition that enlivens stories and ceremonies, or without trickster signatures and discourse on narrative chance—a comic utterance and adventure to be heard or read."[5] Vizenor here alludes to Jean-François Lyotard's *The Postmodern Condition*, defined as "incredulity toward metanarratives."[6] Lyotard suggests that realistic alternatives to dominant ideological structures would be specific "phrases," realistic expressions. Vizenor uses this theoretical frame to show how Native American writers, by their rephrasing of history and identity, cast off especially America's metanarrative of manifest destiny. They replace that vast ideological fantasy of dispossession with specific tribal narratives on specific ground.

These energizing dynamics of identity, place, and community that Owens identifies in modern and ancient cultures may be why Owens's theoretical texts refer so often to the complex ironies of his friend and mentor, Vizenor, who weaves trickster stories of a "comic holotrope," a holistic strategy in stories that can trick even death. "The narrative voices or comic holotrope, the signifier in a trickster narrative, is signified in *chance*," as Vizenor puts it.[7] His indispensable terms will resonate through this reading of Owens.

As a master of theory focusing on Indigenous perspectives through literature, Owens also applied his steady rage for resistance in his remarkably crafted fiction. Where literary expression does tend toward resolution in a narrative arc—in spite of modernist and postmodernist objections to closure—the strength of Owens's mixedblood messages in the novels becomes darkly comic, a set of small triumphs of life and story as resistance to settler colonial death. Owens affirms that contemporary mixedblood authors continue to celebrate their freedom, to "oust the inventions with humor, new stories, and the simulations of survivance," in the words of Vizenor's *Manifest Manners*.[8] As Owens shares this turn toward survivance with Vizenor and other Indigenous writers, his final gift may have been to underline by contrast the aesthetic and ethical values of life-giving freedom in a darkly comic mode.

In framing some of these edges of context for Owens's last fiction, it is worth noting that *Dark River* gestures toward ethnographic content to cast a broad Indigenous cultural background, but Owens does not foreground traditional cultures in this text. Following his lead, I am not delving here into literary ethnography of Apache or Choctaw contexts, rather offering a close reading of Owens's assiduous crafting of imagery that leads to the complex finale. There are nods in *Dark River* to ancient Southwestern tales of Monster Slayer, for instance, and we shall look in detail at how Owens weaves Grandmother Spider intricately through the narrative, but he does so without tribal specificity. Indeed, where Jessie refers obliquely to Monster Slayer, "the boy . . . who slew all the monsters there," Shorty, fifty pages later, affirms, "I'm slaying monsters."[9] Certainly Owens generates mythic dimensions to the story, and we will look at those through his imagistic lens. Yet his fictional purposes, with the protagonist as a Choctaw outsider in an Apache community, allow the narrator to remain, "a stranger" who would "know only the surface,"[10] as we shall see in more detail. Indeed, claiming distance as a value, Jake speaks directly against cultural appropriation,[11] in a clearly authorial intrusion reflecting an ethos of cultural respect: "The people of Black Mountain had stories about beings who lived up in the peaks, but he'd deliberately shut his ears to all that from the beginning. It wasn't his culture, and it wasn't any of his business."[12]

Accordingly, as the text of the novel avoids specular "local color" or cultural display, I will consider a structural, textual analysis rather than an explication of Apache or Choctaw cultural contexts, even as they do resonate in the novel. Here I begin my rereading of the novel with my own discomforts—initially the ending did not work for me, seeming to arbitrarily abandon threads of the plot. Yet the closer I looked, the more I understood its radical logic in the "tradition" of a *nouvel roman*, literally throwing off narrative structures of plot and character to affirm narrative chance. And for Owens to do so within an otherwise seemingly conventional murder mystery further claims levels of iconoclasm that explode not only the genre (a topic for another essay), but, as we shall see, the boundary between life and death.

Where other readers might explore vital cultural and genre resonances, here I will look, first, at the novel's gradual emphasis on specific maternal, grandmotherly aspects of Grandmother Spider. Second, the novel's remarkable finale asks for elucidation of the characters' and the author's individual, and, by extension, Indigenous, sovereignty that chooses to reconstruct the story by narrative chance. And as we will see, both this benign evolution of spider imagery and this reappropriation of self-representation must function through a tone of profound irony. Thus we will focus on mirth rather than myth in Owens's text.

Where we saw him invoking Vizenor's discourse of a "trickster narrative," it certainly would not be wrong to apply Owens's description of "contemporary mixedblood authors" to himself, as he and they "celebrate their freedom" with "new stories." We shall see further, in the anticlimactic finale of *Dark River*, how that narrative dynamic celebrates a special freedom of Indigenous agency to retell the tale.

Thus when Owens "wrote the book" on the Native American novel, *Other Destinies: Understanding the American Indian Novel* (1992), he indeed sketched his own aesthetic, which amounts to a literary land ethic. Speaking of Louise Erdrich's best-selling first novel, in the context of N. Scott Momaday's Pulitzer-winning first novel, he writes,

> This web of identities and relationships arises from the land itself, that element
> that has always been at the core of Native Americans' knowledge of who they are
> and where they come from. Central to Native American storytelling, as Momaday

has shown so splendidly, is the construction of a reality that begins, always, with the land.[13]

In Owens's own work, as in Momaday, Erdrich, Vizenor, and so much of the literature Owens critiqued, the narrative structures of resilience and survivance on the land weave through characters and plots where political or psychological defeat strikes individuals and communities when that land is lost. Dispossession is marginalization. Dispossession is alienation. The literature maps a history and its psychology based in Native ground and its losses. He continues in his discussion of Erdrich: "In Erdrich's fiction, those characters who have lost a close relationship with the earth—and specifically with that particular geography that informs a tribal identity—are the ones who are lost."[14]

Yet in a trickster universe, things are always more complicated than binaries of loss or redemption, tragic or comic, as we see in his further discussion of Erdrich, where Owens quotes another of her statements. In the epigraph above, Erdrich marks the simultaneous sense of strength and fragility inherent in a web of relations. Interdependence and relationality may give life, but they also make it vulnerable: "When you're in the plains and you're in this enormous space, there's something about the frailty of life and relationships that always haunts me."[15] I cite Erdrich's interview here specifically cited by Owens to highlight precisely that their shared sense of an Indigenous web of identities and relationships is not, in many Native writers, merely a comforting matrix for their concerns. This haunting must be an honest if difficult, and certainly pragmatic, recognition of one's smallness, both physical and psychological, "in this enormous space." It is existential, and always political, thus both philosophical and historical.

Owens's broad and personal collisions of individuality and community, frailty and relationality, here bring into focus the simple question of this essay within this larger Indigenous literary context: How does Owens transform stories "about the frailty of life and relationships" into "the core of Native Americans' knowledge of who they are and where they come from" that "arises from the land itself"? How does the land transform frailty into identity?

Where Diane Glancy refers to Owens's "multirootedness of being,"[16] his multi-rooted complexity is both historical and conceptual. As Owens put it, "I have learned to inhabit a hybrid, unpapered, Choctaw-Cherokee-Welsh-Irish-Cajun mixed space in between. I conceive of myself today not as an 'Indian,' but as a mixedblood, a person of complex roots and histories."[17] Amid such complexity, how does Owens translate death on the land into life on the land? Or, better, in his stories and essays, how does he trick death into life? Erasure into agency?

Is it finally a mere mystery? Or is it a joke? A trickster trick? Owens does hint at mystification in his murder mysteries. In an earlier essay on Owens's novel *Bone Game*, I mapped how he enlists Indigenous mystery—as against colonialist mystification—to face death and affirm mysterious life.[18] On the one hand, one may celebrate a leveling perception of mystery, allowing it a place in the experience of life and death. Indigenous spirituality can vitalize rocks, water, trees, all persons. On the other hand, colonial strictures of life and death tend to suffer mystification by hierarchical power relations. The colonizing church mystifies human relations of life and death to serve the colony, the state apparatus of empire. With many variations, such categories of mystery and mystification may be manipulated to fit comic and tragic narrative structures, where Indigenous life triumphs or colonial death triumphs.

This dynamic of choice in narrative turn and structure is one subtext when Owens, Vizenor, and many other Indigenous novelists so often enlist the comic mode to elude oppressive tragedy. Vizenor's famous neologism "terminal creeds" encapsulates even as it devastates the settler colonial metanarrative for the so-called vanishing Indian, and "terminal creeds" names the context cut through by Owens's *Dark River*.[19] In this study, I will enlist Owens's comic dismissal of what he called in his criticism the "'Chief Doom' school of literature,"[20] to map in *Dark River* how he jettisons even Indigenous mystery—because of its romantic baggage—in favor of something akin to arbitrary postmodern choice, or better, "narrative chance."

For Owens, with his family background among agricultural workers in California's central valley, issues of individual mortality and cultural survivance often translate into class conflict. To face directly the "poverty and hopelessness" that "are such unavoidable realities in Indian existence," Owens constructs a murder mystery plot in *Dark River* with a number of subterfuges to throw off "the modernist tradition of naturalistic despair, of which the Indian is the quintessential illustration," as he puts it in his theoretical magnum opus, *Mixedblood Messages*.[21] As we shall see especially in the finale of *Dark River*, through both characterization and bizarre plot shifts, through comic cinematic allusions and incongruous "ruins of representation," to cite Vizenor,[22] Owens rejects what he critiques in "the Indian as a static referent," an easy target for white guilt.[23] He messes with stereotypical representation, both in content and in form. He enlists what could be the postmodern "trace" glimpsed by Jacques Derrida, or the shifting referentiality unveiled by Roland Barthes, pushed further by the "trickster discourse" of Gerald Vizenor, to rewrite the colonial narrative where Indians do have a choice to survive.

In his critique of "Chief Doom," Owens resuscitates an alternative, what he calls "the threat to the white psyche" of American readership,[24] by reimagining an Indian as a moving target in the unpredictable plot, unpredictable and surprising because of Indigenous agency. Thus, instead of standing still as the doomed, stoic Indian facing—then bowing before—the cold winds of manifest destiny, the characters in the novel's finale playfully choose alternatives. This affirmative turn in the anticlimax of *Dark River* is precisely what Owens suggests in *Mixedblood Messages*: to pose a fluid, changeable alternative to "the Indian" in Herman Melville, William Faulkner, and Ernest Hemingway by allowing vital Indigenous figures to "remain unacceptably disembodied and amorphous, internalized and unsignified."[25] By a trick of uncertainty—shall we call it a kind of "frailty"?—Native Americans may be less easily absorbed into America's melting pot. The ground of weakness becomes a strength. Existential frailty in a web of identities becomes a tool of political force.

Such an inversion of the dialectics of power was of course familiar to Owens, as such strategies are generally more visible from the margins than from the center. This radical aesthetic of his final novel, (dis)embodying mystery to elude the colonial machine, echoes in the finale of his earlier novel *Bone Game*, as well, where the smiling mythic gambler walks "slowly away toward the trees."[26] Unlike the easy target of Chief Doom, Owens's traditional Indian in a modern setting remains disembodied, a moving target, a threat. In *Dark River*'s not-so-grand finale, the Apache characters banter ironically and light-heartedly about their own "last cameo" appearances and an alternative "surprise ending" in a casually postmodern, though positive, self-reflection, a Pirandello-esque exposé of authorial manipulation in the characters' voices.[27] Stepping out of the text into authorial context, they step out of the metanarrative that the novel's narrator critiques and into their own chosen "phrases" (to summon Lyotard) or "narrative wisps" (to summon Vizenor, below) and thus into agency. Their tone and their almost gleeful energy again throw off "the modernist tradition of naturalistic despair."[28] We will look more closely at this strategic lack of closure in that final text and context, but first a brief further discussion in another context of the *Dark River* that leads to no ending, that flows on forever. To navigate that river, which we may only glimpse, we must look closer at Chief Doom, who is shorthand for no exit, for no choice, for the vanishing Indian, for lack of Indigenous agency, for manifest destiny.

In *Mixedblood Messages*, Owens offers a devastating if cryptic critique of what he calls the "'Chief Doom' school of literature," based on the character Ikkemotubbe, or Doom, in some of Faulkner's stories, and that resurfaces even in fiction by modern and contemporary Native writers. What we find in the modern versions of "Chief Doom" are caricatures inherited from the centuries-old tradition of the doomed, tragic savage. These "new" Indian novels, by "authentic" Indian authors, articulate in sometimes extraordinarily well-disguised form the familiar stereotype of the vanishing American, the crucial difference being that white people no longer have to shoot or hang the Native, who is quite willing to do the job him- or herself. "Most crucially, they are human beings incapable of asserting any control over their lives, infantilized and cirrhotic, waiting to exit stage west."[29]

Lightly punning on Hollywood Westerns and dime novels—and their full two centuries of pop culture structuring American ideology—here Owens skewers the stoic vanishing Indian stereotype. He exposes the weak, footloose fantasies of a manifest destiny that can only contend with its own projections of a weaker foe.

In his 1998 study, *Mixedblood Messages*, Owens continues his withering scorn, as he sets the stage for his 1999 novel, *Dark River*, and its surprise ending(s) by contrast:

> What do Euramerican readers want to see in works by American Indian authors? They want what they have always wanted, from Fenimore Cooper to the present: Indians who are romantic, unthreatening, and self-destructive. Indians who are enacting, in one guise or another, the process of vanishing. Borrowing from William Faulkner, that epic poet of inexorable, tragic history, I'll call this the "Chief Doom" school of literature. It seems we cannot escape it, even when it is manifested as a form of inner-colonization.[30]

It is striking that Owens has been reflecting not only on Indian stereotypes projected onto Indian representation by the colonizers, but also an internalized oppression within the colonized, within Native writers themselves. Once exposed, this internalization of oppression actually may become a ground of agency—again frailty becomes strength—because it remains within the Indigenous self where choices and narrative chance remain.

Owens concludes a theoretical chapter of nuanced discussion in *Mixedblood Messages* that reports on an array of Native American novelists, from the first, John Rollin Ridge in 1854, through Mourning Dove in 1927, John Joseph Matthews and D'Arcy McNickle in the 1930s, N. Scott Momaday in 1969, Leslie Marmon Silko starting in the 1970s, Louise Erdrich and Gerald Vizenor in the 1980s, and Sherman Alexie in the 1990s—all weaving through a careful discussion of representations of tragedy and despair as they may or may not reinforce the stereotype:

> I believe the most popularly and commercially successful Native American works thus far are marked by a dominant shared characteristic: They are the direct heirs of the modernist tradition of naturalistic despair, of which the Indian is the quintessential illustration, as we see clearly in Faulkner and Hemingway.[31]

Owens is calling for representations of Indians in fiction that do not conform to America's perennial ideology of the vanishing Indian, but he does so while clearly acknowledging the difficulty of finding a different discourse. (Such a "trickster discourse" is a foundation for his admiration of Gerald Vizenor's originality.) By exposing how the veneer of "the modernist tradition of naturalistic despair" tends to perpetuate vanishing—even in "commercially successful Native American works"—Owens guides us to the *Dark River*.

For a close reading of *Dark River* in the shadow of Chief Doom and of Owens's nuanced uses of "frailty" as power, we must begin with irony. Irony is everything in a comic mode that transgresses tragedy. Early on in the novel, we thus meet wisecracking Jessie James (his name its own set of multiple ironic reversals), as the protagonist Jake's young, college-educated friend—who not only is selling vision quests to white people through his VQE, Vision Quest Enterprises, but who insists, straight-faced, that a vision is "guaranteed." Owens riffs on New Age cultural appropriation, made worse by an Indian doing it:

> Jessie looked serious. "Four thousand for a minimum of five days, vision guaranteed. Two for the short, three-day version, no guarantee. Have you seen those great books by Ed McGaa, Eagle Man? He's got sample prayers, something he calls a Lakota Mother Earth Relationship Word List, a sweat lodge recipe, lists of Indian names white people can give themselves, everything you need to be a spiritual Indian."

This ironic checklist for misappropriation of sacred earth relations is punctuated by Jake's concise repartee: "Nobody can guarantee a vision."[32]

Indeed, Jessie's absurd insistence, "Sure I can," becomes absorbed in Owens's web of fiction within a few pages where we find that Jessie, clearly a trickster figure, is "sort of the tribal youth counselor," educating the rez kids with a film series to cut through Hollywood stereotypes such as Disney's *Pocahontas*, even as he plays basketball with them.[33] Jessie explicitly affirms that he's helping the Indian children "develop their sense of irony" for survivance: "I'm just trying to make sure the kids know their roles, develop their sense of irony so they'll know how to function, how to adapt like Russell Means."[34] Irony equals survival for kids in a world where history would erase you.

If Jessie provides more than comic relief in his affirmation of ironic trickster choices of survivance, Owens pushes his role even further to embody the ultimate reversal, or, less grand, the simple defusing or liberating of death. Although he dies just over a quarter of the way through the plot, Jessie continues to discuss the action through to the ending. Not only lightening that darkness, by getting shot in his acrylic wolf costume—when he is mistaken for a wolf—and returning as a wisecracking ghost, Jessie also provides the initial pattern of dialogue for reflexive metafiction in Owens's project to demystify the novel itself, to probe the membrane between literature and life. When the characters interpose their choices on the narrative, it implicates the reader to choose as well.

Further still, Jessie launches the novel's metafictional commentary with self-reflection on his own death—"'I realize we're supposed to be afraid of the dead,' he said. 'But it's okay . . . I'm sort of not really dead or something'"[35]—hilariously understating the sudden links between fictional and spiritual worlds.

In addition to Jessie, especially to structure the ending of the novel, Jake needs another friend, Shorty Luke, who, like Jessie, is a constant vehicle for irony, especially with the running joke as "the other surviving twin."[36] Yet because Shorty is also "one of the Apache elders," as Birgit Däwes points out, he "has taken the responsibility for the story within the novel and thus also has the last word." Däwes points to Shorty's responsibility itself as a natural, "fluid continuum, like the eponymous river" in the narrative.[37] I agree that the novel's form enlists such river imagery, but we see at the ending that there is further content in Shorty's fluid responsibility, a crucial ability, to choose narrative directions. Owens affirms not only natural and cultural affinities between Shorty's identity and the river itself, but also existential and political opportunities in this Indigenous moment of storytelling.

We are first introduced to his integrity, indeed "a feeling of power and authority" in Shorty, playfully, through the sounds of his chainsaw, "his Stihl 026" bucking firewood "in the aspen up the hill. No one else at Black Mountain owned a saw that sounded so good." On this palpable wavelength, Jake's thoughts verify that Shorty, "who knew every corner and crevice of the mountains," is "the only one besides Jessie whom he could remotely consider a friend on the reservation."[38] Both the mountain crevices and Shorty's reliable friendship will prove vital to the novel's nonterminus.

Not only do Jessie and Shorty function, along with Jake, as the author's ironic mouthpieces for social critique, but their doses of comic relief and good-natured outlook balance the main character's often dark, morose, even violent presence. Jake's post–traumatic stress disorder as an (ironically) "adjusted" veteran of the Viet Nam War becomes an early theme that structures Owens's dialectic of frailty and power in a personality of pain and trauma.[39] Reminiscing back twenty years to when he met his now ex-wife Tali, "the topless dancer [who] had become a tribal matron" across these decades, Jake exposes the strength of his weakness in a remarkable road-trip passage:

> The Saguaro Club had beckoned him just as the desert had, and he'd driven toward the tilting red cactus like he'd been driving toward the tilting red sun every day since being discharged in New Jersey. He'd drunk and fought his way across Amarillo to Albuquerque and down to Las Cruces and through Silver City, Patagonia, and Tucson before turning the Chevy pickup north to Phoenix. . . . So he'd circled like Old Buzzard heading north finally to be beckoned aside by the falling cactus and find himself sitting twelve beers later watching the most beautiful woman he'd ever seen take off her clothes on a little stage in a small barroom on a street where rags of paper hung to real cholla cactuses and dark-skinned men and women littered doorways.[40]

This American road ends at the "most beautiful," yet beside "doorways . . . littered" by the down-and-out, here dancing together in Owens's precise juxtaposition of the novel's polarities. Which is stronger? The truth of beauty or the truth of injustice? Openness or darkness? Love or fear? It's the question of the *Dark River*. Owens's minimalist depiction of the ensuing bar fight incited by a drunken Jake not only invokes the violence in this traumatized man, but it leads with flawless fictional rhythm to one of the most romantic—yet still minimalist, and thus humorous— moments in a novel of ironic insights. Unexpectedly, Tali shows up outside his jail cell after the fracas:

Her hands were on her bluejeaned hips, and her black hair hung over the pearl snaps of a sky-blue western shirt. . . . "You're so fucking stupid you must be some kind of Indian," were the first words she said to him. Two months later they were married.[41]

Short and sweet generates a terse irony that by contrast emphasizes the maximus of their abiding love and passion. Their erotic longing and delight are narrated clearly in the novel through Tali's "after-dark visits to his little shack,"[42] certainly to help transform darkness into something welcoming, that is, the central project of the plot.

Owens gives over this work of transforming darkness to feminine forces in the structure of the narrative, from Grandmother Spider, to the flow of the river, to Tali herself. Thus, playing further in this same direction of warmth and "home," Owens's imagery, like Tali's river imagery as a dancer, again links Tali herself through the land itself to the spirits:

The woman who came to him once or twice a month when not even the reservation dogs were barking was a different woman, not a wife. When she came silently to his door, opened it, and glided across to the room where his bed was, he invariably felt as though one of the spirits had come down from the mountain, what the people called *gaan*, and he knew it was a blasphemous thought. That shadowy woman had nothing at all to do with the dancer who had brought him home.[43]

The resonance of "home" becomes pivotal in the plot to the apparent purposes of the novel. Owens weaves "home" for Jake with cumulative imagery of a spider's web.

To offer the plot a tension just shy of fulfillment, so near and yet so far, all of Tali's family have moved into their "home," into this web of relations for Jake, including her "three children, crazy aunt," and "a swarm of other relatives," where she and Jake have built decades of a life on her fictional Black Mountain Apache reservation.

The fact that this web of family relations only partially sustains him sets the pattern for his mixed relations to the spider imagery itself that would weave that web. Although Jake, a Choctaw from southeastern woodlands, gets to know these arid southwestern lands, working for years as the tribal game warden, yet he comes to feel "foreign and strange in the desert. There weren't enough shadows."[44] His expectations here affirm a value in the darkness itself, in "enough shadows" to hold mysteries. Darkness is a goal, as it becomes increasingly associated with the spider.

He even senses that he is in love with the dark river, an "other," rather than with his Apache wife. As the elder, Mrs. Edwards, counsels him,

> I saw it from the beginning. You fell in love with that river, not Tali. I heard them calling to you from the first day. That's why you never had to learn how to live with a real woman again, or real people. You knew that the other was waiting for you down there, and it was easier.[45]

The challenge for this war veteran, as perhaps for all veterans, is to weave back in, to reintegrate into society, "to live with . . . real people" beyond the dark river in the soldier's soul. Yet Owens takes the challenge through a further reversal, into a redefinition and embrace of the darkness itself. Many Indigenous tribes have ceremonies to ease warriors back into the domestic life of their clans, but not so much in modern America. So Jake must find an alternative.

> And after twenty years he had remained a stranger, he knew now, not just among the people of the tribe but even to his own wife. He knew the country, the creeks and dry streambeds, the creases and secrets of the river canyon, the wide mesas, but he knew only the surface.[46]

Linking these natural images with human value, and vice versa, Owens hints at Tali's larger significance, as the flowing feminine principle, in Jake's first glimpse of the stripper earlier in the plot: "and he marveled at the way all of her flowed in a continuous, dangerous circle like the eddy of a fast river."[47] Indeed, the "dark river" of the novel flows as more than a metaphor, weaving together disparate pieces of the plot in its mysteries of stillness and motion. "Nothing was ever simple, except the river."[48] In the dramatic context of a murder mystery, Owens plays with this web of relationality not only to cross boundaries, but actually to restructure the dividing lines and territories across "nations" of the human and the more-than-human worlds.

The dark beauty of the river itself in Owens's crafted prose thus becomes more than a backdrop to the human drama. It works as a character, again contesting ontologies and taxonomies, to drive the plot from the title to the finale. For example, near the end of the drama, one vivid descriptive passage touching the river launches a chapter comprised almost entirely of sharp dialogue between hostages and captors. "Scarcely two hundred yards across, close to the river, the canyon held the darkness grudgingly, while the lighter sky struggled to descend."[49] The problem with a critical term like "pathetic fallacy" is its Eurocentric assumptions that seeing consciousness in nature is a de facto fallacy. In this novel, if a dark canyon and a lighter sky struggle, they do so as part of a world teeming with awareness. Thus Owens immediately follows this descriptive line with the *un*awareness of Jensen, the bad guy, in contrast with the land: "'Okay,' he said. 'We don't know where the hell any of them are.'"[50] Between an animate river, canyon, and sky, on the one hand, and Jensen's impotent cursing, on the other, Owens constructs a perfect juxtaposition of kinds of consciousness. Indeed, the chaotic human dialogue that makes up the bulk of this ten-page chapter is deftly sandwiched between single paragraphs of Owens's naturalistic description, with the concluding paragraph rising to poetic, yet grounded, prose. The rattled dialogue ends with what, if taken out of context, could be a commentary on the human condition. Sam Baca, echoing Jensen at the start of the chapter, says to Two-Bears, "I don't know either. . . . I don't know a damned thing, and it's too late for that explanation you promised."[51] In the paragraph that directly follows, Owens allows the presence of the river to wash the reader, and perhaps the characters, clean of some human confusions:

> The river flowed in a long, gradual curve through the section of canyon they walked, cutting in and pooling deep against rough, black stone cliffs and then rippling into long whitened runnels that spread shallow from one pine-forested bank to another. Oak, chokecherry, locust, and other small brushy trees gathered close to the water, wound with wild grapevines that shone an intense green over the lightening gray white of the river stones along the far shore.[52]

Owens's sentences flow freely here, almost unpunctuated, like the river itself. Whether or not each of the characters benefits from the river flow, it states its presence here, as throughout the text. The steady fact of its knowing presence surrounds human ignorance and structures a fundamental irony of the novel between human disorder and natural order.

Owens's murder mysteries suggest how irony, in both its tragic and comic modes, works by a surprising exposure of relationality, of a set of relations that had not been visible but now comes suddenly to light. The ironic juxtaposition may be verbal or visual. Irony breaks and reshapes boundaries, linguistic, cognitive, social, psychological, even as it exposes them. There are endless examples of the equation between irony and exposure across the literary landscape, from William Shakespeare to Sherman Alexie. Owens employs such ironic surprise at almost every level of this fiction, from dialogue to description to commentary. One of his featured ironies is America itself, with its frail self-assurance, punctured here by the simple fact of tribal gaming, at the expense of old, white retirees. Jake observes the emperor's new clothes:

> The tribal casino blazed pink, green, and gold when he drove by, the lights like ax blades against the surrounding pines. Rivulets of people merged at the edge of the parking lot into a stream that flowed from lot to casino and back again, blue hair, baseball caps, and bald heads shining like various stars. . . . He'd never driven by the casino when it wasn't blazing, day or night. He'd gone inside only once, and had been forced back by the evil of the place. . . . The tribe was making a bundle, doing to the white world what that world had always done to Indians.[53]

The layers of this understated irony of Indian payback are not only hilarious, they are historic and political, a thorough reversal quietly doing its basic economic groundwork under blazing lights of "pink, green, and gold." The triumph of America's empire becomes its own weakness, its own shame.

These ironies in Owens, shifting the ground of American history and identity—where Indians now are the winners—are not incidental to this murder mystery. They are central. This fiction denies many of the Hollywood stereotypes at the now postmodern heart of American manifest destiny. Early on in the novel, as Jake contemplates the casino crowds, he watches as

> one council matron, Benecia Martinez, who lived in a house with no electricity or running water, held a stuffed mushroom with her pinkie finger extended. . . . He knew how much everyone enjoyed such a scene. They were playing the white man, a subtle and satirical amusement on the reservation.[54]

These musings on the part of the protagonist become explicit authorial commentary, where Jake concludes this paragraph: "Indian retribution was patient but inevitable."[55]

Here we have another example of what I have called elsewhere an Indigenous "radical patience," key to narratives by many Native novelists from Leslie Marmon Silko to Gerald Vizenor, where events flow like a river through larger cycles in the cosmos.[56] A trickster, or a storyteller in that tradition, knows those larger cycles and can map the dynamics of those larger tales, beyond the reach of "Chief Doom" in the American narrative.

The concluding pages of the novel lightly toss all of these dynamics up in the air, as Owens peels back panic from even the ultimate reversal: life into death. Let's remember Owens's emphasis on the persistence of the vanishing Indian stereotype, even as it arises in texts by Native American writers. Of some fictional Native protagonists, as we see in his critique of "Chief Doom," Owens, again, observed: "Most crucially, they are human beings incapable of asserting any control over their lives, infantilized and cirrhotic, waiting to exit stage west."[57] Thus it is here, on the issue of "asserting any control over their lives," on agency, that we may find another key to the crazy finale of Owens's final novel.

Let's look at two key elements that navigate *Dark River* toward that finale: first, this question of control in narrative chance; and, second, the question of how to love a spider. Both questions really are about the mystery of death.

Long before the anticlimax, the great dark spider weaves the plot, literally—but the characters, especially the male protagonist's young granddaughter, Alison, will break the pattern at the end—and it is worth emphasizing such a gender power shift here as the spider herself resonates with a triumphant feminine principle as Grandmother. Near the finale, Alison indeed inherits Jake's generational leadership:

> "Now we go home," Alison said [to the conflicted survivors at the river]. "No more stories. We'll follow you, Grandfather." [She says this to Jake's friend, Shorty, "the surviving twin."]
>
> Shorty looked at her carefully for a moment. "No, Granddaughter, it's your turn. You lead."
>
> Alison began walking, with the others following in a single line.[58]

This passing of the baton from aged and tired masculinity to young femininity occurs just six lines before the end of the novel, a turn that indeed further affirms Alison's announcement, "Now we go home." It is worth keeping in mind this final feminist—or, more specifically, neomatriarchal—gesture of the plot as we trace how Jake gradually became tuned to the feminine or maternal qualities of Grandmother Spider in preparation for his dramatic departure. The western Apache, like many tribes, including the Lenape, the Hopi, the Iroquois, and Owens's own Chickasaw, are matrilineal cultures. Hence this slight narrative twist weaves many layers—contemporary and ancient—as Owens structures the finale so that young Alison leads the survivors, "following in a single line," out of the Dark River canyon.

Early in the plot, Owens inserts feminine strength itself as it deals in life and death, to set up this key imagistic line of the feminine in the novel. A brief image of a human grandmother ringing the neck of a rooster, the neighbor's "arrogant old cock," who had "taken a particular liking to Jake,"[59] sets the dramatic stage, and sets the stakes, in opposition for the evolving imagery of Grandmother Spider. This is very first time we see the Apache elder, Mrs. Edwards, who knew "what a name meant" and who can see into Jake Nashoba's PTSD-troubled soul, with his Choctaw surname meaning "wolf."[60] As the rooster's cry fades, a shriek of "particularly deep-throated outrage that had emerged from the muffled sound of a cornered and caught chicken," the narrator muses on "the old, dark-skinned woman with silver braids to her waist . . . starting to pluck the chicken in defiance of the whole community, a community that had admired the rooster greatly."[61] Against any maternal comfort, Jake sees her as his enemy, because she sees his guilty conscience, his "Ghost sickness" from the war in Viet Nam. "But from the first he'd felt that the old woman was his implacable enemy, that she'd seen into his heart at first glimpse and knew his irremediable guilt."[62] The veteran's self-loathing must lift in order to see the grandmother's gifts.

Indeed the novel's mixed imagery of feminine power begins even earlier with Jake's grim memories of his own grandmother's stories, when as a child he was "hardening himself against them. The old woman stank, a smell of sweat, death, old age, forgetfulness, and chewing tobacco. She knew the meanings of those things that cut into the kerf of their lives . . . knew how to answer them, and feared nothing."[63] We shall watch how the plot of *Dark River* gradually softens Jake to her spiderly embrace.

After these human grandmothers, and midway through the plot, the spider herself makes a first major appearance, gradually shape-shifting in tone, though certainly not in a straight line toward love. When Jake, as game warden trying to stop a hunting party turned murderous, climbs on the cliffs above "the Dark" with a threat of rifles that "could train a night scope on him and he'd be dead," he finds a familiar hiding place, in the shelter of a spider protecting him while "everyone hunting him was now an enemy."[64]

The fissure made a shoulder-width chimney all the way to the top of the cliff face. Near the top of the chimney, a circular web stretched pale, shimmering strands across the space, and in the center of the web a great dark spider sat looking down at him, a bright star in the sky on either side of the wide legs.[65]

The image is straight out of arachnophobic horror films. Initially the reader is shocked to see the protagonist scrambling from one danger (guns) to another danger (spider legs), but the plot trains us otherwise. Although Owens allows the reader a reflex reaction of fear and loathing against such horror imagery—"Spiderwebs caught on his hands and swung across his face, and something glowed at him"—he here redirects that tension, in a crucial foreshadowing of the finale, toward something, if not comforting, yet certainly more positive:

> At first there was silence. Then once more he heard the river curling against and twisting around the rock face . . . and then became aware of another faint sound, a barely perceptible keening, songlike and delicate. It seemed to come from directly overhead. He turned his face upward and saw the web of the spider vibrating slightly, the large arachnid plucking the strands of her web.[66]

We are hearing spider music as "songlike and delicate," though here still ironically reflecting "a great dark spider" threat. We are also, with Jake, becoming fine-tuned to spiderly expression, an eight-legged consciousness. This moment and others yet more gentle will soften the anticlimax, nearly one hundred pages later, when "the earth had opened up, and two enormous mandibles framed by spider legs reached out and seized Jake. In a moment he was gone, dragged into a hole that closed at once."[67] Toward such an unexpected resolution in silent death, Owens sets the stage carefully and extensively here for the reader to choose a different reaction to the spider—respect, if not affection. We shall see at the end how the other characters then continue for a couple of pages of denouement—claiming their own respect by asserting their own alternative narrative choices, their narrative chance.

Owens animates such unconventional, benign spider imagery especially in a dream of Jake's walking in deep grass, as the author is clearly setting up the reader for a strangely harmonious, "songlike and delicate" resonance with Jake's final disappearance into the arachnid's arms:

> There was only a small black hole in the ground between the clumps of grass. He began to walk away, but a voice said, "What are you looking for?"
>
> "I'm looking for my own people," he said. "I've been gone a long time, and I have a long way to go."

"Don't you realize that no one can go to that place?" the voice said.

Jake looked down to see a black spider at the top of the hole. "Come into my house, Grandson," the spider said. "Don't be frightened."[68]

Her last line here might be that central theme of defanging the darkness in the novel: replacing fear with—what?—love? The comfort of Grandmother Spider, a divine creative figure in some Indigenous traditions, expands into an erotic fantasy in Jake's dream—again a new layer of connotations that the reader can bring to the final imagery of spiders:

> How can I go into such a tiny hole, Jake thought, but he closed his eyes and when he opened them he was in a warm, lighted room. . . . An old woman stood smiling at him, and around the room lay beautiful young women, all naked with dark, shining hair and smooth, sleek-looking bodies. Their breasts were small and taut, and as the girls rested on backs and elbows watching him, he could see that they were smiling. He thought of his wife.[69]

Owens manages to transform a sexual fantasy, within an Indigenous mythic context of Spider Woman, into a deepening characterization within the plot. Further, when playful banter and teasing ensues, amid "a murmur of laughter in the room" as Jake begins to undress, the old Grandmother Spider speaks to the wound of grief in his veteran's soul: "Now you can rest. You're very tired, poor boy."[70] It is safe to say that ultimately this moment of compassionate juxtaposition between sex and grief not only defuses arachnophobia, it defuses death itself, indeed giving "life" to "death" in a radical reversal that gives light and warmth to a soldier who so deeply needs to rest in peace.

The reversals are almost complete here in Jake's dream, through more strands of imagery that Owens delicately weaves into the plot. The text seems to be delighting with the protagonist. Even the dirt where one would be buried becomes luminous in the dream:

> Jake looked down at the soft dirt of the cave. The girls were lounging bare in the same dirt, but they appeared to be immaculately clean and shining. He sank to his knees and then stretched out on the warm earth and fell into a dreamless sleep.[71]

Here, in another key reversal, the dream ends as Jake falls asleep—reestablishing the prior dream of Grandmother Spider as a waking reality. Sleep and waking interpenetrate, just as death and life must for this plot to unfold. This micro form of Owens's short chapter fits the novel's macro content by familiarizing the unfamiliar, by softening the afterlife. "Don't be frightened."

The fact that Owens, two dozen pages further toward the finale, returns Jake in yet another dream to "the old woman" who toggles preposterously into "a huge black spider . . . its mandibles working actively,"[72] underlines the author's literary efforts to transform a generally threatening arachnid image into a presence that not only is nonthreatening, but is actually benevolent—and further, not only a spider, but a human and humane grandmother in Jake's longing. Owens and the spider even play with alternative reader responses—in narrative chance—explicitly, in a layered dream image where Grandmother Spider has woven dresses for the girls out of the colors of Jake's own belt. This slight shift to alternative plot imagery forecasts the proliferation of narrative chance(s) taken at the finale.

> "See what wonderful dresses I made of it," the spider said, waving two legs toward the girls.
>
> Jake felt himself start to gag, but the feeling went away at once.
>
> "You prefer the other one?" the spider said. Instantly she was the thin old woman again.[73]

This very process of projecting and choosing narrative roles—spider or grand-mother, warrior or lover, death or life—becomes the woven plot itself. And the novel does not shrink from painting these extremes: "I hate you. . . . I love you," Tali declares.[74] Or, "He was the world's enemy. 'I will kill the world,'" Jake muses.[75] Yet they each "prefer the other one," as Grandmother puts it, and choose to take their chances in a dark narrative affirming life.

Thus in his dreams, Jake acclimates himself and the reader to the difficulties of such a choice, and to accept the anticlimax as something far more than a B horror movie, where, again, "two enormous mandibles framed by spider legs reached out and seized Jake."[76] Instead of some dramatic fight at the conclusion, he and we have been prepared to accept his soldier's fate as blessed, even erotic, rest, especially against the worst expectations, as when the actual old Apache woman in the plot, Mrs. Edwards, had declared to her niece, just prior to Jake's second dream:

> Jacob Nashoba was always lost, Tali. . . . There was never anything we could do. . . . Many of us are lost for some part of our lives, but if we are lucky and have help

we can find our way back. . . . But some people never have a chance. They're too far from where they began, too far from their homes, too far from their people. Strangers can't help them. They forget the stories they need. Jacob is one of those.[77]

These grim words set Jake's ex-wife, Tali, on an even more determined pursuit to help him, partly through touch, but they also set in contrast the opposite logic for the book's last line to work against "lost," reflecting on the comforting cocoon of Grandmother Spider: "It is said that Jacob Nashoba went home."[78]

At the end, we never hear from Jake beyond death—in direct contrast with Jessie's speaking and playfully shape-shifting ghost. The text offers a dark silence. What thus is remarkable about this concluding line, in addition to its narrative chance consummating the spider imagery woven around Jake's need for (eternal) rest, is its finality or closure. It arises after the two-page denouement, which we will look at further below, comprised of self-reflexive dialogue, in that process of narrative chance or creative choice. Thus we can extend to the finale what we saw earlier in Gerald Vizenor's aesthetical-ethical-political principle of narrative chance.

> These stories are serious and comic, numerous narrative wisps that controvert hyperrealities. Tribal literatures are burdened with colonialism and tragic world views; however, there is a curious humanism in tribal narratives on minacious consumerism. Serious attention to cultural hyperrealities is an invitation to trickster discourse, an imaginative liberation in comic narratives; the trickster is postmodern.[79]

Just as the threat of "minacious" or menacing "consumerism"—that is, the culture of colonial corporate capitalism in modern America—is liberated and humanized by "tribal narratives," so Owens has liberated and humanized the image of Grandmother Spider, opening the door for Jake as protagonist to go to his just reward in the earth.

In a further shift of narrative energy, of narrative chance, like Vizenor's "imaginative liberation in comic narratives," at the very moment when those "two enormous mandibles framed by spider legs reached out and seized Jake," the text shifts instantly into what may be called a defamiliarizing denouement. Suddenly the secondary characters, all standing on the shore of the Dark River, reflect on the now concluded development of the plot. With Jessie now a (speaking) ghost and with Jake now seized and disappeared (lovingly?) by the spider, with both thus unavailable as narrative points of view, Owens turns to Jake's only other friend, Shorty, to lead us out through his narrative choices—though, as we noted, Shorty soon defers to Alison for the final honors.

As soon as Jake, without a sound, "was gone, dragged into a hole that closed at once," the very next line shifts back from authorial narration to dialogue. Shorty directly comments on his own narrative choices for the text, as narrative chance, referring to the giant spider's abduction of the protagonist, as though he and the characters themselves, not the prior narrator, and not the author, have written this script:

> "My idea," Shorty said [referring to Jake's welcome abduction by the spider].
> "Good one," Jessie [as a ghost] replied admiringly.
> Shorty turned to Alison. "Don't worry, your grandfather has gone home."[80]

Although Owens deftly inserts more narrative action, indeed a brief, martial arts fight scene between the French woman, Sandrine, and "the bad guy," Jensen, yet the self-reflexive dialogue continues. Added to the fictional fun is the fact, again, that Jessie, fully present in this scene, has actually died many chapters previously. Here, after "Sandrine, pirouetting on the ball of her left foot, moved in a full circle until the heel of her right boot struck Jensen hard on the temple"—knocking Jensen's rifle away—the reflexive banter continues as they tie him up. These lines of dialogic metafiction exemplify multiple layers of self-reflexivity, consciousness, and agency in both the plot and the penning of the tale:

> "Maybe we should have lightning hit him while he's tied," Jessie said.
> "Maybe you should go away now, Jessie," Shorty replied. "I think it's time for a poignant scene in which you have to go to the land of the dead, leaving your loved ones behind."
> "No," Alison yelled. "Not yet."[81]

Ultimately affirming their Indigenous agency, the fictional characters thus debate alternative outcomes, their narrative chances, in a pattern of self-reflexive dialogue that actually preceded the "enormous mandibles." The plot even reverses the violence of killing of the bad guy:

"Too predictable," Shorty Luke said. "The minute Two-Bears showed up back there at camp with that rifle and started following you, everybody knew this would happen. Let's try it different. Eighty-six that and do a retake."[82]

Invoking a "retake" as though they are film directors and script writers, the characters themselves are constructing their own narrative, with even the bad guy getting a say, to the extent that narrative chance becomes narrative choice, lightened or enlightened by comic relief. Even spilled blood disappears in a miracle of narrative flexibility.

"You mean I'm not supposed to be shot again?" Jensen said, getting to his feet. "That's a fucking relief." The blood had disappeared from his camouflage shirt except for that around the arrow wound.

"Maybe," Shorty said. "But you shouldn't swear so much, white man."

"What about Jake?" Jessie put in.

"Well, Jake's not predictable, or hackneyed, as they say. Seems pretty original to have him down in a hole like that. He's the hero, right?"

"Maybe the wolf should tear out Jensen's throat," Jessie offered, becoming the wolf as he spoke.

"Spirit wolves don't do that," Shorty said.[83]

In addition to the reflexive references to Jake as "the hero" of the tale, even while it is unfolding, Shorty's repartee to Jessie's more-than-magical-realism as ghost-wolf forms another crucial, ethical context for Jake's rendezvous with the earth between the "enormous mandibles."

Early on, as we saw, the narrative made a keen point about Jake's surname: "Nashoba, 'wolf' in Choctaw, was his name, his grandfather's name, too, so maybe it meant something. Who could know?"[84] Now we read Shorty's affirmation of an ethics beyond the vicious stereotypes of wolves: "Spirit wolves don't do that." Just as Native Americans are burdened by stereotypes enshrined in the Declaration of Independence as "marauding savages," so a wolf is expected to "tear out Jensen's throat." Owens—by his characters' narrative chance—rewrites that wolf script even as it is unrolling, and precisely in a way that shifts the wolf-hero from a savage to a gentle spirit. Thus Jake, the hero, may enter the gentle embrace of Grandmother Spider as a kindred spirit, without resistance, a veteran healed of violence.

And thus Shorty makes illuminating choices that point in conclusion to the mythic dimensions of the actions. When they need something to tie the murderous hands of Jensen, Shorty's passing comment is telling.

> "Tie his hands," Shorty said to . . . Alison.
>
> "With what?"
>
> "There's always something," Shorty said. "There was always something to do it with."
>
> Alison looked around and then walked fifty feet toward the river, returning with an armful of wild grapevines.
>
> "See," Shorty said. "There's always something."[85]

Shorty's cryptic allusion, and more, his implicit trust, elevate the drama to mythic dimensions. "There was always something" available for survival provided in the old stories, in the myths of creation, and in tales of the people's emergence. His simple past verb, "was," alludes to mythic time, then soon contracted into a magical present—"There's always something"—to rely on in the abundance of creation. Shorty relies on that mythic trust, casting us back toward Jessie's earlier reference to the ancient Monster Slayer traditions of Southwestern tribes, "the boy with the bow and arrows came down to the earth and slew all the monsters there. Ha ha ha ha."[86] As always, Owens is understated, and here even minimalist, to balance the vast symbolism in comic mode. Yet in Shorty's moment of trust and practical faith at the conclusion, and in Alison's simple gathering of earth's provisions to defend themselves with wild grapevines, the text now links their postmodern narrative chance, their reflexively articulated choices, to the ancient oral traditional context, an appropriate though almost invisible gesture of mythic summary.

In a fictional cloud of irony, two primary structures have brought us home with Jake in this narrative. First, by weaving benign imagery to soften threats of darkness, Owens manages to invoke a farcical, dire, giant spider, transforming it into a grandmother's embrace. Jake's fear of frailty before death fades as the earth opens to receive him, de facto. Owens challenges the reader to see beyond standard expectations, blending ironic humor, the life and breath of laughter, with the spider of mythic meaning. Second, the characters, launched by Jessie's self-reflexive jokes, propelled by elders' storytelling energy in Shorty, and eventually led by young womanhood in Jake's granddaughter, Alison, actively rearticulate their own identities in the very process of rediscovering their "sense of place as well as community."[87] Frailty transforms into fluid, feminine, creative power of expression. They make their choices to live. On the ground of their reservation, ground that will embrace them all like a spider in death, Owens has brought them full circle to the dark river of imaginative liberation.

NOTES

1. Owens, *Other Destinies*, 4.
2. Ibid., 5.
3. Däwes, "'The Past Was a White Man's Illusion,'" 203.
4. Owens, *Other Destinies*, 20.
5. Vizenor, *Narrative Chance*, x.
6. Ibid., xiv.
7. Ibid., 189.
8. Vizenor, *Manifest Manners*, 39.
9. Owens, *Dark River*, 223, 271.
10. Ibid., 50.
11. For a more thorough discussion of cultural appropriation, see the essays in Moore, "Cultural Property in American Indian Literatures," Fall 1997 issue of *American Indian Quarterly*.
12. Owens, *Dark River*, 28.
13. Owens, *Other Destinies*, 193.
14. Ibid.
15. Erdrich quoted in Owens, *Other Destinies*, 19.
16. Glancy, "Letter to Louis," 291.
17. Owens, *Mixedblood Messages*, 176.
18. Moore, "'*Eran Muy Crueles*,'" 179–200.
19. Vizenor, *Bearheart*, 185. For a more thorough discussion of the comic mode in Native American literatures, see chap. 5, "The Last Laugh: Humor and Humanity in Native American Pluralism," in my monograph, *That Dream Shall Have a Name*.
20. Owens, *Mixedblood Messages*, 82.
21. Ibid., 72, 81.
22. Vizenor, "The Ruins of Representation," 7.
23. Owens, *Mixedblood Messages*, 85.
24. Ibid.
25. Ibid.
26. Owens, *Bone Game*, 241.
27. Owens, *Dark River*, 285.

28. Owens, *Mixedblood Messages*, 81.

29. Ibid., 82.

30. Ibid.

31. Ibid., 81.

32. Ibid., 25.

33. Ibid., 25, 30.

34. Ibid., 31.

35. Ibid., 143.

36. Ibid., 44.

37. Däwes, "'The Past Was a White Man's Illusion,'" 213.

38. Owens, *Dark River*, 19.

39. Ibid., 7.

40. Ibid., 32–33.

41. Ibid., 34.

42. Ibid., 19.

43. Ibid.

44. Ibid., 49.

45. Ibid., 45.

46. Ibid., 50.

47. Ibid., 33.

48. Owens, *Dark River*, 14.

49. Ibid., 244.

50. Ibid., 245.

51. Ibid., 252.

52. Ibid., 253.

53. Ibid., 51, 53.

54. Ibid., 65.

55. Ibid., 66.

56. In my essay "Silko's Blood Sacrifice: The Circulating Witness in *Almanac of the Dead*," I explore the dynamics of the novel's most radical claim, "the disappearance of all things European." The novel plays with a logic that makes such a claim tenable. By a redefinition of time and space, according to the Mayan calendar that forms the basis for the actual Almanac; by the identification of Indigenous lifeways with life cycles of time and space as animist, ancestral spirits; and crucially by the identification of Euro-American, colonialist lifeways with cycles of death. For example, old Calabazas muses on the old promises: "the world that the whites brought with them would not last. . . . All they had

to do was to wait. It would be only a matter of time." Silko's elders advocate what I would call a "radical patience" as resistance. See Moore, "Silko's Blood Sacrifice," 235.

57. Owens, *Mixedblood Messages*, 82.

58. Owens, *Dark River*, 285–86.

59. Ibid., 14.

60. Ibid., 18.

61. Ibid., 14–15.

62. Ibid., 29.

63. Ibid., 4.

64. Ibid., 190–91.

65. Ibid., 190.

66. Ibid., 190–91.

67. Ibid., 284.

68. Ibid., 235.

69. Ibid.

70. Ibid.

71. Ibid.

72. Ibid., 254.

73. Ibid.

74. Ibid., 89.

75. Ibid., 93.

76. Ibid., 284.

77. Ibid., 253–54.

78. Ibid., 286.

79. Vizenor, *Narrative Chance*, 9. Not a definition, I take his "hyperrealities" here to refer to the dominant metanarratives of corporate colonial history, where commodified "realities" are a "hyper" mask that might be exposed by humane trickster attention.

80. Owens, *Dark River*, 284.

81. Ibid.

82. Ibid., 282.

83. Ibid.

84. Ibid., 13.

85. Ibid., 284.

86. Ibid., 223.

87. Owens, *Other Destinies*, 5.

BIBLIOGRAPHY

Däwes, Birgit. "'The Past Was a White Man's Illusion': The Temporal Continuum and Trans/
   Nationalism in Louis Owens' *Nightland* and *Dark River*." In *Louis Owens: Writing Land
   and Legacy*, edited by Joe Lockard and A. Robert Lee, 201–19. Albuquerque: New Mexico
   University Press, 2019.

Glancy, Diane. "Letter to Louis." In *Louis Owens: Writing Land and Legacy*, edited by Joe
   Lockard and A. Robert Lee, 291. Albuquerque: New Mexico University Press, 2019.

Lockard, Joe, and A. Robert Lee, eds., *Louis Owens: Writing Land and Legacy*. Albuquerque:
   New Mexico University Press, 2019.

Lyotard, Jean-François. *The Postmodern Condition: A Report on Knowledge*. Translated by
   Georges Van Den Abbeele. Minneapolis: Minnesota University Press, 1988.

Moore, David L., ed. "Cultural Property in American Indian Literatures: Representation and
   Interpretation." Special issue, *American Indian Quarterly* 21, no. 4 (Fall 1997).

———. "'Eran Muy Crueles': Requirements of Madness in Louis Owens' *Bone Game*." In *Louis
   Owens: Writing Land and Legacy*, edited by Joe Lockard and A. Robert Lee, 179–200.
   Albuquerque: New Mexico University Press, 2019.

———. "Silko's Blood Sacrifice: The Circulating Witness in *Almanac of the Dead*." In *Leslie
   Marmon Silko: A Collection of Critical Essays*, edited by James Thorson and Louise Barnett,
   149–83. Albuquerque: New Mexico University Press, 1999.

———. *That Dream Shall Have a Name: Native Americans Rewriting America*. Lincoln:
   Nebraska University Press, 2013.

Owens, Louis. *Bone Game: A Novel*. Norman: University of Oklahoma Press, 1994.

———. *Dark River: A Novel*. Norman: University of Oklahoma Press, 1999.

———. *Mixedblood Messages: Literature, Film, Family, Place*. Norman: University of Oklahoma
   Press, 1998.

———. *Other Destinies: Understanding the American Indian Novel*. Norman: University of
   Oklahoma Press, 1992.

Vizenor, Gerald. *Bearheart: The Heirship Chronicles*. Minneapolis: Minnesota University Press,
   1990.

———. *Manifest Manners: Postindian Warriors of Survivance*. Hanover, NH: Wesleyan
   University Press / University Press of New England, 1994.

———, ed. *Narrative Chance: Postmodern Discourse on Native American Indian Literatures*.
   Albuquerque: New Mexico UP, 1989.

———. "The Ruins of Representation: Shadow Survivance and the Literature of Dominance."
   American Indian Quarterly 17.1 (1993): 7–30.

Cross-Worlds

The Sight and Sound of James Welch

A. Robert Lee

given interests that alight on patterns of Native self-dislocation with occasional if provisional hard-won recovery, James Welch would not readily be awarded a rosette for writing good-cheer fiction. But he would amply invite one for skills of narration, the command of story rhythm and exactness of detail, the interior mapping of his main players. His five novels, *Winter in the Blood* (1974), *The Death of Jim Loney* (1979), *Fools Crow* (1986), *The Indian Lawyer* (1990), and *The Heartsong of Charging Elk* (2000), each in how they draw on Blackfeet/ Gros Ventre, Oglala Sioux, Crow (ancestral antagonists to the Blackfeet), Navajo, or other tribal legacy, and as mainly carried in figures of mixedblood descent, leave no doubt of adroit orchestration in bridging detail into overall form.[1] For whether situated in time-now or time-was, Welch's neorealist narratives endow their flow of plotline with a hugely distinguishing power of lens. This quality of particularization in eye and ear invites best recognition, not the only but a quite presiding hallmark.

Welch indicates the general perspective of time and place in his poem "Blackfeet, Blood and Piegan Hunters":

If we raced a century over hills
that ended years before, people couldn't
say our run was simply poverty or promise for a better end.

We ended sometime
back in recollections of glory, myths,
that meant the hunters meant a lot
to starving wives and bad painters.[2]

Locale can be township Harlem and the cities of Bozeman, Billings, or Helena, or the Big Sky Montana of Little Rockies, Mission Canyon, Snake Butte, and Milk River, not to mention in *The Heartsong of Charging Elk* the Marseille of *le Midi*. More circumstantially, it can be on- or off-reservation housing, bar or prairie, football field or basketball court, state penitentiary or the European sites of the Buffalo Bill's Wild West show. Eye and ear in each assume character virtually in their own imaginative right, as his poem "Blackfeet, Blood and Piegan Hunters" bears witness in kind with virtually every other contribution to Welch's only verse collection, *Riding the Earthboy 40* (1970).

In play, throughout, is Welch's sense of worlds colliding, or at the very least overlapping. Sightlines are several: tribal worlds within tribal worlds as in the historic past of *Fools Crow*; worlds at the modern interface of America's Native and white worlds as in *Winter in the Blood*, *The Death of Jim Loney*, and *The Indian Lawyer*; America and France in *The Heartsong of Charging Elk*. One readily adds collisions of time, Native pasts negotiating their way into the present, or location, Native prairie to township or penitentiary. Welch, too, has been no reticent in addressing sexual worlds, Native men and women, Native men and white women, or kinship in the persons of Native sons and daughters and adults and children. In each his signature quality of particularization has been essential. Jim Barnes, Welch's Choctaw-heritaged fellow poet, gives emphasis to precisely this quality of exactitude in his "Postcard to James Welch in Missoula":

Remember when you were here . . .
You told us in a glance
the moving days are best, when sounds strike
the inner ear from places only the hawk
can name and some wild damned Indian,
eyes full of rainbows and fast jacks, *Achukma!*[3]

Phrasings like "eyes full of rainbows" and "inner ear" hold for virtually all of Welch's writing together, aptly, with the play of irony that such might indeed belong to "some wild damned Indian."

Winter in the Blood

If N. Scott Momaday's *House Made of Dawn*, the deserved winner of a Pulitzer in 1969, bespeaks landmark, it would be far from injustice to think James Welch's own first novel, *Winter in the Blood*, belongs in the company of a number of contemporaneous Native fictions. These notably, and among others, look to the lyric "homing-in" of Lesley Marmon Silko's *Ceremony* (1977) and surreal-peregrinatory fashioning of Gerald Vizenor's *Darkness in Saint Louis Bearheart* (1968).[4] In Welch's case here was a novel, a novella, born of Montana Blackfeet intimacy, that offers a virtuoso portrait of Native split and dislocation. But for all that it points to the losses, and for sure the pratfalls, of its unnamed narrator and the historic fractures of his family, it also positions them in relation to eventual yet unpietistic resighting and rehearing of tribal remembrance. The upshot is a beautifully styled dark-comic parable wholly in command of its constituent detail.

Midway the bemused narrator makes the near classic observation: "Again I felt that helplessness of being in a world of stalking white men."[5] It confirms all the novel's subtlety of tone, the modern role-reversal of an uncertain heir to Northern Plains hunter himself hunted. As serious as is the vision of the one contemporary Native life, it also holds itself up as laconic comedy of errors. Self-drift, drinking, absurd chance encounter, dream and fantasy, accusing shafts of memory, all shape the trajectory. To this end Welch develops a first-person voice full of quizzicality, at odds with itself, with family, and assuredly with the white world. From his return home past the borrow-pit, with its implication of earth lost or evacuated, to his mother, Teresa First Raise, and her new husband Lame Bull, and through to the epiphanous recognition of the blind Yellow Calf as his true Blackfeet grandfather as against "the half-breed Doagie,"[6] and the funny-serious burial of his grandmother, the narrator inhabits each of his several worlds at once. In none does he prevail, whatever the degree of understanding he has achieved at the novel's conclusion.

The one evokes literal Dodson, Montana, its township bars and commerce, along with his mother's Blackfeet/Gros Ventre Reservation valley holding of hay, alfalfa, and fishing country. Another, more internal, bears "the presence of ghosts,"[7] the haunting line of dynasty that includes the snowdrift drunken death of First Raise, his father, and of Mose, the fourteen-year-old brother mangled and then killed in a cattle roundup whom the narrator might once have saved. Yet another summons his Cree woman, whom he thinks to marry, who unmanningly steals his gun and razor, then haunts him through the memory of her teeth made green by drinking crème de menthe. Nature itself can seem to collude across each, "cockeyed" as Yellow Calf calls it, in which meadowlarks sing in mock-chorus, pheasants gabble, magpies as tricksters argue, a hawk shot by the narrator in childhood is remembered only for its unmoving tongue, his long-time horse Bird dies pulled down by mud, and the fish have disappeared from the river despite the efforts of white agri-scientists at repopulation. Displacement holds sway: "I was as distant from myself as a hawk from the moon."[8]

The story of Amos, the pet duck who survives as its siblings drown, offers the analogy of another family given over to self-drowning. The episode shadows forward to the early tribal widowhood and abandonment of his grandmother; his mother's marriage to First Raise as drinker and who could make white men laugh, yet also a handyman, and who was found dead-frozen in the borrow-pit with his arm pointing homeward; and the narrator's always accusing culpability in the accident and death of Mose. Throughout an Eliotic wasteland note sounds, Montana, if once a Native ecology, then also now dry season, rainlessness, a place for grail and fisher-king.

Each encounter for the narrator adds to the displacement. Who, exactly, is the airplane man from Malta in Phillips County, Montana, clad in white hunter garb, carrying a teddy bear and five boxes of chocolate-covered cherries, and who hires him to get to Canada before his arrest by "the two suits" as a possible FBI fugitive? His own mother's letter to the Harlem priest, with whom she drinks but who refuses Native parishioners burial in tribal ground, he finds himself, almost unself-comprehendingly, moved to destroy. His overnight encounter with the barfly Malvina, one in a line of several women, edges into fantasy, rough yet maudlin and even comic sex, with its bedroom gallery of the woman's photographs. All of these conflate in his hangover reveries, episodes of dream picaresque. The hitchhike back home, in which he gets a lift with a family of Hutterites, exposes him both to a father who asks if "Indians" eat river turtles, having his picture taken like some curio, and a daughter the very instance of anemia, a sickly whiteness.

Only in his understanding of the example of Yellow Calf, and the love and succor he once gave to the grandmother and to Teresa as the child he fathers with her, does the narrator begin to glimpse a way to confront the unbalance of his life. His bad leg, dating back to Mose's death, has localized the larger malaise, life lived at a limp. But Yellow Calf's revelation and the linkage it supplies into a better order of Native being, together with the grandmother's burial, become processes of birth. For even as he wears his father's patched-up suit, Teresa dons red lipstick, coat, high heels, and a black cupcake hat, Lame Bull makes a preposterous funeral speech, and the coffin fails to wedge evenly in the ground, rain has at last fallen again. The old lady's pouch, and with it her arrowhead, he himself returns to the earth. Absurdity, comic-absurdly as befits, has in whatever small degree begun to dissolve.

As for the first time, and true to his age of thirty-two against the endless taunts of being called a boy, the narrator finds adulthood in a historic continuity of name, family, tribe, land, and call to health. He makes a self-promise to have his leg fixed and, a vintage touch of Welch irony, even marriage to his Cree. The signs of dislocation remain, nowhere more so than in the inspired motley and rhetoric at the grandmother's funeral. But they do so also in relation to the signs of resuscitation, life however oddly quilted over death. Which is to suggest that the contrary condition of things persists, without some final, transcendent-spiritual redemption or homing-in but rather a kind of working contingency. *Winter in the Blood* so fuses a beautifully judged sense of carnival into seriousness, the narrator's life as Native comédie humaine, a jugglery, while always underwritten by sober enough reality. Welch creates the novel's cross-worlds with nothing if not a poet's sureness of monitoring eye and ear.

The Death of Jim Loney

The Death of Jim Loney offers a protagonist's life from the outset even less likely to resolve into recovery. Welch's circumstantial touch, again, is assured. The narrative of a Montana mixedblood, displaced in life as environs at the edge of both Belknap Reservation and Harlem Township, is given not just with flair but with beckoning exactitude. Loney, the name an evident play of words, who authors his literal death as against his death-in-life in the shoot-out at tribal-heritaged Mission Canyon, turns finally to face his spirals of inefficacy however brought on by both family circumstance and his own unresisting complicity. A lesser novelist might have trodden into stereotype. The abandonment with his sister by his Gros Ventre mother, Electra Calf Looking, and white drifter-barfly father, Ike Loney, could have edged into stereotypical mixedblood blight. His "white" love affair could have given way to formula, easy transgression. Even the intended or accidental rifle killing of his onetime Native classmate carried risks of acceding to melodrama. In the event Welch writes subtler pathology, self-complexities, the torque of wasteland within carefully situated inside the latticed history of its making.

The narrative stagings, more aptly the ligatures, in how Loney's life unfolds again take on especial calls to sight and ear. An opening tableau, a "smoky night," has him exchanging with a local farmer about the township football game amid mud, the pounding of rain, and a crucially mistaken play at one with his own erroneous spectator life, and then to follow his arising need to "go downtown for a drink."[9] Nighttimes in turn have him dreaming of "a large bird and dark,"[10] the visionary avatar for his absentee parentage—his mother especially. He sees in mind his father as "a weeping man" and the silhouette of a Native woman, his own or another mother, who has lost her son.[11] His dog Swipsey freezes into silence in the ice and has to be dug out. These each supply markers, Jim Loney caught at his own psychological edge as much as at the edges of Harlem.

They also extend into Loney's prime relationships. With Rhea Davis, the beauteous Texas belle who has fled her millionaire family to teach on the reservation, he meets both love and yet a call to spatial escape, to Seattle, that he cannot accept. She concedes that initially he signified fantasy for her, a version of dark Indian warrior manhood. But she also learns better, seeks to take on marriage with him, even though her plan to have them move *à deux* to ocean-coastal Seattle where Loney once served in the military increasingly meets his inevitable delay and resistance. With Kate, the sister who has climbed through professional qualification into a role as successful bureaucrat in Indian Education and seeks to take him back with her to Washington D.C., the same reluctance holds. How to extricate himself from Rhea's fond illusion that "he was lucky to have two sets of ancestors" and that stirs his contemplative riposte that "he had no family and he wasn't Indian or white"?[12] How, as Welch positions him, reflexively to free himself of a self whose internal lock has resisted undoing and only a particular kind of "Indian" death will end?

Both relationships, and Loney's haunting by a quotation from the book of Isaiah of the need for the spiritual in human affairs, take their course inside the novel's measure of sight-and-sound corridor. The way stations are of several kinds accompanied by dips into the "controlled oblivion" he seeks from his drinking.[13] He remembers basketball hoops with Brother Gerard at one of the mission schools, his love of the adoptive "aunt" Sandra (his father's ex-lover) and touch of her hair, his exchange with and final imagined message to the boy Amos After Buffalo from Mission Canyon to which he himself will eventually flee, and the different exchanges in Kenny Hart's and the other township bars. The pictorial image the novel attributes to Loney along with his sister as "two half-breed kids caught in the slack water of a minor river" precisely situates each.[14]

In this respect the denouement especially adds particularity. Invited to go deer-shooting with Myron Pretty Weasel, one-time fellow basketball player but also unliked friend and in contrast to himself the son of a successful Native rancher, their venture becomes both actual and yet phantasmagoric, the shooting of real bullets yet an act of near out-of-body ancestral ritual. Interpretation has rightly seized upon Loney's confusion as to whether he thinks, in the heat of the moment, he is shooting a patrolling bear ("the image spooked him").[15] Pretty Weasel dazzles him in the half-light, modern sport hunter and yet in ursine form sacred totem. Loney shoots both and, implicitly, his own might-have-been incarnation, his own better anima. "I killed a man," he tells Ike, the trailer-resident father he now reaches for and who in turn will give him $60 and a Remington pump gun.[16] Their final meeting enacts starkest father-son sight and sound to be followed by Loney's trashing of the trailer as tell-tale sign that he is indeed the killer of Pretty Weasel.

In his suicidal flight Jim Loney seeks tribal ground "on the reservation."[17] The flight again implies ritual, the remembrance of Amos After Buffalo, Native calendar as against Thanksgiving, and his lost mother now a nurse in New Mexico. Pursuit by the township's law officer Painter Barthelme, and the reservation police Quinton Doore and Lefthand, transitions into yet further ritual. Is he simply criminal fugitive or the far deeper death-shadow that, paradoxically, has given the only substance to his life and finally transformed him into death-facing Gros Ventre brave? As he falls and spins he sees "the beating wings of a dark bird as it climbed to a distant place" even as Welch makes audible the slug from Doore that kills him (Painter witnesses to "the blast beside him" fired by Doore).[18] *The Death of Jim Loney* so closes through the yet one more indicative play of eye and ear in the narrowing vortex of Loney's life. In so doing it gives Welch's novel its own perfect compositional sense of ending.

Fools Crow

With *Fools Crow* (1986) Welch develops the almost unique repicturing of tribal Montana in the late 1860s. He himself has been insistent, however, upon how from the start his interest was in infinitely more than spectatorship or even topography. His resolve lay in articulating a tribally centered dimension of clan rite of passage, belief system, language, word, and naming, in all the lived and filled human detail of historic Blackfeet culture. This sought-for reality he indicates in an interview:

> My main point in writing this book is to present the Blackfeet way of life—daily
> life, hunting, raiding, ceremonies, mores, belief, preparing hides and food—before

the whites made real inroads into their culture. The Indian had a different reality and I try to present that.[19]

Centered on the life of Fools Crow, originally White Man's Dog, and whose change of name marks his coming-of-age as warrior and medicine man, the novel from the outset takes great care to set up a meticulous Native-animist geography. The opening chapter sets terms of reference, atlas-specific while at the same time a cartographic poetry. The Montana Rockies become "the Backbone of the World," the moon "Night Red Light," the sun "Sun Chief," winter "the Cold-Maker," death "Shadow Land," and the ancestral Blackfeet deities "the Above Ones." Shadow nomenclature as may be when given in English transliteration, each, even so, points to a Blackfeet sense of cosmos and nature-cycle born of its own precisely ordering and cultural semantics.

For this is Blackfeet life alive in circumstance, the three bands of the Pikuni, Kainah, and Siksika, and their subdivisions into warrior societies, as well as Fools Crow's family of Rides at the Door, his father, mother, and his wife, Red Paint, and child. Welch attentively delineates a working round of hunt, raid, sweat lodge, courtship, migrations between summer and winter camps, intimacy with Nature and its animals, birds and sounds, diplomacy with other Blackfeet, and, unsentimentally, tribal rivalries and different acts of human pettiness and crime. Time joins seamlessly to place, belief to practice, Blackfeet cosmology to Blackfeet everyday existence. Louis Owens has persuasive grounds for terming the novel "an act of cultural recovery."[20]

Napikwans, white men, operate at a distance, as though situated at the spatial-temporal periphery. Which is not to underestimate the trauma for the tribe of the Baker/Marias River Massacre of 1870, in which 173 Pikunis, mostly women and children, were killed by the military under Major Eugene M. Baker in revenge for the murder of the rancher Malcolm Clarke by the Piegan warrior Owl Child and comrades (Clarke had earlier humiliated Owl Child in a horse dispute). Nor is it to downplay the devastating impact of different waves of white-imported smallpox. Both are given place in Welch's novel, but as incidents, however important, within yet others. The effect is to preempt the usual emphasis of frontier, farm settlement, and the cavalry, with a tribal perspective, a step aside from the "winning" of the west. Rather, tribal memory presides. Fools Crow, for instance, remembers "the stories told by his grandfather of the origins of the constellations. He had been young then and it all seemed simple. There were only the people, the stars, and the blackhorns."[21] Whatever the self-estimate of settlers in their covered wagons, or the cavalry in their forts, as white people they are initially thought of in trickster terms and humor: "At first we thought these nanikwins were animals and incapable of reproducing with human beings."[22]

Blackfeet history, in general, Welch conveys as tough if savvy tribal order, humanly contradictory, and increasingly vulnerable to encroaching white America. Welch, to his credit, eschews any hint of sentimentality. If the Pikunis hold to a warrior etiquette they also have renegades capable of destructive, indeed murderous, action, as in the case of Owl Child and his followers. The situation becomes one of Pikuni continuity yet possible rupture, history as know-how, survival, a way of being, and yet history as also the threat of diminution and erasure. It is a dynamic shrewdly perceived in the observation of the historically actual mixedblood scout Joe Kipp:

> These people have not changed, thought Kipp, but the world they live in has. You could look at it one of two ways: either their world was shrinking or that other world, the one the white man brought with him, is expanding.[23]

Fools Crow's pilgrimage to Feather Woman as shaman, and as led in imagination by the spirit Nitsokou, becomes in effect a search for the understanding of Blackfeet destiny. He is shown a scroll, a parchment of signs and predictions, that serves as prophecy:

> Fools Crow thought of the final design on the yellow skin in Feather Woman's Lodge. He saw the Napikwan children playing and laughing in a world that they possessed. And he saw the Pikuni children, quiet and huddled together, alone and foreign in their own country.[24]

In this "final design" past and future join to set inheritance against dispossession. Eye and ear again give Welch his point of arrival, the sighting of Pikuni children "foreign in their own country," the sound of Napikwan children "laughing in a world that they possessed." This closing configuration as to the Blackfeet people in time and place is historic, chastening. It also again reminds of Welch's power to have his fiction "see" and "hear" lived history, the mosaic seen in its particularity while at the same time made over into a working whole.

The Indian Lawyer

The Indian Lawyer offers a quite different bead on Native fortune. Time and place are modern, explicitly dated as 1988–89 and the Reagan–Bush transition, a Native life ostensibly framed as middle-class success—and yet not quite—in the person of Sylvester Yellow Calf. Stanford-educated and rising attorney in Buster Harrington's upmarket Helena law firm as may be, he was born poor and raised on the Blackfeet Reservation by grandparents as fond substitutes for the mother and father who abandoned him. In due course, his will become quite another kind of reverse or almost reverse trajectory: onetime basketball supremo who thinks to enter politics and then makes a false step, Indian who is established city lawyer in the Montana state capital and then becomes pro bono lawyer for water and land rights on behalf of the Sioux of Standing Rock in the Dakotas. None wholly fits, a man celebrated for on-court prowess success yet who once "fouled out" and caused the game to be lost, caught at both ends. The novel catches the ambiguity to a fault.

Welch keeps the narration to an almost step-for-step Montana thriller format, the one contra-flow and confidence trick elided into the other. That holds whether for Yellow Calf's "performance" of Native identity, Democratic Party state politics, the dance of parole board and parolee, and even the back and forth of the several love affairs. Yet throughout, *The Indian Lawyer* functions also as larger cautionary tale. Mixedblood heritage gets due place, necessarily, but so equally does both reservation and white ethnicity: a Mountain West novel of both Blackfeet-Crow legacy and white class-strata, each in their paradoxical mirroring and counterreflection. To this purpose Welch keeps the situating of his novel as highly particular yet at the same time indicative of more encompassing human nuance.

Landscape takes on implication, whether Prickly Pear Valley "dark with a summer storm" or, for Yellow Calf, "the country was not empty, but remote and secluded, even intimate if you were alone"—lived in by hawk, antelope, or rattlesnake.[25] City and social-circuit come fully coded: the Harrington mansion "built during the 1880s and '90 in Helena by lumber barons, mining kings, prosperous stockmen and merchants."[26] The reservation at Browning's Moccasin Flat signifies "bald poverty," yet under the guardianship of his grandmother Mary Crow is the ancestral family warrior pouch,[27] which Yellow Calf will profess to not understanding, then forget, and then later refind to carry with him beyond Helena. The penitentiary of grey-squared cell and unwindowed detention, with its deadly regimes of drugs, bribery, and rape, plays against the "the clean Victorian office" of Yellow Calf.[28] It would be hard to doubt this role of contextualizing location, the novel's geometry of sight and sound, as backdrop to Yellow Calf's negotiation of the life's hand given him and then taken.

The plotline works the framing correspondences with aplomb. The double-track of Jack Harwood, educated convict serving his time at the Deer Park penitentiary for armed bank-robbery, and of Yellow Calf as Montana Board of Pardons member links through Harwood's wife Patti Ann whom the convict inveigles into a seduction scam as would-be leverage against Yellow Calf. But just as Harwood has been knifed in the prison by the "Indians" who regulate drug and other illicit cellblock traffic ("The trouble was, the Indians thought he still had the money"),[29] Yellow Calf and Patti Ann will be pursued under threat of violence by Harwood's paroled white-trash henchmen. The doors revolve. The novel styles its story as counterflow, a dialectic.

Woody Peters and his lover-sidekick Bobby Fitzgerald so become turncoats who see the chance to make off with the heist money they think hidden and still available from the original Harwood robbery. That the money has in fact paid for Patti Ann's hysterectomy adds the twist of another kind of knife, an end to any might-be imagined parent-and-child family future the border-pathological but highly intelligent Harwood anticipates on his long-ahead release. The wife as agent-to-be, against plan, falls in love with Yellow Calf. Likewise, Yellow Calf will use his lawyer savvy as to probation and prisoner-remand, and his visit to the roadhouse Shanty Bar where he scouts them out, to outmaneuver Peters and Fitzgerald. The doubling, though multiplication might be the apter term, links into the rest of the narrative.

The paradoxes accumulate. Shirt-and-tie smart, besuited, Yellow Calf the might-be congressman for the Democratic Party is also heir to the great-grandfather pictured in deerskin leggings. He can be neither fully the lawyer as "new warrior" as his lover Shelley suggests and that, for his own part, he fancies himself in line with the once only Indian on the basketball team, nor fully the lawyer on equal working status with the white world that had allowed him professional entrance. The love affair with Patti Ann that begins when he is a member of the parole board will lead to his demission. His announcement of a run for Congress is made at the school where he once played Father Christmas, pastiche deepened by the unspeaking of tribal leaders. When a pupil offers him a plywood pipe of peace, it mocks his own Indian-ness, marks the contrast with his grandfather's medicine pouch, and shows up his tilted un-disconnect from Native actual legacy.

Each of the women in his life similarly seeks negotiation of gains and deficits with him, notably Patti Ann who fantasizes and then both loves and loses Yellow Calf. His grandmother, Little Bird Walking Woman, maintains Blackfeet legacy for him, although she was a flapper in her 1920s young womanhood and with a husband who has foresworn all tribal accoutrement as what he designates hocus-pocus in favor of a job in industry. Shelley, senator's daughter, divorcee, and mother of two, contrasts with Patti Ann and her miscarriages, two women who never quite "see" or "hear" him. Lena Old Horn, Yellow Calf's onetime school counselor, is drawn to him romantically even as she stays in a relationship with Stanley Weintraub, the teacher of English, whose nose he will break on a basketball court for how he embodies a whiteness he both seeks and resists. No one relationship in which Yellow Calf is pivotal takes full hold, the unbalance rather than balance of life forces caught winningly by Welch.

Two images especially linger and connect. Yellow Calf remembers seeing a raggedy Indian boy child "paying marbles all by himself" and in which "I saw myself."[30] The closing vignette, playing hoops alone under wind and sleet on a nighttime basketball court in Browning and having given up the prospect of a federal congressional career, returns to the same thread—"He was going one on one against the only man who ever beat him."[31] *The Indian Lawyer* has not always won plaudits, whether from Native literary-nationalist critics who persist in thinking it too readily a portrait of the white man's assimilated Indian or from "mainstream" critics who think the plot altogether overpatterned. Both do a disservice. Welch, rather, fashions a novel that subtly sees and hears, and indeed grounds, contrariety, the "Native" success and yet not of Sylvester Yellow Calf caught between the lawyer who is Indian and the Indian who is lawyer.

The Heartsong of Charging Elk

The Heartsong of Charging Elk opens with an explicit act of sight and sound, that of the title character in his eleven-year-old boyhood participating in the surrender of the Oglala Lakota in 1890 at the Red Cloud Agency in Pine Ridge, Nebraska. Tribespeople led by Crazy Horse and met by Red Cloud ("great war chief . . . Now he was a reservation Indian")[32] belong in the boy's memory of both the inerasably seen and heard. His is the poignant remembrance of the so-called Battle, actually massacre, of Wounded Knee. Despite defeat he watches leaders resplendent in full tribal dress and sings with the captive Sioux as they give ancestral chant ("The whole valley was alive with the peace song"). The soldiery, the wasichus or white people, may surround them, or herd their tribal horses, or fly the cavalry's "white and blue flag."[33] But despite poverty, their bedraggled line, even the tears of Charging Elk's mother, the Sioux look to headdress dignity and proclaim necessary songs of life and survivance. Welch's prologue provides an unerring eye-and-ear frame for the life-portrait to follow.

For ahead will lie the compendious unfolding of Charging Elk's career, the one transition implicated in the other, Great Plains America into European France, youth into near middle-age, with the Atlantic passage brought about by his part in the touring spectacle of Buffalo Bill's Wild West show. Spoken Lakota, in all its brilliance of idiom and immense cosmography, coexists for him with eventual French (and langue d'oc) under the respective linguistic as well as political mantra of *liberté, fraternité, egalité*. The novel so folds fact-fiction history several ways at once. Sioux history moves from inside to outside, an instance of the Red Atlantic as Jace Weaver has called it.[34] The clash of tribal and settler cross-worlds, in turn, finds its ironic simulation in Winning of the West circus spectacle. Charging Elk's life, its contradance, Welch fashions with quite singular dispatch to act in all these respects as embodiment, an intermediation.

The novel, in kind with its predecessors, draws from a huge weave of event, each throughout Charging Elk's life styled in a way to keep his story persuasively grounded by eye and ear. Across the sixteen years from arrival in France in 1893, to his lonesome awakening in a Marseille hospital after a fall from a horse in the arena, through to his cross-cultural marriage and impending parenthood with the farmer's daughter Nathalie Gazier, he lives a life at once memory and almost Gulliver-like encounter. How, at each turn, and as though reverse explorer, to "read," to "hear," and indeed to understand, the discordance of two kinds of Old World? That is no less compounded in the cultural double-take of Cody's circus—"the young Indians enjoyed the spectacle of themselves reflected in the astonished eyes of the French people."[35]

The Sioux language bespeaks Wakan Tanka or the Great Mystery, Nagi or spirit, liberty in the Oglala Plains, Pine Ridge, and the Dakota territories and badlands of Paha Sapa. Charging Elk lives amid buffalo and seasons, his parents Shrub and Double Back Woman, the energy and tease of Lakota society, the Winter Count, his animal helper, and the young man companionship of his kola or bosom companion Strikes Plenty and "their wanderings in Paha Sapa."[36] That of France means in all senses other language, variously Catholic Nativity and western clock, *la famille* and *le raison*, table manners and brasserie, guillotine and cheese. His employments have him at different times portside fish-worker for the René Soulas family, soap factory laborer, prison gardener, and small-farm laborer at the Gazier fruit and vegetable holding. Other zig-zags exert hold. He retains belief that "the real world" lies in the Sioux afterlife as against the present French "dream" with its white colorist jibes at his dark skin,[37] its one imprisonment for market theft of bread and another for murder with abrupt "political" release and award of French citizenry to follow. He will be obliged to decipher, always through his own Indigenous lexicon, a civilization as much otherworld as that met by the settlers, French trappers, and westering gold miners who first entered Sioux lands.

Marseille, "a large city and it smelled of the sea," is "noisy with carts and wagons" as against "the wide open country of the Lakotas."[38] The Eiffel Tower, in Charging Elk's sighting, resembles a "naked iron tree."[39] Marseille's harbor arouses similar imagery: "Not even in Paha Sapa had he seen such a strange forest."[40] Caught out by vagabondage and petty theft in France, his "kaleidoscopic images of loneliness and despair,"[41] he learns for the first time the inside of a cell as against the outside land-space of his home Plains. He can become the cause célèbre of the journalist Martin St-Cyr after killing Chef Breteuil for bordello homosexual drugging and molestation. His subsequent sentence to imprisonment in La Tombe can shadow both the Émile Zola of "J'Accuse" and the Dreyfus Affair and Victor Hugo's Jean Valjean in *Les Misérables*. His thoughts can turn to the snippets that enter his dreams of Black Elk (on whom the novel is loosely based) and Crazy Horse, the Ghost Dance, the federal government ban of the Lakota tongue, the emergent reservations, and the turn-of-the-century dip in Native populations. He can even witness Buffalo Bill as fading impresario, himself the passing parade. To this end each stage in Charging Elk's story exhibits Welch's characteristic specificity of grip.

For these cross-worlds, their cultural mirrors, the novel keeps in precise imaginative alignment through to its close. Above all, the exilic chronicle as Welch offers it will cause Charging Elk to steer his way through lattices of stereotype, whether vanishing Indian ("Even the sacred Paha Sapa had been taken from the people"), savagism ("a whooping, naked savage who scared the children half to death"), or the exotic ("everyone is different from me in your country").[42] None of which, even as he calls on the enduring signage of Lakota legacy and not least in his affecting speech to the court ("he realized that he did not have the French words to explain about evil. It could only be explained in the Lakota tongue"),[43] is to deny friendship with the Soulases, sex with his prostitute Marie, or love with Nathalie. But at the core, body and spirit, his rite of passage as told by Welch in *The Heartsong of Charging*

Elk involves learning the contrast between the plenitude of his Lakota identity and what exactly under Western eye and ear has come to be signified by the word *indien*.

"I always had a sense of economy from my poetry background" runs an observation in one of Welch's early interviews.[44] It speaks appositely to the styling of the novels that he had then so far written while presaging those to follow. In this respect it bears every repetition that if his fiction does not apportion into the postmodern turn, its reflexive turns of circle and narratology, it exhibits a full roster of quite comparable claims. These lie in his story-line sight and sound, the working density in his depictions of cross-worlds, be it dislocation in *Winter in the Blood* and *The Death of Jim Loney*, tribal dynamics in *Fools Crow*, American Dream in *The Indian Lawyer*, or the nineteenth-century transatlantic in the *Heartsong of Charging Elk*. The upshot on Welch's part deserves to be thought as commanding as it has been rare.

NOTES

1. Page references to Welch's *Winter in the Blood*, *The Death of Jim Loney*, and *Fools Crow* are to the Penguin editions.
2. Welch, "Blackfeet," 32.
3. Barnes, "Postcard," 56.
4. "Homing in" has become standard formulation for the returned Native isolate. See Bevis, "Native American Novels," 580–620.
5. Welch, *Winter in the Blood*, 120.
6. Ibid., 159.
7. Ibid.
8. Ibid., 2.
9. Welch, *The Death of Jim Loney*, 3.
10. Ibid., 20.
11. Ibid., 23, 34.
12. Ibid., 102.
13. Ibid., 59.
14. Ibid., 90.
15. Ibid., 129.
16. Ibid., 145.
17. Ibid., 160.

18. Ibid., 179, 178.
19. Cited in McFarland, *James Welch*, 161.
20. Owens, *Other Destinies*, 128.
21. Welch, *Fools Crow*, 93.
22. Ibid., 66.
23. Ibid., 252.
24. Ibid., 386.
25. Welch, *The Indian Lawyer*, 39, 158.
26. Ibid., 40–41.
27. Ibid., 104, 162.
28. Ibid., 17, 75.
29. Ibid., 133.
30. Ibid., 59.
31. Ibid., 349.
32. Welch, *The Heartsong of Charging Elk*, 2.
33. Ibid., 4.
34. Weaver, *The Red Atlantic*.
35. Welch, *The Heartsong of Charging Elk*, 22.
36. Ibid., 23.
37. Ibid., 252.
38. Ibid., 40, 104.
39. Ibid., 40.
40. Ibid., 62.
41. Ibid., 195.
42. Ibid., 195, 328, and 395, respectively.
43. Ibid., 338.
44. McFarland and Browning, "An Interview," 18.

BIBLIOGRAPHY

Barnes, Jim. "Postcard to James Welch in Missoula." In *The Sawdust War*, 56. Chicago: University of Illinois Press, 1992.

Bevis, William. "Native American Novels: Homing In." In *Recovering the Word: Essays in Native American Literature*, edited by Brian Swann and Arnold Krupat, 580–620. Berkeley: University of California Press, 1987.

McFarland, Ron, ed. *James Welch*. Lewiston: Confluence Press, 1986.

McFarland, Ron, and M. K. Browning, "An Interview with James Welch" (February 1984). In *James Welch*, edited by Ron McFarland, 1–19. Lewiston: Confluence Press, 1986.

Momaday, N. Scott. *House Made of Dawn*. New York: Harper & Row, 1968.

Owens, Louis. *Other Destinies: Understanding the American Indian Novel*. Norman: University of Oklahoma Press, 1992.

Silko, Leslie Marmon. *Ceremony*. New York: Viking Press, 1977.

Vizenor, Gerald. *Darkness in Saint Louis Bearheart*. Minneapolis: Truck Press, 1968.

Weaver, Jace, *The Red Atlantic: American Indigenes and the Making of the Modern World, 1000–1927*. Columbia: University of North Carolina Press, 2014.

Welch, James. "Blackfeet, Blood and Piegan Hunters." In *Riding the Earthboy 40*, 32. Reprint, Lewiston, ID: Confluence Press, 1990.

———. *The Death of Jim Loney*. New York: Harper & Row, 1979. Reprint, New York: Penguin Books, 1987.

———. *Fools Crow*. New York: Viking, 1986. Reprint, New York: Penguin Books, 1987.

———. *The Heartsong of Charging Elk*. New York: Doubleday, 2000.

———. *The Indian Lawyer*. New York: W. W. Norton, 1990.

———. *Winter in the Blood*. New York: Harper & Row, 1974. Reprint, New York: Penguin Books, 1986.

Slender Vial of DNA / For Sale

Dismantling Genomic Articulations of Indigeneity in the Poetry of Heid E. Erdrich

Joanna Ziarkowska

n the poem titled "Vial" from the 2008 collection *National Monuments*, Ojibwe poet Heid E. Erdrich refers to an incident from 1996 when Karitiana Indians, an Indigenous group from the Brazilian Amazon, agreed to give blood samples in exchange for medical drugs. However, the promised medications were never delivered. Moreover, with the arrival of the Internet to the isolated community, the Karitiana people incidentally discovered that their blood samples, collected in the 1970s, were still being sold by an American company to scientists around the world for $85 a sample. The profits were not shared with the community. As Larry Rother explains in an article for the *New York Times*, Francis Black, the first researcher who obtained the samples, had died, which made an investigation into the matter difficult. However, officials at the National Indian Foundation, a Brazilian agency that supervises Indigenous groups in Brazil, claimed that his presence on the reservation was not authorized and violated existing regulations. Similarly, in 1996 scientists did not have permission to conduct genetic research.[1] "Vial" is one of many poems that reveal Erdrich's interest in science and its technologies as well as the way it coexists with and oftentimes participates in modern forms of colonialism. More importantly, Erdrich's poetry addresses ethical challenges posed by technoscience, its methodologies, and protocols, especially in the context of genomic research in Indigenous communities, which in recent years has been conducted in a variety of projects such as studies on diabetes, DNA ancestry testing, and molecular anthropology. While the "quirky beauty of science" is often irresistible and enters productive dialogues with Ojibwe epistemologies,[2] Erdrich is also aware of how it is incorporated into highly politicized projects, which engage in bioextractive economies and present-day biocolonialism. While there are consistent similarities between how Ojibwe and scientific discourses explain the world and myriad interconnections among human and nonhuman beings, science's insistence on the superiority of Western methodologies is racist and problematic. Indeed, as Erdrich extensively illustrates, science often decontextualizes and misrepresents Indigenous perspectives and identities, and thus reduces Indigenous people to the status of research objects.

The gravity of the case described in Erdrich's poem is directly tied to the need for recognition of the Karitiana people's (and many Indigenous people's) epistemologies and their foundational element, namely relationality. Goenpul scholar Aileen Moreton-Robinson defines it in the following way:

> Relationality is grounded in a holistic conception of the inter-connectedness and inter-substantiation between and among all living things and the earth, which is inhabited by a world of ancestors and creator beings. It informs our epistemological and ethical premise that social research should begin with an awareness of our proper relationships with the world we inhabit, and is conducted with respect, responsibility, generosity, obligation, and reciprocity. . . . Relationality is an inextricable part of our sovereign knowledges, informing our scholarship to produce innovative social research. As a presupposition it shapes ways of knowing, being, and doing; to be connected is to know, and knowing is *embodied* in and connected to country, but not all knowledge is accessible.[3]

Biocolonialism shuns relationality as both a system of beliefs and a practice and transforms a body into a site of extraction. Interestingly, Erdrich resists the temptation to portray a binary of Western biocolonial science versus Indigenous relational epistemologies. In this chapter I give voice to my admiration for how Erdrich correctly identifies and eloquently responds to ethical dilemmas posed by scientific research conducted without any contribution and often without the consent of Indigenous people while at the same time marvels at the beauty of science. Moreover, rather than presenting them as antagonists, the poet represents scientific discourse and Ojibwe epistemologies as communicating similar messages about the world and myriad interconnections among human and nonhuman beings. Erdrich's poetry collected in *Cell Traffic* and *National Monuments* testifies to her fascination with biomedical processes (for example, microchimerism and nutritional epigenetics) and the intricate processes governing the movement of molecules. At the same time, however, Erdrich is aware of how genomics, the discourse that it uses, and the definitions that it produces pose a potential threat to Indigenous people's cultural and political sovereignty. Thus, I intend to demonstrate how Erdrich's poetry comments on the proliferation of genomic research, its effects on Indigenous communities, and the possible mechanisms of resistance to what Sisseton Wahpeton Oyate scholar Kim TallBear calls genomic articulations of Indigeneity. TallBear's brilliant *Native American DNA* provides an explanation of the fundamental differences between genomic and Indigenous definitions of Indigeneity and how the former intervene in issues of cultural identity and political sovereignty.[4] Moreover, as numerous cases from around the world illustrate, the rising interest in Indigenous blood samples spurred by continental genetic ancestry research is a global trend and reflects a belief that Indigenous blood stores important knowledge about humanity's history and thus must be obtained at all costs. The scientific and, as we will see, economic value of Indigenous blood and body parts draws attention to the second aspect of the pronounced intervention of technosciences in Indigenous lives, namely how they have become a target of biocolonialism. Unlike the extractive colonialism of the nineteenth century, biocolonialism violates Indigenous people's bodies, spiritual beliefs, cultural sovereignty, and the right to participate (or refuse to) in scientific research.[5]

Defining Indigeneity

By addressing the harm inflicted by extracting samples in the Karitiana case, Erdrich draws attention to how unrestricted and unsupervised research in Indigenous communities has become one of many common points on the political and activist agenda of Indigenous peoples around the world. According to Ronald Niezen, the concept of "Indigenous" and "Indigeneity" is relatively recent. It facilitates global networking and mutual recognition of people characterized by "descent from original inhabitants of a region prior to the arrival of settlers who have since become the dominant population; maintenance of cultural differences, distinct from a dominant population; and political marginality resulting in poverty, limited access to services, and absence of protections against unwanted 'development.'"[6] While on one level Indigeneity is tied to the local and regional, it is also a global movement "underpinned by a flexible notion of demands for 'cultural rights' including claims for the political self-representation of marginalized groups."[7] The international circulation of Indigeneity has given traction and recognition to Indigenous peoples' claims in a political and legal sense and forced settler states to consider their voiced demands. For James Clifford, the global dimension of Indigeneity has turned it into "interactive cosmopolitanism: genealogical inclusion of outsiders; trading relations; [and] circular migration."[8] Despite such a dynamic and fluctuating model of Indigeneity, global Indigenous political activism shares similar and widely recognized issues. As Marisol de la Cadena and Orin Starn observe, "land claims, control over cultural heritage, bilingual education, the inclusion and commemoration of indigenous histories in national imaginaries" have arisen as important elements of an Indigenous identity worldwide.[9]

The similarity of these goals is also mirrored in the way Indigenous identities are formulated. In her description of the Indigenous articulation of Indigeneity, Kim TallBear draws attention to how many critics, Ronald Niezen among them, emphasize the temporal dimension of the concept.[10] "Original," "first," "native," and "aboriginal" people are those who inhabited the land *prior to* the arrival of settlers. Thus, the rupture and trauma of colonial invasion are identified as the fundamental and prioritized elements of Indigeneity. What seems to be more important, however, as TallBear and other critics observe,[11] is the way Indigenous people's identities are tied to a place. "They narrate their peoplehoods," writes TallBear, "as emerging in concert with particular land- and/or waterscapes. . . . Landscapes are places *through* which humans and their molecules move and *settle*."[12] Similarly, Juaneño/Yaqui scholar M. A. Jaimes Guerrero asserts:

> In a literal sense, indigenism means "to be born of a place," but for Native peoples, it also means "to live in relationship with the place where one is born," as in the sense of an "indigenous homeland." In this cultural context, an indigenous member has the responsibility to practice kinship roles in reciprocal relationship with his

or her bioregional habitat, and this is manifested through cultural beliefs, rituals, and ceremonies that cherish biodiversity (that is, human culture in relationship to bioregion).[13]

It is precisely the idea of emerging/originating from a place as well as a sense of being connected with it in a complex network of relationality that give rise to an Indigenous identity. Therefore, as Tewa scholar Gregory Cajete repeatedly emphasizes, "It is the land that ultimately defines a Native people."[14]

On the other hand, a genomic articulation of Indigeneity is based on biological descent, thus giving no heed to land ethics and relationality. As TallBear writes, in such a framework, "an indigenous group becomes a biological-based or population-based category in which individuals from different 'tribes' or 'peoples' are sampled in order to build knowledge about broader population histories."[15] The immediate consequence of this insistence on biology is the claim that what unites Indigenous people globally is not a resistance to colonialism and the protection of their traditional cultures but a biochemical analysis of DNA nucleoid markers. Such an analysis facilitates grouping Indigenous people into, first, geographies and then "races," in contemporary scientific discourses referred to as populations to escape associations with the nineteenth-century racist pseudoscience and eugenics.[16] This reliance on biochemical components of blood and biological connections undercuts Indigenous definitions and understanding of kinship and family and social structures that do not always rely on blood-relatedness. For example, in Dakota, Lakota, and Nakota cultures, while connection through blood is important, "a networked set of social and cultural relations" may often override biological relatedness.[17] Similarly, the White Earth Nation, when working on constitutional reform, "decided that citizenship would once again be based on Anishinaabe values, which are rooted in relationships and family,"[18] thus downplaying the importance of blood and the politics of blood quantum. A genomic articulation of Indigeneity ignores such nuanced factors that create expanded networks of kinship relations.

Furthermore, what is even more significant is that the genomic understanding of Indigeneity is constructed upon the "expectation of [the] inevitable disappearance" of Indigenous people.[19] According to TallBear, this claim replicates the logic of the vanishing Indian permeating popular culture with Edward S. Curtis's photograph "The Vanishing Race" as an iconic example. However, if in the nineteenth century American Indians were to be wiped out by the progress of Western civilization, in the twentieth and twenty-first century, the vision is of imminent genetic admixture:

"If admixture is on the rise, indigenous people are—by genetic definition—vanish-ing."[20] Hence the sense of urgency that informs many genomic projects such as the Human Genome Diversity Project (HGDP) and the Genographic Project.

Moreover, despite the negative depiction of admixture as directly leading to the demise of Indigenous people, paradoxically, the genomic articulation of Indigeneity also frames it in a positive light, constructing a "we-are-all-related" narrative. The basis for this logic is the popular theory of "Mitochondrial Eve" (mtEve), the single genetic mother of all people, whose descent is traced to Africa. However, as TallBear rightly points out, this cheerful story completely ignores the implications of European and American colonial history. "Tracing all human lineages to mtEve does not make us all 'African' in any meaningful sense," writes TallBear. "But the claim itself is meaningful because Africa is not simply a name given by some humans to a particular landmass. Enduring colonial perspectives are at play. Africa has long been seen as fundamentally different."[21] What such a narrative demonstrates instead is how the eugenic discourse of "race" is now reconfigured as the seemingly objective and scientific concept of "population."

The examples that TallBear provides succinctly demonstrate how genomic discourse usurps the right to intervene in Indigenous cultural and tribal sovereignty. The widely publicized case of the Kennewick Man shows how a genomic articulation of Indigeneity takes over Indigenous understanding of cultural ties and belonging, and attempts to challenge adopted legislation. When nine-thousand-year-old remains were found near the Columbia River in Washington, the Confederated Tribes of the Umatilla Indian Reservation, the Colville Confederated Tribes, the Wanapum Band, the Yakama Nation, and the Nez Perce Tribe opposed further research and demanded repatriation under the Native American Graves Protection and Repatriation Act (NAGPRA).[22] However, a group of prominent anthropologists, led by forensic anthropologist James Chatters, filed a lawsuit in a federal court, alleging that the tribes were interfering with their constitutional right to study the remains.[23] The rationale employed the well-known argument that genetic research into evolution was ideologically neutral and beneficial to all of humankind. To validate their claims, the scientists attempted to prove that the Kennewick Man could not be traced directly to contemporary Native Americans. NAGPRA requires tribes to document cultural affiliation of the remains, and while it is relatively easy to do so with remains from the nineteenth or early twentieth century (the presence of ritual objects serves as proof, for example), it was not possible in this case. Thus, it was believed that a genetic connection to contemporary tribes might be proved by lineal descent tests that at that time, did not give satisfactory and unequivocal results. The legal dispute lasted for over twenty years. Eventually, in 2015, a group of scientists from the University of Copenhagen, Denmark, published an article in *Nature* stating that the Kennewick Man was in fact related to contemporary Native Americans, including the Confederated Tribes of the Colville Reservation.[24] Finally, on February 18, 2017, the remains were buried in an undisclosed place in the presence of members of five Columbia Basin tribes. The Kennewick Man controversy clearly demonstrated how genetic definitions of identity stand in contradiction to Native American epistemologies and ontologies and showed that there is a danger of DNA testing becoming a legal mechanism for interfering in and rewriting these definitions, thus challenging Native American sovereignty. While the remains were finally returned to the tribes, it was only after a more advanced technology was discovered to prove a genetic connection with contemporary Native Americans. The case sets a very disturbing precedent for the future, since, as Yakama scholar Michelle M. Jacob rightly observes, it "has helped solidify the privileging of DNA testing as the 'gold standard' in producing historical 'fact.'"[25]

Likewise, TallBear's second example, the use of DNA ancestry testing to authenticate Indigenous descent, is equally contentious. With twenty-six million people having taken an at-home ancestry test by the start of 2019,[26] the rising popularity of direct-to-consumer DNA tests and their widespread availability have become a fact. However, as TallBear asserts, the information provided by the test is more nuanced and complex than the DNA-testing companies are willing to admit in their marketing strategies.[27] The widely publicized case of Senator Elizabeth Warren serves as a good example. In response to President Donald Trump mocking her with the name "Pocahontas," Warren released her DNA test results. Supported by Carlos Bustamante, a professor of genetics at Stanford and adviser to Ancestry and 23 and Me, Warren identified herself as Indigenous, simultaneously admitting that she was not an enrolled member of any federally recognized tribe.[28] What followed was a statement by Cherokee Nation secretary of state Chuck Hoskin Jr. in which he said, "Using a DNA test to lay claim to any connection to the Cherokee Nation or any tribal nation, even vaguely, is inappropriate and wrong. It makes a mockery out of DNA tests and its legitimate uses while also dishonoring legitimate tribal governments and their citizens, whose ancestors are well documented and whose heritage is proven."[29] Indeed, what ancestry tests identify is the frequencies of the appearance of mitochondrial DNA or Y-chromosome markers,[30] the object of study of human genome diversity researchers, which have nothing to do with tribal and cultural affiliations. Contrary to what genetic companies promise their consumers, there are neither tests nor markers unique to specific populations: it is impossible to state on the basis of a DNA test if someone is Cherokee or Navajo.[31] Consequently, if DNA tests are used at all by Indigenous tribes in the United States, it is usually a popular parentage test that is employed, and it is done only in individual cases rather than *"across the entire membership."*[32] Despite this, DNA-testing companies advertise their services to federally recognized tribes, claiming DNA tests' applicability in assessing tribal enrollment applications. If such protocols are adopted, writes TallBear, Native Americans become "re-racialized" by "promoting the idea that the tribe is a genetic population."[33] More importantly, shifting more importance to genetic factors undermines the historical and legal basis of Native American sovereignty and may in consequence challenge Indigenous rights to self-governance, land claims, and other privileges provided in treaties and derived from "government-to-government" relations between tribes and the U.S. government.

The impetus given to human genome diversity research, the resultant "gene fetishism,"[34] and the geneticization of Indigenous people have not gone unnoticed by the global Indigenous movement. In fact, they have become an important part of global activism and fueled transnational anticolonial coalitions. As Debra Harry (Numu / Kooyooe / Dukaddo) illustrates with case studies from the United States, Canada, New Zealand, the Solomon Islands, and Brazil, to give a few examples, "Indigenous peoples' DNA is sought for medical, behavioral, large-scale human population studies, and ancient DNA genetic research."[35] What all these diverse projects have in common is the tendency to reduce Indigenous people to the status of research objects and/or the failure to obtain their consent for various research agendas. In response to such practices, in June 2000, the Indigenous Peoples Council on Biocolonialism issued a primer and a resource guide, titled "Indigenous People, Genes and Genetics: What Indigenous People Should Know about Biocolonialism," in which the authors write:

> Indigenous people and nations must prepare themselves to critically evaluate proposals for research involving their people and their territories. Policies which recognize and protect the collective rights of indigenous peoples are lacking. We must accept the responsibility to put into place policies that protect our interests, and we must come to understand the issues so that we can make fully informed decisions.[36]

Indeed, the resource guide emphasizes the silenced facet of ethics (or the lack thereof) in genomic research among Indigenous communities and the absence of policies protecting Indigenous people from abusive bioextractive practices. The lack of efficient protections and the often unequal relation of power between Western scientists and Indigenous people draw attention to how science becomes implicated in biocolonialism.

In many respects, biocolonialism is a part of an old and well-established practice of subjugating and exploiting Indigenous peoples introduced by extractive colonialism. According to Laurelyn Whitt, "biocolonialism may be understood as any activity that . . . through the use of force or coercion (economic or otherwise), involves or facilitates the removal, processing, conversion into private property, and commodification of indigenous genetic resources by agents of the dominant culture(s)." The results of such actions are complex and manifold and include "erosion of indigenous health and well-being, whether physical or spiritual"; "disruption or discrediting of indigenous knowledge and value systems"; "imposition of concepts, practices, and values that further the economic and political interests of the dominant culture"; and the "loss of political and economic autonomy and increased dependency on the dominant culture(s)" (against which TallBear warns).[37] As numerous cases discussed by Whitt, Harry, and TallBear illustrate, biotechnologies have become one of many instruments through which biocolonialism is possible and effective. Moreover, they successfully facilitate the transformation of Indigenous bodies, blood, and tissue into what Catherine Waldby calls "biovalue." "Biovalue," Waldby explains, is

> a surplus value of vitality and instrumental knowledge which can be placed at the disposal of the human subject. This surplus value is produced through setting up certain kinds of hierarchies in which marginal forms of vitality—the foetal, the cadaverous and extracted tissue, as well as the bodies and body parts of the *socially* marginal—are transformed into technologies to aid in the intensification of vitality for other living beings.[38]

What is at stake is not only the advancement of biomedical technologies, the resulting improvement of human (white) bodies, or future patents and profits they are likely to generate but also the processes of the production and validation of knowledge. Since the knowledge such research produces is depicted as indisputably valuable for all humankind and thus prioritized over other systems of knowledge (generally non-Western), Indigenous people are expected to willingly donate their blood samples. Their uniqueness and identity as Indigenous people are thus reduced to the biochemical structure of their DNA, which "has emerged as a new natural resource that, like Native American land in the nineteenth century, can be appropriated by the modern subject—the self-identified European, both the scientist and the genealogical researcher—to develop knowledge for the good of the greater society."[39] This sought-for entity, referred to by TallBear as Native American DNA, has indeed become a desired commodity, capable of providing a sense of Indigenous identity that in turn fulfills numerous ideological functions and cultural fantasies. What Heid E. Erdrich's poetry offers at this point is an intervention in the commodification and exploitation of Indigenous bodies and a depiction of land as instrumental in the construction of Indigenous identities.

Heid E. Erdrich's Poetry of Science

In an introduction to Heid E. Erdrich's volume *Cell Traffic*, Dean Rader writes: "I know of no other contemporary poet whose poetry is so firmly rooted in indigenous cultures but so thoroughly pushes mainstream aesthetic envelopes. She dismantles (and re-mantles) literary forms, she merges science and Native histories, she assembles poems from RSS feeds."[40] Erdrich depicts science as absolutely fascinating, compatible with Native epistemologies, and instrumental in describing everyday processes. Yet, Erdrich never forgets that, as science and technology studies scholar Sheila Jasanoff emphasizes, "science and technology operate, in short, as *political agents*" and are thus subjected to ideologically driven agendas, with studies on ancient human migration patterns serving as a telling example.[41] Accordingly, Erdrich engages with science, especially genomic research, but the implications that she explores are not only negative. Rather, to use Jenny Reardon's words, Erdrich well understands that to address concerns generated by genomic studies, one must be guided by a framework that does not "demarcate science from society, but rather calls into view the ways in which particular orderings of the 'social' world affect the kinds of categories scientists can use to characterize human diversity."[42] Consequently, while her poems on cell traffic in human bodies are motivated by fascination with biotechnologies, Erdrich never forgets that tracing DNA markers in ancestry tests is "no longer just a laboratory technique, but also a political act."[43]

In her take on science's investment in biocolonialism, Erdrich adopts a global perspective to draw attention to how the problem affects Indigenous peoples around the world and constitutes a basis for transnational coalitions.

"Human Map," from the earlier collection *Fishing for Myth* (1997), reprinted in *Cell Traffic*, is a comprehensive summary of science's exploitative approach to Indigenous people. The speaker comments sardonically on quotations from Boyce Rensberger's *Washington Post* article "By Analyzing DNA Samples from 400 Ethnic Groups, Scientists Could Reconstruct Human History," thus juxtaposing Indigenous and genomic articulations of Indigeneity. What this strategy reveals is how these incompatible epistemologies function in a context of unequal power relations, illustrated by Western science's claims to truth-production and a dismissal of alternative perspectives as manifestations of culture or religious beliefs rather than scientific methodologies. Indeed, the language of Rensberger's article, with its simplicity and clinical detachment, promises to offer an objective description of the project motivated by a universal respect for the pursuit of truth. Since "Hidden within / the DNA of each human being is a record of that person's ethnic history,"[44] scientists recognize their duty to uncover evolutionary patterns with a special emphasis placed on a "we-are-all-related" narrative, which displaces Native Americans as the original inhabitants of the continent. To quell any potential doubts, scientists reassure Native people that there is nothing controversial or racist about the project, since "the concept of race long ago lost its scientific / validity."[45] However, considering the manner in which Native people are selected and coerced into participating in the project, one concludes that the concept of race is indeed well and thriving.

The race-oriented agenda of the scientists' project is manifested on the level of power distribution, which is reflected in the way Native people are reduced to the level of research objects. The poem begins with an ironic announcement:

> You will be happy to know someone has asked our cells to tell,
> in their own bloody language, whether or not all Indian tribes
> descend from a single group migrated from Asia.[46]

By drawing attention to the fact that it is the cells, not people, that are of interest, the speaker comments on the continuous objectification of Indigenous people in scientific contexts, a practice that effectively prevents them from being seen as contributors to processes of knowledge production. As early as in 1994 when controversies around the HGDP emerged, Indigenous people condemned such "vampire projects" that "sought . . . to steal their genes, patent them and use them to make drugs that they would never be able to afford."[47] Now, this "Vampire Project" directs its interest toward blood in the speaker's community. The futility of resistance can be detected, as the rationale behind scientific progress always prevails:

> You say you won't go to the blood drive? But the needle's nothing
> new. Bloodshed always determines who inherits a patch of earth. . . .
> Whether we help them or not is no matter. Our blood will out.
> Our bodies' code will crack. They will have their map.[48]

The needle used to draw blood is placed on par with other weapons that shed blood, and coming to collect blood samples mirrors past campaigns of coming to take possession of Indigenous lands. "Bloodshed" is always embedded in such projects, the difference being that in the twenty-first century it is not a military but a bioscientific conquest.

It is no coincidence that Erdrich uses the image of a map to represent this continuum of exploitation. Blood is intertwined with the violence of settler colonial practices, the theft of land symbolically contained in the practice of Western cartography, and now again it is used to disfranchise Native people as even scientists admit that "their findings might be used to support / 'increasingly incendiary claims of land tenure in ethnic disputes.'"[49] The extraction of bodies not land this time is facilitated through the discourse of "civic duty" and the manipulation of information to produce Western-oriented knowledge, and "knowledge," as Sheila Jasanoff reminds us, "has become the primary wealth of nations, displacing natural resources, and knowledgeable individuals constitute possibly the most important form of capital."[50] To yield this new resource, Native people are misinformed about participation:

> Rumor has it
> donations need no consent and any clinic might be in on it—so
> go ahead—Give Blood! It's your civic duty.[51]

Here, Erdrich alludes to the manipulation of an informed consent requirement and situations in which research subjects are either misinformed about research goals or indirectly coerced into participation. With the imagery emphasizing parasitic extraction and the bitter irony detectable in the line, the meaning of the word "donation" becomes distorted and instead shifted toward exploitation. What Erdrich challenges is not science per se, but its methodologies and dubious ethics that dehumanize research subjects and nonchalantly dismiss any other epistemologies. Of this process, the speaker ironically says:

> All the way back to "humanity's dim evolutionary past,"
> without the flashlight, scientists can trace
> "the ancient migrations and ancestral intermixings
> that have shaped every tribe and culture on Earth."
> Still, it's too late to test Sky Woman, whose breath of life exists
> in all creatures, or Thought Woman, who imagines us even now,
> or any of the First Beings who survived by tricks.
> Too late, so they will have to settle for *your* blood.[52]

The introduction of principal characters from Haudenosaunee and Acoma Pueblo creation stories is a powerful way to draw attention to the existence of Indigenous epistemologies that have already generated knowledge about "humanity's dim evolutionary past." In other words, what never occurs to the scientific establishment is that "the assumption that Indian ancestry will be 'discovered' and scientifically 'answered' is insulting to groups who already have strong beliefs regarding their origins."[53] Moreover, from an Indigenous perspective, the stories of Sky Woman and Thought Woman are not narrative artifacts of a bygone culture, but complex concepts that explain not only the creation of all human and nonhuman beings but also the sources of their relatedness. Vanessa Watts (Mohawk/Anishinaabe) asserts that the narrated events are "not imagined or fantasized. This is not lore, myth or legend. These histories are not longer versions of 'and the moral of the story is. . . .' This is what happened."[54] Moreover, numerous Native scholars emphasize that Indigenous epistemologies resist compartmentalization into distinct categories such as philosophy, religion, science, etc., and instead contain all of these functions. They are shaped locally and integrate place-based knowledge and ethics. Therefore, the speaker in the poem emphasizes how creation stories already serve as scientific theories related to disciplines that Western science divides into evolutionary genetics and quantum physics: Sky Woman's "breath of life exists / in all creatures" and Thought Woman "imagines us even now." However, since neither Sky Woman nor Thought Woman can be interrogated (nor can their blood be tested), it is Indigenous people's blood, analyzed with the help of Western methodologies and technologies, that will provide the answer.

Claims in support of the validity of Indigenous epistemologies are followed by Erdrich's vocal objections to representing Native people as "vanishing," which, as TallBear has pointed out, is a key element of the genomic articulation of Indigeneity. "Human Map" directly tackles the idiom of the vanishing Indian that successfully renders research on population genetics urgent and threatened by admixture. Ironically alluding to a series of acronyms used to refer to consecutive genomic projects, the speaker references a long history of scientific interest in and research on Native people, all done to contribute to the welfare of all humankind (except Native people themselves):

> Anthropologists, our friends, support this "needy and urgent
> cause." And who knows? You may be one of the "HIP people"
> (Historically Interesting Population)
> who, they note, are vanishing at an alarming rate.[55]

Reduced to scientific objects and remnants of the past, Indigenous people's survival into the modern era is considered miraculous and interesting only from a scientific/ anthropological perspective. Thus, Indigenous people are again deprived of agency and subjectivity in the Western process of knowledge production. The speaker actively resists such sentiments, by saying: "Vanishing? They make it sound so passive, as if whole peoples / simply fade away."[56] In "Human Map," not only are Native people alive and well, but they also critically (and humorously) challenge the discourse that portrays them as being on the brink of extinction and at the mercy of scientists who will save their blood samples but not their bodies. Census data and various manifestations of Indigenous activism speak the language of regeneration and resistance, not death. As TallBear writes,

> Genetic-based assertions about the impending doom of the indigene contradict
> key indigenous claims. A pivot-point of indigenous organizing is that while peoples
> acknowledge assaults on them and their lands, they view themselves as working
> toward survival as peoples, toward greater autonomy. Not surprisingly, they resist
> terms that objectify them as historical or biological curiosities or vestiges.[57]

The logic of the genetic articulation of Indigeneity and biocolonialism is further explored in "Vial," a poem that relates the story of the Karitiana people. It begins with a compelling and defamiliarizing description of a vial of blood:

> Tube of red
> like a lipstick
> passion's paint,
> paid for, yet
> unpaid for,
> filched like a drugstore compact pinched.[58]

The first stanza draws attention to the aesthetic beauty of blood, its thick substance and passionate color, and immediately establishes an association with beauty products such as lipstick and pressed powder, which, with their appealing packaging, are used for beauty enhancement and, more importantly, are products that can be purchased, "paid for," or "filched." This juxtaposition is indeed striking since, unlike lipstick, blood is not or should not be a product subject to the rules of financial transactions. And yet it is. In the second stanza, by comparing a "slender vial of DNA" to a "glass finger," Erdrich demonstrates that for the Karitiana people (and in many Indigenous and non-Indigenous cultures), blood is still perceived as integral to the body, even when removed, and carries spiritual value. Using examples from the Solomon Islands and New Zealand, Harry demonstrates that "Indigenous peoples have a relationship with DNA akin to that which [they] have with [their] ancestors—one of reverence, respect, and responsibility."[59] While for scientists, research centers, and pharmaceutical companies, blood can be decoded, transformed into blood products, commodified, sold, and purchased, for the Karitiana people, it remains an integral part of their bodies and essential for the community's health and integrity. Specifically, Erdrich draws attention to how blood is instrumental in the passage to the afterlife and therefore irreplaceable:

> Rich and red
> blood of hunger
> bled in fear of the next world wanting
> the body whole,
> each drop accounted for.[60]

Therefore, it is justified to assume that the decision to donate blood was not easy and only taken with a view to receiving medical help. Cheating the Karitiana people out of medicine is represented not as an isolated event, but as a scientifically sanctioned practice of biocolonialism. In an alliterative enumeration tracing what happened to the blood samples once they were collected, Erdrich reviles the rationale used in the scientific world to justify such practices:

> For Sale
> to non-profits
> yet non-bought
> non-paid for.[61]

As Rother explains, Coriell Cell Repositories, a nonprofit group located in Camden, New Jersey, stores human genetic material, the Karitiana people's included, and offers it for research. In a telephone conversation with Rother, Joseph Mintzer, the then president of the center, denied profiting from the distribution of the samples.[62] However, the samples did become products distributed and sold online, and the profits never reached the community. Hence, Erdrich's piercing juxtaposition of blood samples being "non-bought" (since voluntarily donated) and also "non-paid for" (not in money but in medications that the community was promised, or in an exchange) emphasizes the perfidy of such practices that clearly take advantage of the unequal power structures inherent in the dealings of scientists with Indigenous tribes, especially those in remote areas of the world with limited access to information and legal counsel. Thus, "Vial" also draws attention to the urgent need of legal frameworks that would protect Indigenous people from such practices in the future. As Ryan Rhadigan observes, "Whether ultimately codified into law, or used conceptually to structure and facilitate the development of more respectful, collaborative, and consensual, research frameworks, recognitions of indigenous people's rights to genetic resources as property can help to improve and democratize scientific practices."[63]

If the pursuit of truth is presented as humanity's ultimate goal, it can only be achieved through the application of scientifically sanctioned methods. As TallBear and Jacob have affirmed, such claims have numerous shortcomings. For instance, excessive reliance on genomic analysis to authenticate Indigenous identity ignores the complexities of cultural and historical factors and poses a tangible threat to Indigenous peoples' cultural and political definitions of self-determination. The danger of embracing genetic testing as a legal means of authenticating Indigenous (or ethnic) belonging is exemplified by the Kennewick Man case, whose artistic and subversive potential Erdrich explores in a series of three poems.[64] The first one, "Kennewick Man Tells All," begins with an epigraph from a *New Yorker* article (from June 16, 1997) in which James Chatters, the forensic anthropologist who first studied the remains, says: "We didn't go digging for this man. He fell out—he was actually a volunteer. I think it would be wrong to stick him back in the ground without waiting to hear the story he has to tell."[65] Indeed, as Suzanne J. Crawford extensively documents, the arguments against reburial repeatedly evoked the concept of Kennewick Man as a storyteller who desperately wanted to tell his story.[66] If so, Kennewick Man emerges as a perfect "Native informant" since "he can be read through empirical processes to provide scientifically verifiable data. He cannot speak for himself but must be spoken for. And even better, he cannot mislead researchers through misinformation or poor translations, as living Native 'informants' are wont to do," writes Crawford.[67] Erdrich's strategy to counter such objectifying discourse consists of two elements. First, she endows Kennewick Man with a voice and agency and, second, she draws attention to science's unstable claim to be able to "explain all":

> Ladies and Gentleman of the press—Kennewick Man will now make a brief
> statement
> after which he will answer questions as time permits.
> I am 9,200 years old
> I am bone.
> I am alone.[68]

Evoking a press conference setting, Erdrich acknowledges the extensive coverage of the case in the press as well as the immense importance ascribed to genetic and radiocarbon testing. However, the climax never arrives as Kennewick Man reveals little, or rather he chooses to indulge in personal ruminations rather than hard scientific data. The ridiculousness of relying solely on science is brilliantly rendered in the anticlimax of the scene and the puns that allude to the situation: stating that Kennewick Man will answer all the questions if "time permits" is truly humorous in the context of how much time he spent buried in the river. More importantly, however, by admitting that he is alone, he rejects the passive identity of a research object and instead assumes agency and a personality. Indeed, his brief performance is about affect rather than scientific facts. He is transformed from a specimen into an individual, separated from his culture and land and therefore suffering. He is alone and yet no longer alone, since Erdrich establishes a personal and intimate connection by acknowledging his humanity. By thus reframing what Kennewick Man communicates, Erdrich lampoons the idea that investment in Western sciences is the only narrative capable of ordering and explaining worldly phenomena.

"Kennewick Man Attempts Cyber-date" continues the process of transforming the remains, a desired object of scientists, into a living individual, subject to his own desires. In the poem, Kennewick Man is confronted with technologically oriented problems of the twenty-first century. Responding to his newly emerged needs, he attempts to arrange a date on the Internet. He needs to confront the dilemma of self-representation and the careful balancing of reality and self-fashioning:

> So when Cyber-date asks me what I look like,
> I am no liar.
> Not like I expect to match a hottie.
> Not looking for "Barbie and Kennewick Man."[69]

While the allusion to Kennewick Man's physical appeal is humorous for obvious reasons (BARBIRE and KENNewick Man), it is also not accidental here. Like "Kennewick Man Tells All," the poem is preceded by a quotation from James Chatters in which he refers to artist Thomas McClelland's reconstruction of Kennewick Man's face from a plaster cast of his skull. Looking at the face, Chatters immediately sees a resemblance to actor Patrick Stewart.[70] Chatters's comment is by no means innocent here as it alludes to two separate ideas governing evolutionary history. First of all, in the coverage of the case, the popular media, quoting the scientists working on the case, often emphasized Kennewick Man's "Caucasoid" characteristics. Thus, using the Kennewick Man to prove that it was people of European origin who first inhabited the American continent challenges the status of Native Americans as the original inhabitants and dismisses their claims to tribal lands and sovereignties. It is the same logic that is present in the "we-are-all-related" narrative that incessantly emphasizes the theory of the common origins of humanity. Secondly, the enthusiasm with which many people accepted the idea that the Kennewick Man is of European origin is explained by the fact that he does not look Native according to the existing stereotypes and cultural fantasies. Crawford asserts that "Authentic Indians" as projected by whites—"[the] one[s] with the land, [who] wear buckskin and feathers, live in tipis, dance with wolves, and hunt buffalo while riding bareback"[71]—are difficult to find today. "Through Kennewick Man," writes Crawford, "white popular culture can appropriate the role of the 'Authentic Indian' that Native Americans have not adequately embodied."[72] Consequently, like the genomic articulation of Indigeneity, the perpetuation of the "Authentic Indian" stereotype secures white culture's grip on the definition of Indianness.

Is Kennewick Man ever aware of the complex issues enveloping his existence? While the cyber format of dating clearly does not appeal to his sensibilities, he does want to "smell a woman's neck again!"[73] Thus, in the last stanza, he needs to complete the application:

> Or just fill all required fields.
> To simply state: My age
> My race
> My God.[74]

Erdrich cleverly points out how, in the case of the Kennewick Man, these seemingly simple questions cannot be answered, even (or especially!) with the help of science. Moreover, the identification of race becomes even more complicated considering the long history of white people's insistence on the right to delineate racial boundaries, with blood quantum in the case of Native Americans, the "one-drop" rule for African Americans, and the changing status of the Irish in the history of immigration laws. Thus, not only does science fail to "tell all," as Kennewick Man's decoded body is expected to, but it also remains oblivious to a rich body of Indigenous epistemologies that already contain theories of human origins and migrations. If "My God" is Kennewick Man's exclamation rather than a question about religion, science's pretense to infallibility confounds him enormously. In her analysis of Erdrich's investment in NAGPRA, Poremski asserts that by humanizing Kennewick Man, Erdrich "voices the bones" and thus achieves the effects for which NAGPRA was created: respect paid to the dead as well an emphasis on "relationships based on familial and human ties rather than material value."[75] It is in a reconstruction of Kennewick Man's personality and body that Erdrich locates the most effective strategy of resistance to the objectification of Native people's bodies in Western science.

As a poetic counterpart and predecessor of *Native American DNA* by Kim TallBear, Erdrich's poetry addresses the complex problem of attributing the power to determine and authenticate tribal belonging to DNA testing. In "DNA Tribes" the speaker begins by drawing attention to the omnipresence of technoscientific discourses, their claims to infallibility, and the nagging requests for participation represented by spam email and pop-ups. This is juxtaposed with images of nature, here represented by the red-eyed vireo, which are governed by elegant simplicity:

> The red-eyed vireo calls:
> Here I am. Where are you?
> Like some bizarre bio-mimic,
> Web ads pop up while I email
> asking: Native American DNA—What Tribe Are You?[76]

Beginning with the image of a vireo, a line from a nursery rhyme, and continuing with biomimetics, Erdrich juxtaposes the world of nature and the world of technology, the latter in caricature form. The vireo performs a dance of deception to hide the true location of its nest:

> The red-eyed vireo calls,
> misleading us to relocate,
> following its flight
> away from nestlings tight in twigs,
> to get us lost in a bog.[77]

The bird only appears to be lost,

> asking all along if we even
> know our own locale:
> *Here I am. Where are you*?[78]

Its seemingly chaotic movement is a clever ruse to keep away potential intruders. DNA testing ads, mimicking a similar dance (popping up), pose an analogous question about the location of belonging: "What Tribe Are You?" The answer, it is promised, is contained in a ridiculously simple act:

> All's I'd need to do is swab
> and mail away
> cells my ancestors took
> millennia to perfect.[79]

However, the use of the conditional form reveals that the speaker is not so easily deceived. In the last stanzas of the poem, the speaker dismisses the false promises of genetic testing: belonging is not solely in the genes. Rather, it is a culturally defined and land-based concept:

> As if that could fool us,
> Make us forget the nesting grounds,
> The red eye cast backward
> To the place always known as home.[80]

The collective "we" never doubts that while the ancestral home is indeed contained and transmitted in cells, it is not something that can be traced or identified by a biochemical test. By establishing Native identity as contingent on land (as home), with its distinct histories, geographies, and networks of interdependencies between human and nonhuman beings, Erdrich resists the alluring and yet reductive discourses of genetic ancestry tests. While described as relevant in tribal belonging disputes, genetic tests are unable to account for complex cultural concepts of kinship and relatedness. Rather, the genomic articulation of Indigeneity with DNA ancestry tests as its most poignant example attempts to hijack Indigenous rights to self-definition.

In Erdrich's poetry, scientific and genomic discourses are not antithetical to Ojibwe epistemologies. Diagnostic imaging technologies and biochemical analysis of blood give access to the world of movement and mobility, both important concepts in Ojibwe culture, on the molecular level. Indeed, Michi Saagiig Nishnaabeg artist and scholar Leanne Betasamosake Simpson emphasizes how mobility leads to productivity and the forging of unexpected coalitions: "We've always moved throughout our territories and through the territories of others with the practice of diplomacy, moving with the consent of other nations."[81] In "Microchimerism," Erdrich recreates the same dynamics of movement that has a potential for regeneration:

> Your cells and hers
> flowed back and forth—
> blood river.[82]

This juxtaposition of water and blood, the way in which they flow and the way in which they are life-giving substances, is a common theme in Erdrich's poetry, inspired by her knowledge of the Ojibwe language. Indeed, Anishinaabe scholar and educator Margaret Noodin explains how water and blood are conceptually and linguistically interconnected:

> The center of *Anishinaabewakiing*, or Anishinaabe country, is the life-giving *gaming*, the "vast water." The roll of "g" against "m" is still heard when people speak of Lake Superior as *Gichi Gumee*, the biggest, most *kchi*, of all seas. . . . Beyond the water are *miskwaasini'ing*, the swamp, and *mashkodent*, grassland. In these words are echoes of *miskwa* (blood), *mashkiki* (medicine), and *mashkawizi* (strength). The middle ground between the bays and rivers is important and an indelible part of Anishinaabe culture.[83]

Clearly, there are linguistic similarities among words describing the Anishinaabeg habitats, and these in turn are connected to all the things that are necessary to thrive and create a sustainable universe. This ancient wisdom does not stand in opposition to what Erdrich finds so fascinating in science. "Careful readers [of Ojibwe literature]," writes Noodin, "will see connections between Western science and indigenous narratives, between maps of land and the etymology of language and culture."[84]

What resonates most compellingly in Erdrich's poems is her attendance to land-based ethics, which, as TallBear emphasizes, is the most important precept of the Indigenous articulation of Indigeneity. It is not the chronology of settler colonialism and the question of who arrived first and where but a thorough connection to the place of origins and dwelling. In "The Theft Outright" (which is also a dialogue with Robert Frost's colonialist "The Gift Outright"),[85] Erdrich emphasizes how everything begins with the land that is a source of life, culture, and identity:

> We were the land's before we were. . . .
> We were the land before we were people,
> loamy roamers rising, so the stories go,
> or formed of clay, spit into with breath reeking soul—.[86]

In Ojibwe ontology, it is the land that creates communities and fosters relationships between human and nonhuman beings. On the one hand, the land is sacred and yet strikingly corporeal in the way it mirrors the workings of the human body: "red rocks" bring to mind

blood clots bearing boys, blood sand
swimming being from women's hands, we originate,
originally, spontaneously as hemorrhage.[87]

Indeed, Erdrich repeatedly compares the land to the human body, insisting they are both animated by blood as a life-giving substance. Land is imagined as having a body that is later shared with the people made out of water and earth. She writes:

We were the land before we were a people,
earthdivers, her darling mudpuppies, so the stories go,
or emerging, fully forming from flesh of earth—.[88]

This comparison further emphasizes the sacredness and sturdiness of the connection between the land and the people who inhabit it, thus establishing land-based origins and ethics as fundamental components of Indigeneity. Moreover, Erdrich's investment in the Indigenous body as originating from and dependent on the land reinforces the juxtaposition that TallBear introduces with the commodification of Indigenous bodies in the scientific (and capitalist) context. Using the imagery of pillage and dispossession, Erdrich demonstrates how lands and bodies are now violated like land used to be and for the same imperialist purposes.

And yet, despite the violence of settler colonialism, the connection between land and people survives, embedded and replicated in Indigenous philosophies and lifestyles. As Simpson explains,

This is in part because within Nishnaabeg thought, the opposite of dispossession is not possession, it is deep, reciprocal, consensual *attachment*. Indigenous bodies don't relate to the land by possessing or owning it or having control over it. We relate to the land through connection—generative, affirmative, complex, overlapping, and nonlinear *relationship*.[89]

Indeed, Erdrich painstakingly demonstrates how Christian and Western precepts of land use differ from Indigenous land ethics, and consistently draws an image of attachment to land that is experienced instinctively, on the level of the body, and across generations. In "Grand Portage," Erdrich illustrates how the land becomes a witness to and an object of settler colonial transformation intent on capitalizing on natural resources and the Indigenous knowledge of how to access them. The title is an English translation of Gitchi Onigaming, an Ojibwe term for the "Great Carrying Place," an eight-and-a-half-mile portage trail that served as a passable route to the meeting and exchange point of Native Americans, explorers, and fur traders representing the North West Company.[90] In 1958 the site was designated a national monument, which, as Erdrich observes, draws attention to the arbitrariness of selecting which literary, cultural, historical, and geographical phenomena deserve the label "monumental." For the speaker, the grandness of the place lies in the awe-inspiring continuity of the space, unshaken by the violent intrusion of traders, settlers, and later tourists. This is communicated with an anaphoric "here" beginning each stanza. Gitchi Onigaming remains monumental not due to the presidential designation but because "There [exists] the true path, the mark, the monumental." The speaker feels part of this continuum and fully identifies with the original inhabitants:

> Here is the path my people walked
> hauling immense trade canoes,
> the semi-truck of centuries past.[91]

The possessive pronoun "my" communicates a sense of belonging to the ancestors and the land. This feeling is traced in geography and Indigenous bodies.

It is not enough for Erdrich to draw connections between the land and the people on spatial and temporal levels. In "Define Chimera," Erdrich uses the phenomenon of microchimerism to demonstrate how a discourse of contemporary science becomes an apt idiom to communicate the relationality of all beings. Microchimerism, extensively studied in the context of bidirectional cell traffic during pregnancy, denotes "the presence of small, though diverse, cell populations or of minute amounts of cell-free DNA, from a 'donor' within the 'recipient.'"[92] Donor cells frequently persist in the recipient's body for as long as twenty-seven years postpartum and become engrafted in the tissues, such as bone marrow, spleen, and liver blood.[93] Thus, microchimerism challenges the idea of clear-cut boundaries between organisms, organs, cells, and DNA. Erdrich creatively approaches microchimerism to convey relationality as a constant movement and transfer of molecules that travel in time, space, and bodies:

> facts to your everyday chimera, composed (as each we are)
> of body, spirit, mind—
> of earth and water, of fire and air.[94]

Here and in several other poems Erdrich utilizes genetic science to speak about Ojibwe epistemologies, which succinctly attests to her fluency in deconstructing the oppressive character of the genomic articulation of Indigeneity and her ability to create an efficient metaphor for intergenerational relatedness and the embodied dimension of Indianness connected with human beings, nonhuman beings, and nonorganic matter.[95]

In an introduction to the edited collection *New Poets of Native Nations*, Erdrich writes:

> Here is poetry of a new time—an era of witness, of coming into voice, an era of change and of political and cultural resurgence—a time shared within this anthology in poetry forceful and subtle, hysterical and lyrical, ironic and earnest, sorrowful and joyful, and presented in ways harder to define, but made of the recent now, the lived realities that poets of Native nations write.[96]

The idea behind the anthology is also an accurate summary of Erdrich's own poetry, in particular her works devoted to commentaries on the uses and abuses of genomic science in research on Indigenous communities. By challenging assumptions that Native people and cultures are remnants of the past, irrelevant in contemporary social, political, and scientific contexts, Erdrich disrupts the discourse of genomic articulation of Indigeneity, which, as TallBear eloquently argued, obliterates Indigenous presence from scientific projects and agendas. The poetry in *National Monuments* and *Cell Traffic*, "forceful and subtle, hysterical and lyrical, ironic and earnest, sorrowful and joyful," constructs an alternative scenario in which Indigenous people are included in technoscientific discussions as participants in research work and in which sovereign nations decide which research projects are in their cultural, political, and ethical interests. Thus, Erdrich recognizes the importance of tribal self-determination and each community's rights to protect their land-based economies and cultures, the two aspects of contemporary Native life that are frequently challenged from political, legal, and scientific perspectives. On the other hand, while respecting tribal nationalism and the importance of cultural values, Erdrich possesses a profound understanding of how issues of land claims, sovereignty, threats posed by unsupervised research, and biocolonialism are fundamental for Indigenous people worldwide. Such common causes are identified by Erdrich as the sources of transnational coalitions that draw attention to the mechanisms of settler colonialism as a global phenomenon and, more importantly, to the ways of dismantling such oppressive narratives and systems.

NOTES

1. Rother, "In the Amazon."
2. Erdrich, *Cell Traffic*, 200.
3. Moreton-Robinson, "Relationality," 71–72; emphasis added.
4. TallBear, *Native American DNA*.
5. Whitt, *Science, Colonialism, and Indigenous Peoples*, 24–25.
6. Niezen, *The Origins of Indigenism*, 19.
7. De la Cadena and Starn, "Introduction," 11.
8. Clifford, "Varieties of Indigenous Experience," 209.
9. De la Cadena and Starn, "Introduction," 10.
10. TallBear draws the concept of articulation from cultural studies and sociocultural anthropology. See Clifford, *Routes* and "Indigenous Articulations."
11. See Burkhart, *Indigenizing Philosophy*; Cajete, *Native Science*; Kimmerer, *Braiding Sweetgrass*.
12. TallBear, "Genomic Articulations of Indigeneity," 512.
13. Jaimes Guerrero, "'Patriarchal Colonialism' and Indigenism," 66.
14. Cajete, *Native Science*, 205.
15. TallBear, "Genomic Articulations of Indigeneity," 516.
16. TallBear, "Anthropology, Genomics, and Whiteness," 42. For the nineteenth century, see chap. 2 in Reardon, *Race to the Finish*.
17. TallBear, "Native-American-DNA.com," 238.
18. Doerfler, *Those Who Belong*, xxii.
19. TallBear, "Genomic Articulations of Indigeneity," 516.
20. Ibid., 518.
21. Ibid., 519.
22. TallBear, "DNA, Blood, and Racializing of the Tribe," 86.
23. Beckenhauer, "Redefining Race," 189.
24. Rasmussen et al., "The Ancestry and Affiliations of the Kennewick Man," 458.
25. Jacob, "Making Sense of Genetics, Culture, and History," 285.
26. Regalado, "More Than 26 Million People Have Taken an At-Home Ancestry Test."
27. TallBear, *Native American DNA*, 67–103.
28. Cillizza, "Elizabeth Warren's Native-American Heritage Reveal."
29. Khalid, "Warren Apologizes to Cherokee Nation."
30. MtDNA is inherited from genetic females and Y-chromosomal units of DNA are inherited from genetic males as only male individuals have the Y chromosome. In *Native American DNA* TallBear provides a comprehensive summary of the structure of DNA and the

process of identification of nucleotides (39–45).

31. TallBear, *Native American DNA*, 82–83.

32. TallBear, "Genomic Articulations of Indigeneity," 524.

33. TallBear, "Genomic Articulations of Indigeneity," 525.

34. Haraway, *Modest_Witness@Second_Millennium,* 141.

35. Harry, "Indigenous Peoples and Gene Disputes," 147.

36. "Indigenous People, Genes and Genetics."

37. Whitt, *Science, Colonialism, and Indigenous Peoples*, 23.

38. Waldby, *The Visible Human Project*, 32.

39. TallBear, *Native American DNA*, 136.

40. Rader, "The Poetry of Participation," xi.

41. Jasanoff, "Ordering Knowledge, Ordering Society," 14.

42. Reardon, "Race without Salvation," 307.

43. Brodwin, "Genetic Knowledge and Collective Identity," 139.

44. Erdrich, *Cell Traffic*, 180.

45. Ibid., 181.

46. Ibid., 180.

47. Kowal, "Orphan DNA," 578.

48. Erdrich, *Cell Traffic*, 180, 181.

49. Ibid., 180.

50. Jasanoff, *Designs on Nature*, 4.

51. Erdrich, *Cell Traffic*, 180.

52. Ibid.

53. Beckenhauer, "Redefining Race," 189.

54. Watts, "Indigenous Place-Thought and Agency," 21.

55. Erdrich, *Cell Traffic*, 180.

56. Ibid.

57. TallBear, "Genomic Articulations of Indigeneity," 518.

58. Erdrich, *National Monuments*, 65.

59. Harry, "Indigenous Peoples and Gene Disputes," 190.

60. Erdrich, *National Monuments*, 65–66.

61. Ibid., 65.

62. Rother, "In the Amazon."

63. Rhadigan, "Moving Bodies," 71.

64. These are "Kennewick Man Tells All," "Kennewick Man Swims Laps," and "Kennewick Man Attempts Cyber-date." I concentrate on the first and the third as they are most

closely connected to the issues that I am exploring here.

65. Erdrich, *National Monuments*, 59.

66. Crawford, "(Re)Constructing Bodies," 215.

67. Ibid., 220.

68. Erdrich, *National Monuments*, 59.

69. Ibid., 62.

70. Ibid.

71. Crawford, "(Re)Constructing Bodies," 222.

72. Ibid., 223.

73. Erdrich, *National Monuments*, 62.

74. Ibid.

75. Poremski, "Voicing the Bones," 27.

76. Erdrich, *Cell Traffic*, 9.

77. Ibid.

78. Ibid.

79. Ibid.

80. Ibid.

81. Simpson, *As We Have Always Done*, 197.

82. Erdrich, *Cell Traffic*, 12.

83. Noodin, *Bawaajimo*, 1–2.

84. Ibid., 2.

85. Consider the fundamental differences in Frost's and Erdrich's treatment of the land contained in the first lines of their poems. For Frost, land is taken possession of whereas for Erdrich it is a relationship of care that connects people and the land: "The land was ours before we were the land's" versus "We were the land's before we were."

86. Erdrich, *National Monuments*, 31.

87. Ibid.

88. Ibid., 32.

89. Simpson, *As We Have Always Done*, 43.

90. Grand Portage National Monument, "History and Culture."

91. Erdrich, *National Monuments*, 12.

92. Gleicher, "Pregnancy-Related Cell Traffic," 341.

93. Tan et al., "Fetal Microchimerism," 1443.

94. Erdrich, *Cell Traffic*, 14.

95. I discuss microchimerism in Erdrich's poetry in more detail in Ziarkowska, *Indigenous Bodies*.

96. Erdrich, "Introduction," xi.

BIBLIOGRAPHY

Beckenhauer, Eric. "Redefining Race: Can Genetic Testing Provide Biological Proof of Indian Ethnicity?" *Stanford Law Review* 56, no. 1 (October 2003): 161–90.

Brodwin, Paul. "Genetic Knowledge and Collective Identity." *Culture, Medicine & Psychiatry* 29, no. 2 (June 2005): 139–43.

Burkhart, Brian. *Indigenizing Philosophy through the Land: A Trickster Methodology for Decolonizing Environmental Ethics and Indigenous Futures.* Michigan State University Press, 2019.

Cadena, Marisol de la, and Orin Starn. "Introduction." In *Indigenous Experience Today*, edited by Marisol de la Cadena and Orin Starn, 1–30. Oxford: Berg, 2007.

Cajete, Gregory. *Native Science: Natural Laws of Interdependence.* Santa Fe: Clear Light Publishers, 2000.

Cillizza, Chris. "Elizabeth Warren's Native-American Heritage Reveal Was Just as Bad as You Thought It Was." *CNN Politics*, December 7, 2018. https://edition.cnn.com/2018/12/06/politics/elizabeth-warren-native-american/index.html.

Clifford, James. "Indigenous Articulations." *The Contemporary Pacific* 13, no. 2 (2001): 468–90.

———. *Routes: Travel and Translation in the Late Twentieth Century.* Cambridge, Mass: Harvard University Press, 1997.

———. "Varieties of Indigenous Experience: Diasporas, Homelands, Sovereignties." In *Indigenous Experience Today*, edited by Marisol de la Cadena and Orin Starn, 197–223. Oxford: Berg, 2007.

Crawford, Suzanne J. "(Re)Constructing Bodies: Semiotic Sovereignty and the Debate Over Kennewick Man." In *Repatriation Reader: Who Owns American Indian Remains?*, edited by Devon A. Mihesuah, 211–36. Lincoln: University of Nebraska Press, 2000.

Deloria, Vine, Jr. *God Is Red: A Native View of Religion.* 3rd ed. Golden, CO: Fulcrum Publishing, 2003.

Doerfler, Jill. *Those Who Belong: Identity, Family, Blood, and Citizenship among the White Earth Anishinaabeg.* Minneapolis: Michigan State University Press, 2007.

Erdrich, Heid E. *Cell Traffic: New and Selected Poems.* Tucson: University of Arizona Press, 2012.

———. "Introduction: Twenty-One Poets for the Twenty-First Century." In *New Poets of Native Nations*, edited by Heid E. Erdrich, xi–xvi. Minneapolis: Greywolf Press, 2018.

———. *National Monuments.* East Lansing: Michigan State University Press, 2008.

Gleicher, Norbert. "Pregnancy-Related Cell Traffic, Microchimerism and Autoimmunity: The Possibility of Reducing Autoimmune Disease Prevalence." *Expert Review of Obstetrics & Gynecology* 2, no. 3 (May 2007): 341–45.

Grand Portage National Monument, Minnesota. "History and Culture." National Park Service, accessed September 2, 2020. https://www.nps.gov/grpo/learn/historyculture/index.htm.

Haraway, Donna J. *Modest_Witness@Second_Millennium. FemaleMan©_ Meets_OncoMouse™: Feminism and Technoscience*. New York: Routledge, 1997.

Harry, Debra. "Indigenous Peoples and Gene Disputes." *Chicago-Kent Law Review* 84, no. 1 (2009): 147–96.

"Indigenous People, Genes and Genetics: What Indigenous People Should Know about Biocolonialism." Indigenous Peoples Council on Biocolonialism, June 2000. http://www.ipcb.org/publications/primers/htmls/ipgg.html.

Jacob, Michelle M. "Making Sense of Genetics, Culture, and History: A Case Study of Native Youth Education Program." In *Genetics and the Unsettled Past: The Collision of DNA, Race, and History*, edited by Keith Wailoo, Alondra Nelson, and Catherine Lee, 279–94. Brunswick: Rutgers University Press, 2012.

Jaimes Guerrero, M. A. "'Patriarchal Colonialism' and Indigenism: Implications for Native Feminist Spirituality and Native Womanism." *Hypatia* 18, no. 2 (Spring 2003): 58–69.

Jasanoff, Sheila. *Designs on Nature: Science and Democracy in Europe and the United States*. Princeton: Princeton University Press, 2005.

———. "Ordering Knowledge, Ordering Society." In *States of Knowledge: The Co-Production of Science and Social Order*, edited by Sheila Jasanoff, 13–45. New York: Routledge, 2004.

Khalid, Asma. "Warren Apologizes to Cherokee Nation for DNA Test." *NPR*, February 1, 2019. https://www.npr.org/2019/02/01/690806434/warren-apologizes-to-cherokee-nation-for-dna-test.

Kimmerer, Robin Wall. *Braiding Sweetgrass : Indigenous Wisdom, Scientific Knowledge and the Teachings of Plants*. Minneapolis, Minnesota: Milkweed Editions, 2013.

Kowal, Emma. "Orphan DNA: Indigenous Samples, Ethical Biovalue and Postcolonial Science." *Social Studies of Science* 43, no. 4 (2013): 578–97.

Moreton-Robinson, Aileen. "Relationality: A Key Presupposition of an Indigenous Social Research Paradigm." In *Sources and Methods in Indigenous Studies*, edited by Chris O'Brien and Jean M. Andersen, 71–72. New York: Routledge, 2017.

Niezen, Ronald. *The Origins of Indigenism: Human Rights and the Politics of Identity*. Berkeley: University of California Press, 2003.

Noodin, Margaret. *Bawaajimo: A Dialect of Dreams in Anishinaabe Language and Literature*. East Lansing: Michigan State University Press, 2014.

Poremski, Karen M. "Voicing the Bones: Heid Erdrich's Poetry and the Discourse of NAGPRA." *Studies in American Indian Literatures* 27 no. 1 (Spring 2015): 1–32.

Rader, Dean. "The Poetry of Participation: On the Work of Heid Erdrich." In Heid E. Erdrich, *Cell Traffic: New and Selected Poems*, xi–xvi. Tucson: University of Arizona Press, 2012.

Rasmussen, Morten, et al. "The Ancestry and Affiliations of the Kennewick Man." *Nature* 523

(June 2015): 455–58.

Reardon, Jenny. *Race to the Finish: Identity and Governance in an Age of Genomics*. Princeton: Princeton University Press, 2009.

———. "Race without Salvation: Beyond the Science/Society Divide in Genomic Studies of Human Diversity." In *Revisiting Race in a Genomic Age*, edited by Barbara A. Koenig, Sandra Soo-Jin Lee, and Sarah S. Richardson, 304–19. New Brunswick: Rutgers University Press, 2008.

Regalado, Antonio. "More Than 26 Million People Have Taken an At-Home Ancestry Test." *MIT Technology Review*, February 11, 2019. https://www.technologyreview.com/2019/02/11/103446/more-than-26-million-people-have-taken-an-at-home-ancestry-test/.

Rhadigan, Ryan Joseph. "Moving Bodies: Sovereignty, Science, and Indigenous Ontology in the Poetry of Heid Erdrich." MA thesis, University of California, Los Angeles, 2013.

Rother, Larry. "In the Amazon, Giving Blood but Getting Nothing." *New York Times*, June 20, 2007.

Simpson, Leanne Betasamosake. *As We Have Always Done: Indigenous Freedom through Radical Resistance*. Minneapolis: University of Minnesota Press, 2017.

TallBear, Kim. "Anthropology, Genomics, and Whiteness." In *DNA and Indigeneity: The Changing Role of Genetics in Indigenous Rights, Tribal Belonging, and Repatriation. Symposium Proceedings. Intellectual Property Issues in Cultural Heritage (IPinCH) Project*, edited by Alexa Walker, Brian Egan, and George Nicholas, 39–44. Burnaby, BC: Simon Fraser University, 2016.

———. "DNA, Blood, and Racializing of the Tribe." *Wicazo Sa Review* 18, no. 1 (Spring 2003): 81–107.

———. "Genomic Articulations of Indigeneity." *Social Studies of Science* 43, no. 4 (2013): 509–33.

———. *Native American DNA: Tribal Belonging and the False Promise of Genetic Science*. Minneapolis: University of Minnesota Press, 2013.

———. "Native-American-DNA.com: In Search of Native American Race and Tribe." In *Revisiting Race in a Genomic Age*, edited by Barbara A. Koenig, Sandra Soo-Jin Lee, and Sarah S. Richardson, 235–52. New Brunswick: Rutgers University Press, 2008.

Tan, Xiao-Wei, et al. "Fetal Microchimerism in the Maternal Mouse Brain: A Novel Population of Fetal Progenitor or Stem Cells Able to Cross the Blood-Brain Barrier?" *Stem Cells* 23, no. 10 (2005): 1443–1452.

Waldby, Catherine. *The Visible Human Project: Informatic Bodies and Posthuman Medicine*. London: Routledge, 2000.

Watts, Vanessa. "Indigenous Place-Thought and Agency amongst Humans and Non-Humans (First Woman and Sky Woman Go on a European World Tour!)." *Decolonization: Indigeneity, Education & Society* 2, no. 1 (2013): 20–34.

Whitt, Laurelyn. *Science, Colonialism, and Indigenous Peoples: The Cultural Politics of Law and Knowledge.* New York: Cambridge University Press, 2009.

Ziarkowska, Joanna. *Indigenous Bodies, Cells, and Genes: Biomedicalization and Embodied Resistance in Native American Literature.* London and New York: Routledge, 2021.

A Futurism That Sees No Future

Recognition in Ayi Kwei Armah, James Welch, and Corwin Clairmont

Kathryn W. Shanley

Work for this chapter was initially guided by the premise that such a thing as a world literature exists and, with that, that Native American literature (also assumed to exist) can (and should) theoretically and pedagogically find a place within the canon of world literature. Yet, to approach the subject fully, I must begin by acknowledging that so much goes unsaid in those ideas, despite my belief that it's possible! Bringing a "local" literature, albeit continental in geographic scope, into the massive category of world literature suggests that a culling for certain qualities has taken place, and for crème de la crème values, according to First-World standards. Quaintness might fit in as well. Quality to a local people, however, means different things differently than it does on a global stage, if for no other reason than that a local people feel, walk upon, suffer, and dream the palimpsest of local history for which there are or perhaps need not always be words.

In that spirit, I acknowledge that I live and work in the homeland of the Salish and Pend d'Oreille peoples, and hail from the homelands of the Nakoda, Dakota, and Lakota, in northeastern Montana.[1] Locals also benefit more directly from having their history shaped as an amalgam of oral and written texts and given back to them for their lived experiences going forward—that is, a storyteller of a place brings threads of current happenings together with memorial events and culturally symbolic frameworks. At best, efforts to bring Indigenous literature into the rubric of "world" involve aligning with a politic that seeks to shift the paradigm of how both "the world" and "literature" *can*—indeed, *should*—be seen as inclusive: the human condition writ large. In the process of imagining inclusion, we hope to expand understandings of global citizenship and of what constitutes civilization and indigeneity—two woefully loaded terms.

Montana meets Ghana in this essay as the term "Indigenous" attempts to encompass something of a common experience in postcolonial world(s) of the last fifty or sixty years. The individuals caught within the legacy of colonialism and imperialism feel the consequences of control over homelands and resources in a way that it takes decades for the metropole intellectual realms to absorb and reflect upon deeply. For example, it was not until 2007 that the United Nations Declaration of the Rights of Indigenous People (UNDRIP) was affirmed by a majority vote, with the United States, Canada, New Zealand, and Australia voting against it. The first draft was finished in 1985, but (as some might argue) the declaration was hundreds of years in the making. Tellingly, Indigenous rights needed to be acknowledged and defined *above and beyond* the U.N.'s recognition of human rights that happened after World War II in 1948. Many stages and types of recognition (or rights) reverberate back and forth over time to produce genuine change and the healing of / reckoning with historical trauma. As nuanced ways of articulating what Indigeneity means and has meant under settler colonialism evolve, indeed, as the very terms of such evolution develop, future hope may be possible. In this essay, I discuss a type of historical recognition of Third- and Fourth-World (formerly) colonized individuals, and I offer a reading of their voices and positionalities as being more crucial for their spatially situated nature than for their "stage" in a discourse of articulated postcolonialism.[2] I briefly compare the works of two writers, continents apart in the late 1960s and early 1970s—Ayi Kwei Armah (Ga / Fante, Sekondi Takoradi, Ghana, Africa) and James Welch (Blackfeet/Gros Ventre, Montana, United States, North America). I then compare their visions to that of contemporary Salish artist Corwin "Corky" Clairmont fifty-plus years later. At moments of profound hopelessness, when individuals see no return to supposed better (former) times nor to future more healthful and regenerative times than are possible in the seemingly hopeless present, recognition of that positionality alone stands as a resistance. Dare I say, guarded hope. While the positionalities of these three Indigenous men can be seen as remarkably alike, Clairmont's perspective moves out of the individual conscious-ness and provides literal space for contemplating the position in which Indigenous postcolonial individuals can find themselves and the global connectedness among Indigenous peoples whose lands suffer under exploitive extractive industries.

All three speak as if they are alienated and helpless, despite their being situated as individuals in territories supposedly liberated. Their homelands are no longer controlled by their own peoples: Welch in northeast Montana in two novels, *Winter in the Blood* and *The Death of Jim Loney*; Armah in his novel set in Ghana, *The Beau-tyful Ones Are Not Yet Born*; and Clairmont in his exhibit based on a journey from Montana to Alberta, Canada, *Two-Headed Arrow / The Tar Sands Project*. Although rarely compared, writers from Africa in this period took up themes comparable to those of their Native American counterparts, especially regarding recognition and representation. The cross-pollination relates to a shift in global consciousness and, to some extent, shared texts and theories, however difficult those influences may be to identify and track. The exchange of knowledge may be less through literary sources than through mass media. As a Native child growing up on the Fort Peck Reservation in the late 1950s and early '60s, all I knew of African life came through newsreels at the Saturday matinee, Tarzan movies, and *Little Black Sambo*, a popular children's book of the time. (We didn't know Sambo was South Indian.) Despite colonial themes and overtones, the knowledge engendered sympathies for the Native peoples from Africa in that young Montana Native girl.

About that time, Nigerian writer Chinua Achebe published *Things Fall Apart* (1958), a novel of how the Igbo tribal sovereignty begins to disintegrate through the lethal destroyer-alliance of the missionary and the government. Achebe extends the themes of colonization into bureaucratic domination in *No Longer at Ease* (1960). Later, James Welch would write a similar culture-on-the-cusp-of-apocalyptic-change novel, *Fools Crow* (1986), set in Blackfeet (Pikuni) Country, but no direct link between Welch and Achebe can be made. According to Welch's wife Lois, he had never read *Things Fall Apart*; no copy had ever come into their house.

By the late 1960s, when Armah and Welch began writing, the academy had just begun to recognize "true" literature could come out of those places seen as hearts of darkness, or as the homelands of noble, destroyed or defeated peoples. As I write, it is almost one hundred years after the Negritude movement began and over fifty years since the so-called Native American Renaissance got its start, yet political struggles to gain sovereignty continue, just as visual and literary representation fight to gain an equal footing. Notably, the Indigenous writers/artists within the scope of this essay hold remarkably similar positions fifty years apart.

A crucial Indigenous rights discourse began in 1962 as the global consciousness started to shift. Indigenous writers were just beginning to be invited onto the world literature stage, though they were continuing to experience othering and domination in most aspects of daily living. Nonetheless, an educated intelligentsia was expected to speak. Calls for the "voice" of Indigenous people carried its own appropriative, ironic edge. For example, Franz Fanon posits, in *Black Skin, White Masks*, "Why write this book? No one has asked me for it."[3] His words beg the question: Why did Fanon feel compelled to write, if he could not assume a willing audience? Was he merely posturing? Who is the "one" in "no one"? In dialectical terms, while "one" might represent "the master," the black writer, "the slave," represents the Black Man. Fanon's question obviously reflects Fanon's need for presence, a desire to be a part of a whole, to have a voice and recognition, a desire for "the other" to display an openness to him in all his uniqueness and, significantly, his blackness. Fanon goes on to say, "There is a zone of nonbeing, an extraordinarily sterile and arid region, and an utterly naked declivity where an authentic upheaval can be born. In most cases, the black man lacks the advantage of being able to accomplish this descent into a real hell."[4] In other words, authentic beingness (apart from the affective dilution of double consciousness) is not available to "the black man," which I read as the "subaltern." As Glen Sean Coulthard notes in *Red Skin, White Masks* about Fanon, he "turns our attention to the cultural practices of critical individual and collective self-recognition that colonialized populations often engage in to empower themselves."[5] I see the posture or positionality expressed in Fanon and later in Welch and Armah, and even later in Clairmont, as far from a "transitional" state in a postcolonial process, as Coulthard identifies is the view held by many Fanon scholars. Rather, I suggest "we are still here," and that that may *still be* one of the most radical positions possible under rapacious capitalism. Fanon's posture matters as a crucial antiracist/anticolonial, existential space that continues.

Key to understanding these two Indigenous writers, Armah's and Welch's positions while continents apart, are the following questions: What kind of advantage empowers someone to descend into a "real hell," and why would one want to do so? Is birthing "authentic upheaval" worth it? Or is the experience to be had there an end in itself—that is, a compulsion arising from a deep obsession to be cleansed, perhaps, wiped clean? Fanon steps beside himself to remark: "Man [*sic*] is a *yes* that vibrates to cosmic harmonies. Uprooted, pursued, baffled, doomed to watch the dissolution of the truths that he has worked out for himself one after another, he has to give up projecting onto the world an antinomy that coexists with him."[6] In an existential moment so characteristic of his time, Fanon frames a positionality that will carry forward for decades, a comingling of racial trauma and despair with hope for ritual regeneration through an epistemic nakedness.[7] Hence, the answers to the questions I pose center on the paradox/conundrum of a subject who is marginalized by constructs of race and the heavy weight of colonial history. His (all pronouns apply) historical moment (the vague "no one") calls upon him to speak, but speak only of his emptiness, his nonbeing. A voicing of voicelessness—the antinomy—gives rise to the drama of a descent into a hell of dispossession, defamation, and homelessness at home.

When we look back at that literary moment, we might be tempted to mock its staged despair, but the seeds of hope contained in it resonate with people like me who grew up on American Indian reservations. Bill Ashcroft illuminates what those seeds grew into: "The postcolonial nation, a once glorious utopian idea, was now replaced in the literature, particularly in Africa, by a critical rhetoric that often landed authors in gaol. But gradually, for instance in Africa through writers such as Ayi Kwei Armah, Ngũgĩ wa Thiong'o, or Ben Okri, and latterly women writers such as Chimamanda Adichie, Sade Adeniran, and Unomah Azuah, post-independence despair has been giving way to broader constructions of future hope."[8] Affective space to breath the real as well as the reenacted cushions the blows for future generations, and mitigates against the craziness of feeling erased. Even if one is consciously living out a cliché of oneself, the person may carry the deep need to dwell in the old or unreal space while allowing embryonic selves to form, which may mean being a spectacle.

Individual Indigenous Spaces across Time and Continents

Ayi Kwei Armah is a Ghanaian writer whose parents were Fante speakers and is a descendant from a royal family in the Ga tribe. He attended the Achimota School in Ghana and later got a scholarship to attend the Groton School in Massachusetts, where he was only the second black student to attend the school. After that, he attended Harvard, earning a degree in sociology, and went on for a master's in creative writing from Columbia. His privileged perspective arises from a genuinely global exposure to a set of ideas. In contrast, James Welch moved around Indian

Country of the Pacific North as a youth, since his father worked for the Bureau of Indian Affairs, eventually graduating from high school in Minneapolis. He spoke of his father as a Blackfeet (Anskapi Pikuni) speaker who at one time served on the Blackfeet Tribal Council when all business was conducted in the Blackfoot language.[9] His mother was Gros Ventre (Aaiiinin) from the Fort Belknap Reservation in the northeast Plains region of Montana. Although Welch later in life traveled through the United States and Europe, residing periodically for a term teaching in university settings, for the most part he lived in the urban area of Missoula, Montana. Armah also returned to Africa and eventually ran a publishing house out of his home. Similar to one another, both men seem to value Indigenous places or nearby communities, however troubling existence there may be for the Native inhabitants, including the many corruptions of governments, tribal and otherwise. In writing about the broad category of Indigeneity and trying to draw useful comparisons, being a cultural outsider may be their only commonality, but these two men eventually became part of an Indigenous intelligentsia of outsiders. They did not know then what lived experiences they had in common, making their similar mindsets remarkable.

One of the most striking similarities between the authors' first novels is that both *The Beautyful Ones* and *Winter in the Blood* have nameless narrators. In Armah's novel the protagonist through a third-person narrator is referred to as "the man" or "the watcher," while in Welch's *Winter* the narrator who speaks in the first person is simply not named by himself or by any other character. The compellingly confessional tone of his observing self signals an outsider/witness stance, made all the more real by a self-deprecating dimension. In a sense *Winter*'s narrator's voice mimics the voice created by ethnographers in as-told-to "Indian" autobiographies, for example, Paul Radin's narrator in *Autobiography of a Winnebago Indian*—a well-known colonial artifact of salvage anthropology. *Winter*'s narrator, too, is a watcher, and in the film made from the novel, the filmmakers chose to name him Virgil.[10] They took the name from the famed author of the *Aeneid*, which depicts a band of survivors who seek a new home and a new life as they flee ruin and death. While the theme of rebirth carries throughout the *Aeneid*, *Winter*'s narrator bumbles his way back and forth between small-town bar life and his home on the family ranch where he no longer feels he belongs. The tragicomic tale gestures at awkward rebirth, and lacking true companionship, he actually talks very little to other characters; we know him through the elegiac articulations in his head about all that he sees and does.

In *The Death of Jim Loney*, Welch's second novel, the plot structure itself takes on the form of an epochal shift, from the Dispensation of Law to the Dispensation of Grace, and Jim Loney, who enters the narrative just before Thanksgiving and dies on Christmas Eve, resembles a Christ-figure unable to be born. Liminality defines Loney, just as his aloneness indicates his place apart from community and/or the "last" of a people, as in a tragic manifest destiny–inspired B Westerns. Loney's death by cop in the end (just before Christmas) serves as punishment in his own cultural terms for his having killed his friend.[11] Christ's redemption cannot become a reality, just as the Western cannot allow "the Indian" to survive westward expansion.

Popular culture, in other words, figures into Indigenous postcolonial depictions as a visual backdrop to the authors' respective identities. In Armah's protagonist's life, the figure of "jungle" Africans—Tarzans, as it were—evokes ideas of the black man on the wrong end of a racial disparagement, related to nature: a man more monkey than human, unevolved and destined to be overcome by extinction of cultural evolution. For Welch, Hop-along Cassidy, in the form of a life-sized cutout, "plugs" the narrator and his brother dead from the sidewalk outside the movie theatre. Cowboys as seemingly innocuous as Hop-along Cassidy, in his white pants and neat neck scarf, kill Indians in the narration of manifest destiny as that story of white supremacy plays out and as the European American settler colonialism spreads across the continent. "Savagery," in the old world or words, or "Indigeneity," in the new, all too frequently occupies the binary opposite to "civilized" in Western thinking, even when the imagery can seem so trivial as not to be taken seriously—for example, when Donald Trump mocks Elizabeth Warren with the moniker "Pocahontas." Such baggage comes along with any American Indigenous attempts at self-representation, or to use Aimé Césaire's construction, it is nearly impossible for an Indigenous person simply to be seen as a man who cries out, rather than being seen as a dancing bear.[12]

Bringing Indigenous literatures to the table of world literature, as something other than discovering orphaned cousins, should highlight both a distinctness in the particular literary tradition and its commonality with other literatures; those things are essential for recognition. As historian and philosopher Isaiah Lorado Wilner so aptly states, to understand "Indigenous influence," we need "to move beyond the theme of brute power to grasp the theme of idea power: the agency to reinvent thoughts and perceptions. Through their idea power—their agency as makers, shapers, and long-distance communicators of worlds of thought—Indigenous people contributed to the formation of global consciousness: the modern perception that the world is one and that all people belong equally to it."[13] The experience of standing on the brink of recognition as postcolonial individuals and as literary traditions more or less representing formerly colonized peoples can be captured more readily through a nonpolemical, nonnostalgic witness posture. That's true even though the urge to preach and to express an anguished desire to "return" to a home that no longer exists, if it ever did, may be palpably evident though silent—that's the point, to reach an empathetic reader.

In *Winter* and *The Beautyful Ones*, neither protagonist seems to understand the new world order of bribes (Armah) or gridded agricultural enterprises, farming and ranching, in Montana (Welch), although Armah's novel focuses on the failed promise of nationalism more explicitly than does Welch's. Because the men can neither fit into their worlds nor live by an alternative set of ideals, each man suffers and seeks out guidance from an elder. Armah's "the man" visits "teacher," a reclusive philosopher who offers no solutions but lends a sympathetic ear; teacher, in fact, is more alienated than the man. In *Winter*, the nameless narrator seeks out an old man, Yellow Calf, also more alienated than the narrator, who was a mentor to his late father First Raise. Yellow Calf tells him to lean cockeyed into the wind. Although Yellow Calf eventually turns out to be the narrator's grandfather, neither sentimentality nor kinship guides their relationship. The advice offered by each of the two novels' elders does not shine a path to a less-problematic future—no intergenerational transmission of knowledge is possible. Similarly, other characters in the novels do not offer the protagonists direction.

One of the most poignant scenes from *The Beautyful Ones* occurs when the man, Maanan (an enlightened tribal woman), and Kofi Billy sit looking out on the ocean after smoking wee.[14] Kofi Billy (a crippled tribal man) says,

> I see a long, long way . . . and it is full of people, so many people going so far into the distance that I see them all like little bubbles joined together. They are going, just going, and I am going with them. I know I would like to be able to come out and see where we are going, but in the very long lines of people, I am only one. It is not at all possible to come out and see where we are going. I am just going.[15]

Being "only one" fits with the idea of cultural markings being lost. In a sense, they inhabit the existential "hell" of which Fanon speaks. What follows is a simple declaration of the moon as beautiful. And later the man who is narrating the event says of himself and Maanan, "There was nothing either of us could say after that. We sat with Kofi Billy, knowing the accident that had broken him was pushing forward from the calm below, but knowing of nothing we could do, and unable to say anything in the hope of calming fears too deep for an outsider to feel. Then after some time Maanan got up."[16] The three of them have touched so powerfully on their shared despair—its poignant grip—that they have nothing to say to one another after that. "There was not much talk after that, not between the three of us, for Kofi Billy hid himself from the world, and said nothing. . . . Maanan was trying for happiness again, in those ways that were to destroy her so utterly in the end."[17] The "Sunday after" the threesome's wee-time together, Kofi Billy's body is found hanging from a sheet.

The men in both novels also struggle to connect meaningfully with the women in their lives. In describing the changes happening with the disintegrating cultural center and the adoption of the white man's ways, the narrator in *The Beautyful Ones* states, "Even the women were becoming mean."[18] In the end of the narrative, as the man escapes and heads home, he thinks, "of everthing he was going back to—Oyo the eyes of the children after six o'clock, the office and every day, and above all the never-ending knowledge that this aching emptiness would be all that the remainder of his own life could offer him."[19] The man's wife Oyo, like Teresa, *Winter's* narrator's mother, wants a man who knows how to prosper in the new world order. *Winter's* narrator wonders what has made Teresa so mean. Teresa's man, Lame Bull, has little tolerance for other Native men who do not have his kind of ambition to acquire wealth. In regard to *Winter's* narrator's love life, he heads off in the beginning of the novel after his Cree girlfriend Agnes who has stolen his gun and his electric razor to hock them. When she finally talks to him, she tells him she wants to go to school to become a secretary. She, too, is lost in the new world. Familial alienation comes with the destruction of cultural, social, and economic order—no longer at ease in a homeland, no ownership through belonging, no future.

Yet the two protagonists contrast one another in that Armah's "man" at best presents a weak hope and/or a weak search for utopia, as H. C. O'Connell argues, while *Winter's* narrator seems to be redeemed comically by a naïve hope, evident when he fantasizes finding Agnes and buying her a crème de menthe in hopes of restarting their future together.[20] That said, I do not regard utopian thought as characteristic of Indigenous thinking; rather, such generalizations give me the heebie-jeebies. Underlying the deep principles Indigenous peoples hold in valuing interconnection with the rest of the world, they see that great mystery and fabulous chance undergird human existence. The schematic of utopia represents an oppositely directed energy, presuming or even arrogating a totalizing view of the world. Gaining power from or sharing it with nonhuman entities more appropriately describes an Indigenous form of agency.

Gold also figures into each of the two writers' lives. Ghana, also referred to as the Gold Coast, has a long history of gold mining, including Indigenous gold mining, but in the late nineteenth century, "colonialism and the introduction of modern mining methods enabled European mining companies to gain control" over the country's industry.[21] The aftermath of such resource extraction and exploitation of human beings undergirds Armah's narratives and continues to be a significant factor of life for the Ghanan economy.[22] Similarly, Welch's mother's people suffered from a gold rush that led to their dispossession of large parts of their homelands.

The Fort Belknap Reservation serves as the setting for James Welch's first two novels, and it is the home of the Aani iih (Gros Ventre) and Nakoda (Assiniboine) peoples. Gold was discovered in the nineteenth century on Fort Belknap treaty land, but through the pressure put on the Indigenous people by both government officials and "friends" of the tribe, they were forced to give up that part of their territory as miners flooded into the area. Tellingly, the man *Winter*'s narrator's mother Teresa marries after his father First Raise is found dead in a ditch is named Lame Bull, who carries the same name as the tribal man who signed the treaty that resulted in the peoples' dispossession. (Of course, the fictional incident and the actual Lame Bull family's lives must not be confused.)

Although what is referred to as the Zortman-Landusky Mine is now closed, the environmental contamination from the open-pit, cyanide leach mine makes it a Superfund site for cleanup to the tune of several million dollars a year. The environmental exploitations leading up to the times Welch's and Armah's novels are set (sometime in the 1960s) were not featured explicitly in the novels; I would argue that is due to a combination of factors: the existential literary style of the day that relies on a limited single-consciousness perspective, à la Albert Camus, and the demands of drawing a portraiture of postcolonial liminality and impotence. In addition, I am not sure either author was, as they say, "politicized," as in touch with detailed perspectives about the mining history in their areas. Economic development after colonialism, Indigenous colonies' resources, and intrusive foreign capital figure in both novelists' work in ways that need a fuller treatment than I can offer here.[23] Clairmont's journey becomes all the more important as an example of "raised consciousness" in contemporary times, and he stands as one who nonetheless continues the witness stance. Throughout the years since the mine opened, the neighboring tribal people have not prospered from its presence in their traditional homelands. Quite the contrary; challenging socioeconomic conditions persist.

By the end of the two authors' novels, their protagonists require rituals of renewal and rebirth, but tellingly they are thwarted in their ceremonial efforts to cleanse themselves. The man, the watcher in *Beautyful Ones* is forced to help his corrupt friend Koomson escape his pursuers. Those involved in a government coup threaten to punish Koomson for his kleptocratic role as a corrupt elected official. The man helps him by stuffing him down the hole of a public outdoor toilet—the only possible escape route—and going down after him, washing out to the ocean as does excrement. The narrator in *Winter* struggles to pull a "stupid" cow out that has gotten stuck in the mud. "I wanted to ignore her. I wanted to go away to let her drown in her own stupidity."[24] In the end his horse Bird goes down, and he cannot save the cow.

In *The Death of Jim Loney*, the protagonist commits suicide by cop—a mean reservation cop—as he finds it impossible to leave the reservation and yet impossible to stay. He carries a Kafkaesque guilt about accidently shooting his friend Pretty Weasel when they were out hunting. As a Christ figure, Loney dies even before he can be born. A measure of "cleansing" may be possible for these men, but rebirth? No. They do not transcend their stuck place. In regard to such cultural liminality, Wangari wa Nyantetu-Waigwa remarks that such protagonists' predicament is "not a failed initiation, accompanied by its abundant discontinuity and incoherence, but with a suspended liminality—and therefore with hope of continuity and birth."[25]

Ayi Kwei Armah and James Welch in their geographical contexts create protagonists who embody the philosophical perspectives expressed by Fanon, in their descents into their respective existential hells. They insist upon taking a look at the paradox of power and powerlessness in postcolonial spaces that have not yet become new or renewed (problematic as such concepts may be). These two writers come together around many commonalities in both their situations and in the themes, images, and plot features of their early fiction, as discussed above. Most notably for the purpose of this chapter, the novelists' main characters' internal dialogues serve as means of recognition without response—in other words, they are talking to themselves, but talking nonetheless—representing a particular type of Indigenous grit and resiliency. In their time, they were not backed by decolonizing movements, such as the #NoDAPL (No Dakota Access Pipeline) activist effort to stop the building of an oil pipeline on Indigenous homelands.

That said, it would be hasty to draw a conclusion that progress has been made since the 1970s in terms of Indigenous efforts to prevent contamination on their homelands, to draw such conclusions based on the idea of Indigenous ability/willingness to articulate fears of an apocalyptic future. As James Anaya, former special rapporteur for the U.N. on Indigenous Peoples notes: worldwide extractive industries in their "drive to extract and develop minerals and fossil fuels (oil, gas and coal)" must be seen alongside the fact that "what remains of these natural resources is situated on the lands of indigenous peoples."[26] The scope of that issue is beyond my focus here on a way of seeing, a literary/artistic mode of witness; basically, I urge caution about not allowing rhetorical assertions of presence, even literal grounding in place to stand for genuine recognition and restored agency. The demand for domestic sources of energy have only accelerated since the 1970s.

Standing Ground with Corky Clairmont's *Two-Headed Arrow / The Tar Sands Project*

As a person who frequently identifies cynicism as a shield of the weak, I do believe that hope lies in slowly changing the vocabulary of discussions and illuminating and articulating suffering. Global solidarity matters. The UNDRIP passed in 2007 asserting Indigenous equality; the most dramatic years for launching the declaration occurred in the late 1960s and early 1970s with social justice movements such as the Alta affair, in Norway, where Sami people protested the building of a hydroelectric dam in their homelands, and the Occupation of Alcatraz, where a group of Native Americans in the U.S. San Francisco Bay area laid claim to the abandoned federal prison for their cultural use, as their treaty rights guaranteed. Rebellions against colonial rule occurred at that time throughout Africa as well. Countries such as Ghana, Angola, and many others began shaping their own governments, reconstituting homelands in ways more respectful to their cultural traditions; in similar ways Native Americans laid claim to sovereignty in the form of fishing and hunting rights. In American pop culture, Vine Deloria Jr., leading American Indian intellectual of the twentieth century, published *Custer Died for Your Sins: An Indian Manifesto* (1969). A year later, he published *We Talk, You Listen: New Tribes, New*

Turf. In literature, N. Scott Momaday's novel *House Made of Dawn* (1969) won the Pulitzer Prize for literature.

Without imagination, we would be incapable of empathizing with other living beings, let alone taking meaningful action to build good worlds that alleviate the suffering of others. Importantly, though, imagination does not reside only in the head—it resides in what is metaphorically called "the heart." It fires in those gut-wrenching moments when ideas and feelings about situations larger than and seemingly outside of ourselves lock together into place. Far from daydreaming or merely being the mind's wanderings, imagination is comprised of undeniable moments of holistic recognition. That is how imagination becomes memorable. In the title of Corky Clairmont's conceptual exhibit *Two-Headed Arrow / The Tar Sands Project*,[27] we see forces of the mind/body/world at work synergistically. He is pulling together everyday objects like Gummy bears and garbage bags and juxtaposing them with aesthetically appealing interactive pieces like a giant tic-tac-toe board and intriguing photos—all for the purpose of leading participants on a journey through a set of ideas. By doing so, he revitalizes viewers' imaginations to see contemporary environmental justice and Indigenous peoples' issues anew. Those ideas, Indigeneity and environmental justice in Native North America, when coupled in and through the imagination, enliven a new set of choices.

In this exhibit, Clairmont spatializes some big ideas and, in the process, poses extraordinarily challenging questions to viewers about themselves and the world. Spatial cognition, which can be defined as learning to think with and through material, profoundly embeds new knowledge within its practitioners and invites creative new possibilities. Perhaps the most important question in this exhibit, however, is not new: Who bears responsibility for the environmental degradation caused by corporations? Add to that: Who benefits from the destruction of an ecosystem, a destruction as collateral to oil as a reward, and who cleans up afterward? Who/where are Indigenous people of northern Alberta today whose homelands have been destroyed? Do their lives matter? (Yes, I mean, "matter"!) Why, why not? How does seeing the Athabasca Tar Sands from an Indigenous point of view change exhibit goers' minds/hearts? And, finally, who speaks for the Bear People, the Turtle and Fish Peoples, the Wingeds, and other nonhuman beings whose lives have been altered seemingly irreversibly by the extraction industry project?

In answer to the question about responsibility, when confronted, few among us would deny we all have a responsibility to live in a balanced way within our "natural" world, but remembering that we too are "natural," and that no single thing that exists is truly set apart from the whole. Valuing interconnectedness gives that question of responsibility more urgency. (Human egos arrogate exceptionalism, it seems.) Along a similar vein, many of us do not recognize that we benefit—at least in the short term—from the destruction of the Tar Sands ecosystem. The extraction project has a forty-year-old history of working against maintaining a healthful environment, steadily destroying the place and its peoples. Where have we been while all of this is going on? Sunco and other corporations earn the profits, and most notably the United States benefits more than Canada does. Spatial cognition involves the assemblage of relationships that we bear witness to as we follow Clairmont's memorial journey and allows those questions and ideas to soak in—no easy escape affords itself. The high number of products made from oil, beyond petroleum for automobiles and other vehicles, cannot be ignored. Oil and gas are us.

By spatializing his experience of traversing the landscape from Missoula, Montana, to Fort McKay, Alberta, the artist allows us meditative space/time to imagine we stand, walk, and travel with him in his pondering of the devastation as well as the interconnectedness. His grappling with the questions often takes the form of visual evidence and juxtaposition, and humor figures in also. Tiny Gummy bears seem to lay claim to the travel as well as the consumerism of place. Our participation in the journey takes us out of our comfort zones. We become witnesses along with Clairmont. And perhaps the most haunting question raised by the spectacle entails the ultimate responsibility to clean up the mess left behind and the seriousness of considering what losses to human and nonhuman alike may be permanent, not recoverable. Our responsibility cannot be avoided.

Because Corky Clairmont is an enrolled member of the Confederated Salish Kootenai Tribes who grew up on the Flathead Reservation, he invites us to see the world along his road trip to, from, and at the Tar Sands site through his Indigenous perspective. And although he would be the first to admit he does not speak for other Indigenous people, we can trust that he has an understanding of what "homeland" means. We can, therefore, readily surmise that he is tackling the question regarding what has happened to the Indigenous people of northern Alberta whose homelands are being and, in many senses, have been destroyed. Do their lives matter? If yes, to whom? If not, why not? Obviously all life matters, but as Jennifer Huseman and Damien Short argue, what we see today comes from a history of encounter and negotiation that goes back to the Royal Proclamation of 1763. Instead of mass murder as occurred during the colonial period, bureaucratic slaughter is resulting in order to effect "a slow industrial genocide,"[28] where the destruction of Indigenous people of northwestern Alberta's social communities lead toward their annihilation as culturally distinct people, free and able to sustain themselves. Their world once provided abundantly to make that life possible.

Who better to ponder those questions than Corky Clairmont. He not only brings his own cultural Salish background with him, but he also comes with an extensive history as an artist/activist. He has seen U.S. and Canadian policies toward the Indigenous peoples of their respective countries play out for the last five decades, during his own lifetime. The imposition of Kerr Dam in the 1930s on the people of the Flathead Reservation, along with several other U.S. policy decisions about tribal land, eliminated their subsistence life by disturbing the river's flow, inviting increased non-Native settlement, and limiting the tribal people's movement through the region for hunting, fishing, and gathering food. Decimation of wildlife such as bison beginning in the mid-1800s also contributed to the subjugation and impoverishment of Salish, Pend d'Oreille, and Kootenai peoples. Clairmont knows that history by heart. The exhibit encompasses his lifelong journey as a tribal citizen, activist, and artist ever refining the crucial political statements about tribal self-determination interwoven with his fine aesthetic acumen for color, form, and composition.

Moreover, working around the edges of powerful political ideas is not new to Clairmont. Practically his entire artistic life has involved a melding together of words and images, as his work resides most easily in what is termed "conceptual art." For example, Clairmont coined the infamous and resonant word "Submuloc" during the Columbus Quincentenary in 1992 ("Columbus" spelled backward), done as a way to gesture toward rethinking Columbus's colonial enterprise and the imperialist history built up around the valorization of the "discovery" of Indigenous lands.[29] Rather than a fantasy of sending Europeans back across the Big Water, Submuloc represents a movement to reverse the gaze, Natives looking into the soul of settler colonialist America. Gerald Vizenor, Anishinaabe author, chooses, as Clairmont does, to celebrate Indigenous survivance, Vizenor's coined term that stands for an affirmation of resilience and creativity in the face of oppression—rather than a denial of the full experience multifaceted cultural cross-encounters bring. Vizenor's novel *Heirs of Columbus* playfully creates characters who save Columbus from himself by teaching him about Indigenous spiritual healing.

Clairmont's meditative and investigative journey from Missoula to Fort McKay is described so well by Stephen Gluecker when he notes, "Through imagery,

Clairmont shows that the bears know no borders, nor does the air or climate or aquifer. Indigenous people did not know these borders. Missoula is tied to the tar sands region by several factors, a shared environment, the commonality of all the climate, fish, wildlife, and humans that occupy that environment."[30] Clairmont's journey notably takes a precise shape around the prime number nineteen, literally the number of stops he takes along the way to document the trip. In addition to illustrating the extraordinary care the artist takes with detail, the prime number used also draws attention to how singular, indivisible, and distinct a person's journey is. Of prime importance, one might argue, is the meaning-making. Yet, ironically, the prime number nineteen also draws attention to the arbitrary nature of both borders and numbers—the Western European practice of gridding in squares as well as in creating taxonomies of hierarchy. Such divisions preoccupy our thinking rather than empower us to see the primary importance of fluidity and connection, of borderlessness.

For all the hard edges and bounded space in the objects and images in Clairmont's display, binaries become readily blended through thematic unity and overlap—the "dinosaur hides" standing for ancient life on earth, now used as trash and the T road sign, along with the word "Chewz," just two examples. The two-headed arrow (the arrow being a stereotypical Plains Indigenous symbol) visually indicating an either/or literal outward direction, up or down, at the same time as it threatens the viewer with the seriousness of consumption—we are what we eat, what we chew, and what we swallow—it is both literal and metaphorical.

As we look to the future, as we face old and new crossroads of decision, the guidance of many Indigenous activists and intellectuals can show us new paths. As noted above, in 2013, James Anaya, United Nations Special Rapporteur on the Rights of Indigenous Peoples, chose the topic of extractive industries and Indigenous peoples for the focus of his annual report. He identified five points through his year-long study: First, that resources associated with Indigenous people either because they control those resources or because they live in places where resources exist means extractive activity brings "increasing and ever more widespread effects on indigenous peoples' lives."[31] Second, that Indigenous people are "open to discussions about extraction of natural resources from their territories in ways beneficial to them and respectful of their rights."[32] Third, extraction measures may be incompatible with peoples' own directions and designs for their future. Fourth, the "business model" employed by many in the extractive industry "is not fully conducive to the fulfillment of indigenous peoples' rights, particularly their self-determination, proprietary and cultural rights in relation to the affected lands

evokes the stereotypes. The systematic dismantling of the use of Indigenous identity in sports mascots shows some progress in shifting ever so slightly away from racist thinking.

13. Isaiah Lorado Wilner, "Transformation Masks: Recollecting the Indigenous Origins of Global Consciousness," in Indigenous Visions: Rediscovering the World of Franz Boaz, edited by Ned Blackhawk and Isaiah Lorado Wilner, 3–41 (New Haven, CT: Yale University Press, 2018), 3.

14. "Wee" is a slang term for marijuana in Ghana.

15. Armah, *The Beautyful Ones*, 74.

16. Ibid.

17. Ibid., 75.

18. Ibid., 76.

19. Ibid., 183.

20. See O'Connell, "A Weak Utopianism of Postcolonial Nationalist Bildung."

21. Ofosu-Mensah, "Historical Overview," 6.

22. "The minerals mined in Ghana account for 37% of the country's total exports, with gold comprising 90% of total mineral exports. Miningglobal.com estimates Ghana's gold reserves to be 1,000 metric tonnes." "Top Five Gold Mining Countries of Africa from Ghana to Burkina Faso," NS Energy, August 28, 2020, https://www.nsenergybusiness.com/news/top-gold-mining-countries-africa/

23. See Kennedy, "Indigenous Capitalism in Ghana," for a discussion of the ways local peoples most often get shut out of capitalist growth and profit.

24. Welch, *Winter in the Blood*, 166.

25. Nyatetu-Waigwa, *The Liminal Novel*, 130.

26. Anaya, "Extractive Industries and Indigenous Peoples," 3.

27. The exhibit went from March 27, 2018, until August 11, 2018, at the Missoula Art Museum (MAM), in Missoula, Montana. The nine-hundred-mile journey to the Tar Sands in Alberta upon which the project is based began at MAM.

28. Huseman and Short, "'A Slow Industrial Genocide,'" 217.

29. Huseman and Short, "'A Slow Industrial Genocide.'"

30. Gluecker, "Two-Headed Arrow," 88.

31. Anaya, "Report to the Human Rights Council," 2.

32. See Kennedy, "Indigenous Capitalism in Ghana" for discussion of how high capital profits and community participation interface in complicated ways when Indigenous peoples choose to create partnerships in development.

33. Anaya, "Report to the Human Rights Council," 3.

34. Huseman and Short, "'A Slow Industrial Genocide,'" 218.

35. Ibid, 221.

36. Wolfe, "Settler Colonialism," 388.
37. Ryan, "Regimes of Waste," 51.

BIBLIOGRAPHY

Achebe, Chinua. *Things Fall Apart*. New York: Penguin, 1994.

Anaya, James. "Extractive Industries and Indigenous Peoples." United Nations General Assembly, Human Rights Council, July 1, 2013. http://unsr.jamesanaya.org/docs/annual/2013-hrc-annual-report-en.pdf.

Armah, Ayi Kwei. *The Beautyful Ones Are Not Yet Born*. Oxford: Heineman Educational Publishers, 1988..

Ashcroft, Bill. "Introduction: Spaces of Utopia." *Spaces of Utopia: An Electronic Journal*, 2nd series, no. 1 (2012): 1–17. https://ler.letras.up.pt/uploads/ficheiros/10634.pdf.

Brody, Hugh. *Maps and Dreams*. Vancouver: Douglas & McIntyre, 1981.

Césaire, Aimé. *Notebook of a Return to the Native Land*. Edited by Annette Smith; translated by Clayton Eshleman. Hanover, NH: Wesleyan University Press, 2013.

Coulthard, Glen Sean. *Red Skins, White Masks: Rejecting the Colonial Politics of Recognition*. Minneapolis: University of Minnesota Press, 2014.

Fanon, Franz. *Black Skin, White Masks*. New York: Grove Press, 1967.

Gluecker, Stephen. "Two-Headed/Tar Sands Project: A Masterwork at the Missoula Art Museum." In *Corwin Clairmont: Two-Headed Arrow/The Tar Sands Project*, 88, 91. Missoula, MT: Missoula Art Museum, 2020.

Gordon, Lewis R. "Through the Zone of Nonbeing: A Reading of Black Skin, White Masks in Celebration of Fanon's Eightieth Birthday." *C.L.R. James Journal* 11, no. 1 (Summer 2005): 1–43.

Huseman, Jennifer, and Damien Short. "'A Slow Industrial Genocide': Tar Sands and the Indigenous Peoples of Northern Alberta." *International Journal of Human Rights* 16, no. 1 (2012), 216–37.

Kennedy, Paul. "Indigenous Capitalism in Ghana." *Review of African Political Economy* 4 (1977): 21–38.

Kowalik, George. "Post-postmodernism, the 'Affective Turn,' and Inauthenticity." *Humanities* 12, no. 1 (2023): 7.

Mills, Jennifer. "Destabilizing the Consultation Framework in Alberta's Tar Sands." *Journal of Canadian Studies* 51, no. 1 (Winter 2017): 153–84.

Nyatetu-Waigwa, Wangari wa. *The Liminal Novel: Studies in the Francophone-African Novel as Bildungsroman*. New York: Peter Lang, 1997.

O'Connell, Hugh Charles. "A Weak Utopianism of Postcolonial Nationalist Bildung: Re-reading Ayi Kwei Armah's *The Beautyful Ones Are Not Yet Born.*" *Journal of Postcolonial Writing* 48, no. 4 (2012): 371–83.

Ofosu-Mensah, Emmanuel Ababio. "Historical Overview of Traditional and Modern Gold Mining in Ghana." *International Research Journal of Library, Information and Archival Studies* 1, no. 1 (August 2011): 6–22.

Ryan, Connor. "Regimes of Waste: Aesthetics, Politics, and Waste from Kofi Awoonor and Ayi Kwei Armah to Chimamanda Adiche and Zeze Gamboa." *Research in African Literatures* 44, no. 4 (Winter 2013): 51–68.

Sands, Kathleen. "The Death of Jim Loney: Indian or Not?" *Studies in American Indian Literature* 5, no. 3/4 (Fall 1981), n.p.

Smith, Alex, and Andrew Smith, directors. *Winter in the Blood*. Ranchwater Films, 2013.

Vizenor, Gerald. *Heirs of Columbus*. Hanover, NH: Wesleyan University Press, 1991.

Welch, James. *Fools Crow*. New York: Viking Penguin, 1986.

———. *Winter in the Blood*. New York: Harper & Row, 1974.

Wilner, Isaiah Lorado. "A Global Potlatch: Identifying the Indigenous Influence in Western Thought." *American Indian Culture and Research Journal* 37, no. 2 (2013): 87–115.

———. "Transformation Masks: Recollecting the Indigenous Origins of Global Consciousness." In *Indigenous Visions: Rediscovering the World of Franz Boaz*, edited by Ned Blackhawk and Isaiah Lorado Wilner, 3–41. New Haven, CT: Yale University Press, 2018.

Wolfe, Patrick. "Settler Colonialism and the Elimination of the Native." *Journal of Genocide Research* 8, no. 4 (2006): 387–409.

Atonement and Forgiveness as Reparatory Justice in Louise Erdrich's *LaRose* and Fernando Aramburu's *Homeland*

Aitor Ibarrola-Armendariz

R eparatory or restorative justice has drawn the attention of numerous sympathizers in recent times as an auspicious way to amend some of the problems within the current judicial systems.[1] Originally pioneered by religious leaders, who claimed that it was a much more humane and morally preferable way of ironing out crime, reparatory justice maintains that criminal behaviors are not just an offense against some abstract entity—be it society or the state—but also, and mainly, against individuals and human relationships. Unlike retributive justice, which tends to focus on punishing offenders, reparatory justice believes that what should be prioritized is repairing the harm produced by any criminal violation.[2] Furthermore, restorative justice prefers to put the key decisions about how the crime should be dealt with in the hands of those directly affected by the misdemeanor, rather than in those of legal experts and court officials. Because it usually involves ordinary people, most specialists would agree that the process of this type of justice should be governed by simplicity and voluntariness—which, again, are usually absent in retributive legal processes.[3] For its defenders, restorative justice reveals important advantages over more conventional ways of understanding crime and justice, among which its emphasis on community values, the protection of the victims' interests, or its much less repressive character are often mentioned.

Sullivan and Tifft, for example, have emphasized the healing potential of reparatory justice and its capacity of generating a fairer and healthier society.[4] To put it briefly, this type of justice could be said to offer a radical alternative or a new "paradigm" allowing communities to deal with criminal offenses in ways that would favor the following principles: centering on the victim, reparation of the harm done, offender accountability, reconciliation, community orientation, informality, and inclusiveness.

Although it is sometimes believed that restorative justice is a concept and practice that has only developed and expanded during these last five decades, the truth is that it has a much longer history, with its roots deeply planted in traditional patterns of curbing crime and conflict in different cultures. As Braithwaite observes in the first chapter of his book on this type of justice, in periods before the emergence of modern states, it was very common to conceive crime in more personal terms and to focus more closely on reparation and reconciliation, rather than on punishment.[5] It was only in the second half of the eighteenth century that a punitive system of criminal law developed mostly as a result of the European colonization of other parts of the globe. Western legal practices displaced in this way more informal and community-based forms of justice and conflict settlement such as family group conferencing, victim–offender mediation, peacemaking schemes, or sentencing circles.[6] Even though these practices could be used in conjunction with more formal criminal justice processes and could be carried out at different stages of those processes, what characterizes them is that they involve the participation of "all people with a stake in a particular offence [offenders, victims, and their respective communities], who come together to resolve collectively how to deal with the aftermath of the offence and its implications for the future."[7] It has only been since the mid-1960s that we have seen a revival of some of these ancient conflict-resolution traditions, especially in places where long-lasting hostilities between different human groups pervade. In the wake of a variety of political and social movements, such as the victims' movement, the restitution movement, the informal justice movement, the women's movement, or peacemaking operations, a renewed interest in traditional systems of conflict resolution and community reconciliation developed. While it is a fact that in some instances the aspirations of proponents of reparatory justice have been deemed overambitious, it is also true that the reforms they have proposed could result in remarkable benefits for victims, offenders, and their communities at large.[8] Of course, this does not mean that pursuing the ideals of restorative justice is not without its problems. Johnstone, for example, has remarked that these ideals tend to be extremely conservative, and according to Daly, some of the claims made by advocates of this alternative type of justice seem too idealistic.[9] Nevertheless, and despite sporadic evidence to the contrary, it is clear that in specific contexts reparatory justice has proved successful in smoothing the path toward a form of doing justice that places victims at the center of the process, as well as empowering other stakeholders in ways that would be unimaginable in a retributive system. In fact, one of the major problems faced by restorative justice is that due to its somehow "subversive" nature, sometimes it is seen to collide with the ideological and administrative provisions of the more conventional justice systems.[10]

As pointed out above, reparatory justice seems to be particularly appropriate in contexts in which, besides the possible violations of the law in the present, there is a legacy of abuses from the past that usually complicate the cases. It is unquestionable that past abuses such as colonialism, political repression, cultural genocide, or slavery put an additional burden on justice systems, which cannot simply disregard these historical grievances when considering present-day offenses. In Barkan's opinion, there is no way in which the judicial system of certain countries could obviate the existence of those long histories of injury and marginalization of particular human contingents, if true justice is to be pursued.[11] In these contexts, it is crucial to bear in mind the kind of exclusion and the lack of recognition of past traumas that specific groups have suffered on account of their race, gender, class, or ideology. Besides a much-needed exercise in historical revisionism, these groups also need to see their human rights protected by the implementation of judiciary procedures that better serve their interests when conflicts and contentions come up.[12] In this sense, a number of experiments carried out beginning in the 1970s have shown that strategies such as family group conferencing, victim–offender mediation programs, or sentencing circles are more effective in these kinds of settings than the typical processes of retributive justice systems. This may be because members of vulnerable groups tend to be less familiar with the formal proceedings of retributive judiciary systems, and their cultural baggage may in fact incapacitate them to function according to some of the basic assumptions in those systems. Zernova has noted, for example, that Native Americans are usually much better equipped to participate in traditional sentencing circles than they are to take part in contemporary criminal trials:

The importance of circles also lies in the fact that they help to prevent the culture shock which many First Nation people experience when they have to appear in court. When native people follow their traditional ethic during court appearances (such as avoiding making eye contact, showing anger and confronting or criticizing others), their behaviour is regularly interpreted as indifference or uncooperativeness. Circle processes circumvent these problems because they create settings where people can behave in a culturally appropriate fashion.[13]

Countries and regions with a history of sociopolitical conflicts all around the world have resorted to reparatory justice as a complement or an alternative to criminal prosecution often applied to minority and juvenile offenders. Canada, New Zealand, Northern Ireland, South Africa, or the United States are well known for having promoted experiments in which the principles of atonement and reconciliation were thought superior to the penalizing practices of their formal courts. These principles seemed to make more sense in contexts in which the concepts of offender, victim, or even crime needed to become more flexible or less formally defined in the light of earlier grievances that often explained, at least partly, some misdeeds.[14] The main assumption behind many of the aforementioned experiments was that the retributive system was paying little attention to factors—such as the victims' tribulations or the community's distress—that were critical in the proper resolution of the cases and the conviction that a restorative justice would bear better results. Of course, these experiments were implemented in highly diverse settings, and consequently, the kinds of strategies used in each case were different depending on the roles assigned to individual participants, their families, mediators, or even the whole community.[15]

In the following pages, I will be delving into two works of fiction—one by a Native American author and the other by a Basque writer—that foreground the importance of restorative justice in sociopolitically volatile contexts. As the following two excerpts from the novels clearly evince, despite the willingness of some of the characters to use principles such as atonement and reconciliation to try to recover the stability of the community, their attempts at peacemaking are not without significant difficulties:[16]

Landreaux put the small suitcase on the floor. Emmaline was shredding apart. She put the other bag down in the entry and looked away.

They had to tell him [Peter Ravich] what they meant, *Our son will be your son,* and tell him again.

... It's the old way, said Landreaux. He said it very quickly, got the words out yet again. There was a lot more to their decision, but he could no longer speak.[17]

He confirmed it to himself: asking forgiveness takes more courage than firing a weapon, than setting off a bomb. Anyone can do those things. All you have to be is young and credulous, with hot blood. And it isn't only that you need balls to sincerely make up for, even if it's only verbally, the atrocities you've committed. What stopped Joxe Mari was something else.[18]

The chapter looks in some detail into the key stages of the restorative process in the two novels. Thus, it begins by describing the calamitous events that cause a profound disturbance in the two small communities and the tough effects it has not only on the two afflicted families, but also on the members of those communities. As will soon become apparent, some of the ideas provided by historical and cultural trauma theory will be invaluable to better understand why those tragic events reverberate so intensely throughout the two local populations.[19] After that, close attention will be paid to the animosity and vengeful attitudes that emerge in the characters' relationships and that cause vicious circles of hate to imperil the cohesion of the community. Indeed, most of the main characters—with a few exceptions—are invaded by yearnings for retaliation as a way to recover their mental and emotional equilibrium. The second half of the chapter will discuss the central role played by atonement—and reparation—both as parts of particular cultural heritages and as a resilience strategy in the process of trying to heal the wounds and to rebuild the damaged rapport between the families. Howard Zehn has insisted that the main aim of these reparatory practices is to help the victims in the aftermath of a violation, as well as assisting offenders to reintegrate in society and humanizing the justice system as a whole.[20] Finally, a few conclusions are drawn regarding the usefulness of certain reparatory strategies represented in the novels to combat grief, alleviate collective trauma, and fight retaliatory impulses. It is true, however, that these alternative ways of doing justice are not without their limitations, as also becomes evident in the texts, and that as Cohen and others have argued, community-based justice may also reveal shortcomings that should be taken into account.[21]

Sudden Catastrophes and Community Disruptions

Louise Erdrich's *LaRose* and Fernando Aramburu's *Homeland* were both published in 2016 to much critical acclaim.[22] Erdrich's novel won the prestigious National Book Critics Circle Award in the United States, while Aramburu's was awarded, among others, the Premio de la Crítica (2016) and the Premio Nacional de Narrativa (2017) in Spain.[23] Moreover, Aramburu's novel was soon turned into a successful HBO miniseries, which has also received several international awards. Besides their great popularity both with the general reading public and the more specialized critics, the two novels share an interest in the kinds of consequences that a tragic event has on two small communities, the former one being an Ojibwe reservation in North Dakota and the latter an industrial town in the Basque region in northern Spain. Despite the conspicuous differences between the settings and the key events in the two novels, there are interesting similarities in the way local families and communities respond to the unexpected catastrophes that disrupt them from the start.[24] *LaRose*, like the two earlier novels in Erdrich's "Justice Trilogy," opens with an awful mishap that is going to shake the foundations not only of the families more directly implicated, but also of the rest of the Native community. While hunting a deer near the edge of his land, Landreaux Iron accidentally shoots his neighbors' five-year-old son, Dusty Ravich, when the ungulate suddenly jumps aside. Of course, Landreaux is horrified when he realizes what he has just done, for not only have the two families been intimate friends for a long time—sharing clothes, food, and rides into town—but Dusty was the best friend of Landreaux's youngest son, LaRose. The opening vignettes of Aramburu's novel also inform the reader that Txato Lertxundi, an entrepreneur, was killed some years earlier, in this case intentionally, in a terrorist operation.[25] Although initially we only learn about Txato's tragic fate indirectly, by seeing how it has affected the lives of his closest kin, it soon transpires that his murder at the hands of some members of ETA in 1988 stands at the very heart of everything else happening in the novel.[26] In an attempt to explain the immediate success of the novel, Fernando Vallespín wrote that "many of us have lived with the news of ETA attacks. The novel describes a hermetic society, . . . impregnated with violence and in which you need to surrender to the prevalent reactions. There lies its appeal."[27] In this sense, both novels focus on the kinds of repercussions that the two pointless deaths, Dusty's and Txato's, have on the two already vulnerable and unstable communities.

Jessa Crispin rightly remarked that despite the Ojibwe reservation's persistent struggles with poverty, addiction, ill health, and despair, "the repercussions of the young boy's death are felt throughout the community";[28] and the same thing could be affirmed about Txato's murder in *Homeland*. Undoubtedly, it is the two families involved in the bloody incidents who see their lives most deeply affected, since the relationships between the parents in particular quickly begin to deteriorate as none of them is sure of how they are "going to go on living."[29] Although the four pairs of parents show evident signs of mental volatility during the grieving process, it is probably Nola and Bittori, Dusty's mother and Txato's wife, respectively, who have the most difficult time coping with the aftermath of their demises:

> I'm not the way I was when you were alive. I've become bad. Well, not bad. Cold, distant. If you come back to life, you won't recognize me. And don't think your darling daughter, your favorite, has nothing to do with this change in me. She drives me crazy. The same as when she was a girl.[30]

Both Bittori and Nola Ravich have been good friends of Miren and Emmaline Iron, respectively—in fact, Nola is Emmaline's half sister—but intense resentment emerges between the two pairs of mothers as their families are deeply afflicted by the tragic events and their views on Native and Basque identity also prove very different. To make things worse, Bittori's relationship with her daughter, Nerea, becomes particularly strained after Txato's death, and Nola also has a hard time with her remaining child, Maggie, whose haughty and rebellious personality does not help her mother much in terms of filling the huge void in her life. Despite their kins' best efforts to mitigate their agony, neither Bittori nor Nola seem able to control the outrage they feel. See, for example, Nola's reaction to her husband's caresses: "He stroked her shoulder. She pulled violently away. The black crack between them seemed to reach down forever now. He had not found the bottom yet."[31]

Interestingly, Emmaline and Miren, wife and mother, respectively, of the alleged offenders, seek advice and consolation from the local priests, who are influential figures in the human landscape of the reservation and the small town. In the case of the Irons, Father Travis Wozniak tries to assuage the couple by offering them the typical religious explanations for the catastrophe: "*Incomprehensible, His judgments. Unsearchable, His ways.*"[32] Since this is of little succor to Emmaline and Landreaux, they look for assistance in an Ojibwe tribal tradition by performing a ceremony at the sweat lodge where they are granted a vision: "They had sundanced together. They talked about what they had heard when they fell into a trance. What they had seen while they fasted on a rock cliff. Their son had come out of the clouds asking why he had to wear another boy's clothing."[33] After this transcendental experience, the couple decide to give up their own five-year-old son, LaRose, in an attempt to compensate for the pain inflicted on their neighbors, the Raviches. This is the act of atonement depicted in the quote above and that, as that passage clearly shows, is surrounded by all sorts of qualms and uncertainties. Miren's visit to the Catholic priest in her town, though, antecedes the main catastrophe in the novel, as she noticed that her family had begun to fall to pieces when her favorite son, Joxe Mari, left for France, as most ETA members did when they were being hounded by the police. The chapter in the novel in which we hear about Miren's conversation with Don Serapio is aptly titled "Blessing," since rather than questioning or condemning her son's incorporation into the terrorist organization, the priest encourages Miren to support her son in his struggle for the liberation of the Basque Country:

> Remove all doubts and remorse from your mind. This struggle is ours, mine in my parish, yours in your house, working for your family, and Joxe Mari's struggle, wherever he is, is the just struggle of a people in their legitimate wish to decide their own fate. It is the struggle of David against Goliath, a struggle I've talked about often during mass.[34]

Most readers and critics have found the character of Don Serapio rather detestable, for not only does he justify the use of violence to try to solve the political conflict, but he also tries to dissuade Bittori from returning to her hometown after ETA declared a definitive ceasefire in 2011, with the excuse that her presence may "get in the way of the peace process."[35] Unlike Father Wozniak, who repeatedly attempts—although without much success, it must be said—to relieve the pain and rebuild the ties between the two afflicted families, Don Serapio proves to be a very toxic figure who, rather than helping to heal the wounds in the two families, prefers to make the chasm between the two increasingly larger.[36]

Needless to say, the plight of the victims' families, Nola Ravich and Bittori in particular, is even worse, since they can turn to neither Native traditions nor the Catholic Church for assistance. Unfamiliar with the workings of Native American customs, the Raviches are quite bewildered by the Irons' gesture of sacrifice and atonement. Deeply perturbed by suicidal thoughts, it is Nola who benefits the most from the company of LaRose, on whom she begins to dote obsessively. Although she and Peter Ravich come to love LaRose dearly, they are never completely comfortable with the arrangement. Peter suspects, for example, that Nola does not see LaRose so much as an "unspeakable gift" of sacrifice, but rather as a compensation that would make the Irons experience the grief that they themselves are suffering. As Peter explains to Landreaux, there is also the pain that Emmaline and LaRose must be going through on account of their unnatural parting:

> "I know it does. Help. As long as we're with LaRose, we're thinking about him, and we love him. He's a decent boy, Landreaux, you've raised him right. Him being with us helps Nola. Helps Maggie. It does help . . . but what's it doing to him? I mean, he's holding Nola together. Big job. Meanwhile this is probably tearing Emmaline apart."[37]

Although Landreaux has been told by his wise friend Randall that he did the correct thing in following the Ojibwe ways and should be worried about neither LaRose nor Emmaline, he eventually accepts Peter's suggestion, and his youngest child is allowed shared visits with his birth family. Even if LaRose's charming personality helps both families, the ill feelings among the main characters continue.[38] Likewise, despite her son's and daughter's endeavors to bring some peace and comfort to her mind, Bittori is also disturbed by memories and emotions that transform her existence into a kind of nightmare. Although Xabier and Nerea, her children, advise her not to return to her hometown to protect her from her dismal past, she still pays secret visits to the house where she had spent the happiest years of her life:

> No sooner had she gotten among the houses when she began to have difficulty breathing. Asphyxia. Not exactly. It's an invisible hand that squeezes her throat whenever she returns to the town. She walked along the sidewalk, neither hurrying nor slow, recognizing details: in that doorway, a boy told me he loved me for the very first time in my life; taken aback by the changes: those streetlamps do nothing for me.[39]

For most readers of *Homeland* and *LaRose*, one of the main achievements of the novels is their immensely rich cast of tormented characters whose mental poise depends on their capacity to face current trials, but who also live under the pressure of a very turbulent history. As Erdrich puts it in the novel, "Loss, dislocation, disease, addiction, and just feeling like the tattered remnants of a people with a complex history. What was in that history? What sort of knowledge? Who had they been? What were they now? Why so much fucked-upness wherever you turned?"[40] Most theorists of historical trauma, such as Brave Heart and Sotero, would certainly agree with this description of the disorientation that invades the collective consciousness of a human group after they have experienced gross abuses or other forms of historical violence.[41] One of the immediate consequences of the tragedies at the core of the novels is precisely that, as the next section shows, families are broken and their sense of communal safety and shared heritage is seriously damaged, since personal grudges and hostility take up most characters' thoughts and energies.

Inevitable Grudges and Resentment

Both Aramburu and Erdrich are remarkably artful at establishing direct connections between the local environments, the characters, and their historical memories, which weigh down on them in ways that can be suffocating.[42] In *Homeland*, the silence and ostracism of the whole village before and after Txato is executed becomes quite unbearable to him and his family: "From one day to the next, many people in the town began to ignore him. And it wasn't only that they didn't say hello. That was nothing. They refused even to look at him. Lifelong friends, neighbors, even some children. What could innocent children know?"[43] In *LaRose*, several distressing events of the present, such as the fears of disasters with the turn of the century, the run-up to the Iraq war in the news, or Dusty's tragic death, are played out against recollections of the protagonist's grandparents and even earlier generations. As Mary Gordon has noted, "With a touch so light as to be almost casual, Erdrich includes details of Indian history that force the reader to acknowledge the damage that has extended through generations."[44] At one point of the novel, young LaRose is being told by his maternal grandmother, Mrs. Peace, about the disastrous effects that attending boarding schools had on her mother and her people in general:

> Chamberlain. Flandreau. Fort Totten and Fort Totten. We left our name in those schools and others, all the way back to the first school, Carlisle. For the history of LaRose is tied up in those schools. Yes, we wrote our name in places it would never be found until the building itself was torn down or burned so that all the sorrows and strivings those walls held went up in flames and the smoke drifted home.[45]

Miriam Schacht has analyzed in great detail the presence and significance that Indian boarding schools have in Erdrich's fiction and concluded that although we sometimes hear about Native children receiving food and education in these institutions, in most instances, their work involves brutal physical abuse, violent cultural erasure, and deep emotional trauma.[46] The effects of all of these become evident in the older generation in *LaRose*, who develop vengeful feelings and resentments toward each other very much as a result of the psycho-wounds inflicted by that system in their tender years. It could be argued that the Arrano Taberna, a local tavern, is also seen to play a similar role in *Homeland*, as it is presented as the breeding ground where Basque youngsters are heavily ideologized before they become members of the separatist movement.[47] It is also here where important information about the terrorist organization—concerning protests, targets, actions, etc.—is circulated and where anybody wishing to get in touch with its clandestine members will usually go. In short, it is a space in which a great deal of brainwashing and ideological repression take place that then extend their tentacles to clench the behavior of most people in the community.

One of the issues that has caught the attention of—and fascinated—readers and critics alike in both novels is how families and individuals who had been close friends in the past develop feelings of animosity against each other in a short period of time. This is best illustrated by the almost irrational hostility that burgeons between the two pairs of matriarchs, Bittori and Miren in *Homeland*, and Nola and Emmaline in *LaRose*, after the two shootings occur. Especially in the case of the former pair, we are told in several vignettes of the intimate friendship and complicity that they had enjoyed in the early days of their marriages:

> "Can you imagine if we had become nuns?"
>
> They laughed. Sister Bittori. Sister Miren. They had their hair done, they rehashed the village gossip, they understood each other without listening, since they usually spoke both at the same time. They criticized the priest, that skirt chaser; they flayed the neighbor ladies; about the house and bed they told everything. Joxian's hairy back, Txato's lascivious mischief. They told it all.[48]

Naturally, readers are somehow surprised when two friends who had shared so much are torn apart almost overnight by the realization that they stand at opposite ends of the political conflict.[49] One could expect Bittori's extreme anger after her husband's unfair assassination, but Miren's overreactions to her old friend's secret visits to the town after that event are harder to explain: "They're planning something. Don't you [Joxian, her husband] see that? They've intruded into our lives and now we've got them right here with us, in our bedroom, even in our bed, they've managed to get us talking about them all the time."[50] Something similar can be observed to happen to Nola Ravich in *LaRose*, whose hatred for her half sister only gets worse after the Irons decide to give up their son: "How generous you are, Emmaline, what a big-time traditional person to give your son away to a white man and almost white sister who is just so pitiful, so stark raving."[51] Evidently, in both cases the bitterness pouring forth between the two pairs of women is not merely related to the more recent adversities in each community, but it runs deeper in the historical rifts that have existed between different cultural and ideological factions within those contexts.

It is no coincidence in this sense that both authors should decide to throw us into a fairly distant past in order to revisit episodes that have left an indelible imprint on the minds and collective consciousness of the groups.[52] Thus, in Erdrich's novel, we are told the story of the first LaRose, an Ojibwe girl sold by her mother in 1839 to Mackinnon, the proprietor of an isolated trading post. Although the young girl is protected by the clerk at the post, Wolfred, he can do nothing to prevent the trader from physically and sexually abusing her. Nevertheless, after some time, the first LaRose takes revenge and kills the monster—with the help of the clerk—by using her Native knowledge of poisonous plants. Even if she goes voluntarily to residential school, fights off tuberculosis, and finally marries Wolfred, it is never clear whether the couple ever manage to overcome the trauma that the murder of the trader left in their minds: "Wolfred followed her gaze and saw it, too. Mackinnon's head, rolling laboriously over the snow, its hair on fire, brightly twitching, flames cheerfully flickering. Sometimes it banged into a tree and whimpered."[53] Likewise, Aramburu takes us to a few incidents in the families' shared history in *Homeland*, which are seen to awaken ghosts that will be troubling them for a long time. This is particularly true about the family of the alleged perpetrator of the crime, who have great difficulty in admitting that they have been the ones causing the severance of the ties with their old friends. It has already been mentioned above how rancorous Miren becomes when she learns that Bittori has returned surreptitiously to their town and that Arantxa, her daughter, has given to Xabier, Bittori's son, a toy bracelet that Txato had bought for her when they were just kids, more than thirty years earlier. Likewise, Joxian, Miren's husband, is distraught by his memories of the great times that he had had with Txato cycling, playing Mus, or cooking meals and eating at the gastronomic society in the old days.[54] Even Gorka, Joxian and Miren's youngest offspring, feels troubled by how unfairly the family of ETA's victim is being treated, not just by them, but by the whole community:

> "Exactly. Because I'm just as big a coward as he [his father] and so many others are these days. In my village people are probably saying in low voices so no one hears them that this is savagery, useless bloodshed, you don't build a nation that way. But no one will lift a finger. . . . That's the price you pay to live in peace in the land of the silent."[55]

It has been said above that it is the two pairs of mothers who see their psycho-social stability most deeply affected by the resentment that the shootings arouse in all of them. However, the fathers are also caught up in that cycle of hostile feelings that prevents them from seeing each other and the world in an objective way. Ian McKee and N. T. Feather have noted that it is the maintenance of dignity and self-esteem that usually drives people into acrimony and even revenge, when they feel that they have been wronged and, therefore, some sort of authority has been taken from them.[56] This is easily observable in Joxian when the graffiti against Txato appearing around the village—and his wife—pushes him to build an invisible wall between his former friend and himself. Even more ostensibly, despite their earlier mutual affection and support, Peter Ravich, who is otherwise a good-hearted man, develops hateful feelings toward Landreaux, also inveigled by his wife: "A sinuous contempt gripped him and he thought of the rapture he would feel for an hour, maybe two hours, after he brought down his ax on Landreaux's head. Indeed, he'd named his woodpile for his friend, and the mental image was the cause of its growing size."[57] It is interesting, though, that the clearest examples of characters driven by malice in both narratives are not those directly touched by the tragic events. In *LaRose*, Romeo Puyat, who is described by Father Wozniak as a satanic presence on the reservation, nurses a grudge against Landreaux because of an accident they had together when they were running away from a boarding school in their childhood, and which left Romeo disabled. Furthermore, Romeo is convinced that Landreaux stole Emmaline's heart from him. Although Landreaux believes that he is outside the reach and interest of this noxious character, he is not: "Landreaux was so full of himself, so high on himself that even now he did not remember those old days of theirs. Far back when they were young boys hardly older than LaRose. That's how far back and deep it went, invisible most times like a splinter to the bone."[58] Romeo's role grows in importance in the second half of the book, as the story nears its climax, since his sinister intentions are seen to threaten the slow recovery process of the two families. He puts together an intricate plan to finish with Landreaux by convincing Peter Ravich that Dusty's death was not a mere accident. In fact, Romeo's malevolent plot only fails at the very last moment thanks to LaRose's miraculous intervention when Peter Ravich is more than ready to unleash his bottled-up anger against Landreaux.[59] Likewise, in *Homeland*, there are several characters, besides those directly involved in the critical offenses, who also contribute decisively to complicating the healing process of the community as they set all sorts of obstacles in that path. There is, of course, the aforementioned interference of the local priest, Don Serapio, who advises Bittori to stop coming to her house in the town: "Just for a while, until things settle down and there is peace. God is merciful. For what you've suffered here, you will be rewarded in the next world. Don't let rancor take possession of your soul."[60] But other characters and institutions adopt a similarly cynical attitude, particularly when they anticipate that their part in the story will be belittled by the new direction that events seem to be taking. There is Patxi, the owner of the Arrano Taberna, or the union workers in Txato's company. All of them hold a grudge against those characters—especially the victims, but also a few offenders—who are making significant efforts to redeem and repair the damage that has been done in the past.[61]

The Role of Expiation and Forgiveness

It can hardly be denied that the general atmosphere in both novels is rather somber with references to drug addiction, menial employment, adolescent anxiety, and old-age discontent in *LaRose* and marital estrangements, political divisiveness, and ethno-cultural stigmatization in *Homeland*. However, it is also evident that these problems are often leavened with the occasional joys and ordinary pleasures of family and social life. During an interview with Claire Hoffman, Erdrich observed that despite the obvious signs of tragedy and grief in her novel, she always intended to represent the everyday lives of people: "I think that's the way life is. I think we experience the most ordinary circumstances and the heightened realm of experience when huge things happen to us. We also have to tend to what people are going to eat, where they are going to sleep, all of the small things."[62] And surely, much attention is paid by both authors to the food their characters eat, the hobbies they enjoy, or the traditional customs some of them follow: going to church, sharing stories, or playing card games. It is precisely the fact that in the face of terrible adversities these people seem to find some extemporary ways and resilience stratagems to bring back peace and harmony that is most striking to outsiders of these cultures. One intriguing point to be made about both books is that the main disruptions do not originate beyond the boundaries of the given community but are generated within the particular group—and even within specific families. Connie Jacobs has claimed on this point that the circular narrative structure of Erdrich's novels is generally motivated by a family's history "and the reverberations of its history upon the life of the community."[63] As pointed out earlier on, this is easily noticed in the case of the two main families in each novel who happen to share a common cultural heritage but relate to it in entirely different ways, thus producing the huge abyss that lies at the crux of the books. In fact, most of the resentful feelings explored above derive from those ideological and cultural fissures between many of the key characters.[64]

Several reviewers and critics have noted that both *LaRose* and *Homeland* are, primarily, about the possibility of expiation and restitution, even in cases in which the damage inflicted on others appears to be completely unbridled. Dusty's and Txato's deaths leave the four families deeply disoriented in both novels and, for these critics, are closely related to the larger tragedies that both communities have historically lived through.[65] As has already been suggested, there are clear hints both in the surviving victims' and the perpetrators' reactions that earlier ghosts are awakened by the two disasters that initially hinder any form of expiation or reconciliation. Nevertheless, it is interesting to underline that it is the families who have caused the grievance who feel responsible for taking the first steps in terms of reparation. While the Raviches and the Lertxundis seem too deeply scarred by the losses, the families of the offenders find resources in their very diversity and cultural traditions to face the challenges that the occasions pose. On the one hand, the Irons count on their strong cultural heritage, a very lively family, and, of course, the most important asset of all, the protagonist of the book: "They had resisted using the name of LaRose until their last child was born. It was a name both innocent and powerful, and had belonged to the family's healers. They had decided not to use it, but it was as though LaRose had come into the world with that name."[66] Although Landreaux and Emmaline are initially worried that their youngest son would suffer a great deal by being transferred into a new family, the child proves to be up to the task of healing the serious wounds in his surrogate family. As several reviewers of the novel have noted, "LaRose radiates the faint hues of a mystic, the purest distillation of his foremothers' healing abilities, but he remains very much a child, grounded in the everyday world of toys and school and those who love him."[67] Likewise, behind her extremely vulnerable appearance after suffering an ictus in 2009, Arantxa, Joxe Mari's elder sister, proves to be the most courageous member of her family as she is the first one to ask for forgiveness when she gives Xabier the toy bracelet: "Arantxa, visibly nervous, spoke about solidarity, sorrow, shame, and at the same time brusquely placed on the desk a green-and-gold object that at first Xabier didn't recognize."[68] Very much like LaRose in Erdrich's novel, Arantxa will play the decisive role of an arbiter and mediator between the two conflicted families along the arduous process of trying to bring back harmony and conciliation to themselves and the community at large.[69]

Law scholars such as Elazar Barkan and Felipe Gómez-Isa have insisted that reparation should not be understood as a panacea that will solve all the problems of afflicted groups. In fact, they argue that the reparation of the damage caused is not as important as the very process that takes place around that restitution.[70] Indeed, it is quite clear that the acts of expiation or compensation enacted by the Irons in *LaRose*, when they surrender their son to the Raviches, and by Joxe Mari in *Homeland*, when he spends the best part of his life in jail, are not enough to reconstruct the families and community. Although it is a fact that LaRose seems to have an immediate restorative impact on some of the characters—Nola and Peter, most clearly—it takes a while for most of the others to feel themselves pacified by the interventions of this "adorable charmer." Evidently, one significant advantage that LaRose has over the rest of the characters in the novel is that besides the love and care that he receives from his two sets of parents, he is also in close communion with the elders of the tribe—especially, his maternal grandmother—and even with some forebears, via visions: "It was a group of people. Half were Indians and half were maybe Indians, some so pale he could see light shining through them. They came and made themselves comfortable, sitting around him—people of all ages."[71] LaRose manages to become an ambassador or a kind of conciliator between the two families mainly because he is attentive to the particular needs of each of his closest kin and tries to provide them with what they require. In a similar manner, Arantxa does not just offer comfort and succor to the victims of her brother's unspeakable crime, who are brought to believe that an end to their pain may eventually be possible, but also rehabilitation for the members of her family who were on the victimizing side of the events.[72] In a letter to her incarcerated brother, she succeeds in softening his heart and pushing him to consider asking Bittori for forgiveness by comparing their existential predicament:

> You've got your jail, I've got mine. My body is a life sentence. One day you'll be released. We don't know when, but you will get out. I'll never get out of mine. There's another difference between us. You're there because of what you did. What did I do to deserve it? ... She [Bittori] says she's struggling to stay alive as best she can because she's hoping for a human gesture from you. She wants nothing else.[73]

According to Dinah Shelton, it is people who insist on dwelling perpetually on past grievances and develop "a culture of victimization" that have the most difficult time facing the future without asperity.[74] This is definitely the case for characters such as Miren or Romeo, who are so deeply enthralled in their individual and family grievances that it is difficult for them to conceive that any type of harmony may be retrieved. Nonetheless, thanks primarily to LaRose's and Arantxa's restorative and healing skills, the younger generation in particular seems to be able to develop new perspectives and strategies to deal with the future. The cases of Maggie and Hollis, Romeo's son, in *LaRose* and of Gorka and Xabier in *Homeland* are highly revealing in this regard, since they finally seem able to look into the future without the kind of acrimony that we still hear in their progenitors. In fact, even those characters most deeply hurt, such as Nola and Romeo or Bittori and Joxian, are seen to experience a partial recovery in the closing chapters of each book.[75] During one of their habitual conversations at Polloe cemetery, Bittori informs her dead husband of her victory in having finally persuaded Joxe Mari to ask forgiveness:

> And she told him, standing at the grave site, under her umbrella, that without Arantxa, without her generous mediation, she would not have succeeded in closing the circle. She softened the terrorist, convinced him to take the step he'd taken. How did she do it? Well, because she loves him. He's her brother, that I understand.[76]

Some analysts have considered the characters of Arantxa and LaRose rather implausible, since not only are they incredibly proficient at reading the needs of the other characters around them, but they also show almost superhuman skills in teaching others to empathize.[77] Arantxa's influence on her two brothers, as well as her parents, in the second half of the novel is beyond any doubt. Similarly,

LaRose proves to be able to see beyond what everybody else can see. Peter Ravich, his surrogate father, realizes this a bit too late, after he has pulled the trigger of his rifle several times against Landreaux, although "Nothing happened": "The picture of those small capable boy hands now fills Peter. Those hands curving to accept the bullets. Loading and unloading his gun. . . . LaRose saving him now, saving both his fathers."[78] Both Erdrich and Aramburu have resisted the idea that they are endowing their mediators with talents that transcend the powers that one would expect from an ordinary boy and a middle-aged, handicapped woman. As the authors see it, these characters simply represent the embodiment of some of the moral virtues in their communities, among which restitution as a form of atonement and asking for forgiveness are central. In this sense, LaRose is the perfect materialization of a tradition among the Ojibwe—and many other tribes—by which adopting children from other families could help to preserve the balance and the very survival of their peoples. As the novel clearly shows, the hero gradually learns to make the best out of his disconcerting situation suspended between two deeply hurt families.[79] In a similar vein, despite her difficult condition as a disabled person, deprived of free movement and the capacity to communicate orally, Arantxa demonstrates that she is "the best of all the members in her family" by being able to persuade even the most intractable personalities in it—Joxe Mari and Miren, in this case—of the need to invoke pardon for past offenses.[80]

On Reconciliation Processes

It could be argued that the readers' first impression after concluding *Homeland* and *LaRose* is that both novels hone in on rather singular geographical locations and very concrete historical moments. Yet, as several reviewers have remarked, Aramburu and Erdrich manage to paint a much larger canvas as their pictures grow immensely thick with history and social mythology.[81] As mentioned earlier on, although the Basque writer focuses his attention mainly on the months after the ceasefire and the situation of victims and perpetrators at that time, we are repeatedly taken into a past that helps to explain their current circumstances. At one point near the end of the novel, Xabier and Nerea worry that they may be becoming accomplices of the new policy promoting oblivion; however, both agree that they should not: "And we aren't. Our memories can't be erased with high-pressure hoses. You'll see, though, that we the victims will be accused of refusing to look toward the future. They'll say we're seeking revenge. People are saying just that."[82] That unfair and visceral reaction is quite common among characters who prefer not to admit that they have contributed to making the schisms in their society even bigger, such as Miren or Romeo. Erdrich is also fond of showing how objects, events, and even people contain layer upon layer of history that needs to be considered in order to try to find solutions to ongoing woes. Jacobs has underlined the need to get acquainted with Anishinaabe history and myth to be able to understand the kind of tactics some of her characters choose to confront some of their existential crossroads. The title character of her novel, for example, after an unequal fight with the Fearsome Four who had offended Maggie at school, realizes the power he can obtain from just having his name and origins:

> There are five LaRoses. First the LaRose who poisoned Mackinnon, went to mission school, married Wolfred, taught her children the shape of the world, and traveled the world as a set of stolen bones. Second, her daughter LaRose, who went to Carlisle. This LaRose got tuberculosis like her own mother, and like the first LaRose fought it off again and again. Lived long enough to become the mother of the third LaRose, who went to Fort Totten and bore the fourth LaRose, who eventually became the mother of Emmaline, the teacher of Romeo and Landreaux. The fourth LaRose also became the grandmother of the last LaRose, who was given to the Ravich family by his parents in exchange for a son accidentally killed.[83]

As Wan has rightly explained, names in many Native American traditions are carriers of identity, status, and heritage, and much of the clout that "the last LaRose" needs to survive his arduous challenges derives directly from his eponym.[84] This is something that readers, but also members of his community, take a while to comprehend.

Besides informing us of the importance of the hero's moniker and the survival skills of most of its carriers, the passage above also tells us of the injurious influence of boarding schools in Native American history. As Joseph Gone has observed, that impact has left "a harrowing legacy of distress and disability for contemporary Native peoples" and a kind of trauma that cannot be easily assimilated.[85] In addition to the altruistic gesture of surrendering her beloved son in an attempt to seek reconciliation, Emmaline Iron is also the founder of an "on-reservation boarding school" to help all those parents who go through cycles of failure and deprivation: "The radical part was that, unlike historical boarding schools, this one would be located on the reservation. Pre-K through grade 4. After that, kids could board but go to regular school."[86] From Emmaline's perspective, this crisis-intervention project tries to provide dependable household structures, to combine education with traditional cultural practices, and especially, to offer coping strategies for those who see their lives muddled by sudden disruptions arousing old fears. Needless to say, this is the case of the two central families in the novel, who will need that type of community assistance to go through the tortuous "trauma process" of dealing with Dusty's demise and the subsequent adoption of the hero.[87] As their forebears tell Dusty and LaRose during one of the latter's visions: *"We love you, don't cry. Sorrow eats time. Be patient. Time eats sorrow."*[88] Martínez Arrizabalaga remarks that apart from dealing with the pernicious presence and impact of the terrorist group on the life of the community, *Homeland* covers a number of related issues that should be borne in mind in any analysis of how to bring peace and balance to the community. She refers, for instance, to the "dominant presence of the separatist left in small towns; the social isolation of families who lived under the pressure of the paramilitary organization; the silence of a majority of the society; . . . the essential process of revision of that past and the painful hints at the possibility of a so-called reconciliation."[89] Author Óscar Esquivias rightly concludes that the novel offers a realistic portrait of a whole society by means of an insightful—but also intimate—rendering of a set of characters that are perfectly drawn and who are somehow brought together at the end of the novel by Bittori's quixotic request for forgiveness.[90]

A number of scholars have argued that one of Louise Erdrich's and Fernando Aramburu's main strengths as writers is their skill in representing the violent clash between two different cultures and world views, and to still advance an evenhanded view of history in which the boundaries between saints and sinners, progressivists and fundamentalists, civilized and savages are constantly scrutinized and problematized.[91] At one point of *LaRose*, the young hero is hearing "old stories" from Ignatia Thunder, one of the elders of the tribe, and he feels quite frustrated because he cannot find a clear "moral" in those tales: "'Moral? Our stories don't have those!' Ignatia puffed her cheeks in annoyance."[92] In fact, something of that sort could be said about the two novels under analysis, since they only provide tentative solutions to the complicated dilemmas that most of the characters face. Both *Homeland* and *LaRose* delve into the various responses that a highly diverse set of human beings give to grievances that can be either very recent in time or throw us back into historical traumas that have hardly been properly processed. As this chapter has shown, responses may range from ill-intentioned revenge plans to others that rely on atonement and forgiveness to try to bring human relationships back to harmony. In appearance, it is those characters who use the latter strategies that seem to get the upper hand in the end, but one cannot be completely sure that those reparatory strategies would have worked under any other circumstances—especially in the absence of characters such as Arantxa or LaRose. The public embrace between Bittori and Miren in the closing lines of *Homeland* is a perfect example of the ambiguity and tentativeness that surrounds the restorative practices enacted in each case: "The encounter took place at the music kiosk. It was a brief embrace. They looked each other in the eye for an instant before separating. Did they say anything? Nothing. They said nothing."[93] It is hard to say whether all the raw emotions that the reader has seen unleashed throughout both texts are really brought under complete control at the end of the narratives.

It seems evident, though, that both Aramburu and Erdrich have been able to articulate alternative forms of justice and restitution in cases in which past traumas and intergenerational wounds emerge. Obviously, as some specialists have remarked, it is not as if applying compensatory and reparatory practices were without their own difficulties.[94] They have demonstrated that complex issues related to legitimacy, nonretroactivity, or redistribution are likely to get in the way when serious violations of human rights and humanitarian law (such as political terrorism or the disregard of Native sovereignty and culture) are seen to require reparatory action.[95] In this sense, only minor steps have been taken in the direction of compensating victims for the suffering caused by terrorist attacks or helping American Indian communities whose traditions have been historically desecrated by the imposition of other institutions.[96] However, Shelton, Ulrich, and others have insisted on the need to develop new models of reparatory justice that can help afflicted communities to fight against both the lethal effects of past injustices and the disruptions produced by more recent abuses.[97] Erdrich and Aramburu offer in their 2016 novels illuminating and thought-provoking attempts at representing the mediating and restorative actions that may have beneficial results in environments where, more often than not, retributive justice has proved mostly ineffective.

NOTES

1.　See Umbreit, *Crime and Reconciliation*, Zehr, *Changing Lenses*, Ulrich, "The Moral Case for Reparations," or Sullivan and Tifft, *Restorative Justice*. This is particularly true in

Western countries, but also in many African, Asian, and South American countries.

2. See Cayley, *The Expanding Prison*, 287–95.

3. Howard Zehr in part 4 of his classic study *Changing Lenses* (177–205) speaks at some length about these remarkable differences between restorative and retributive judicial systems.

4. See Sullivan and Tifft, *Restorative Justice*, 167–91. This is particularly evident in communities that have a long history of conflict and different types of abuses.

5. Braithwaite, chap. 1 of *Restorative Justice*, "The Fall and Rise of Restorative Justice," 3–28.

6. Sullivan and Tifft cover some of these practices in chapter 3 of *Restorative Justice*, 57–80.

7. Paul McCold, "Restorative Justice," 20, is here quoting Tony F. Marshall.

8. See Zehr, *Changing Lenses*, 215–19.

9. See Johnstone, *Restorative Justice*, 25–32, and Daly, "Restorative Justice," 55–58.

10. See Sullivan and Tifft, "Introduction," 2–3.

11. See Barkan, *The Guilt of Nations*, especially the preface, ix–xiv. See also Ulrich, "The Moral Case for Reparations."

12. Martínez de Bringas, *Exclusión y victimización*, "Introducción."

13. Zernova, *Restorative Justice*, 17.

14. See Umbreit, *Victim Meets Offender*, especially chap. 2, "What Have We Learned from Previous Studies," 15–28.

15. See Zernova, *Restorative Justice*, 8–28.

16. This is a point that repeatedly comes up in discussions of reparatory justice. See, for example, Braithwaite, *Restorative Justice* or Daly, "Restorative Justice."

17. Erdrich, *LaRose*, 16.

18. Aramburu, *Homeland*, 573.

19. See Sotero, "A Conceptual Model of Historical Trauma," 93–96, and Brave Heart, "From Intergenerational Trauma to Intergenerational Healing," 2–5.

20. Zehr, *Changing Lenses*, 195–213.

21. Cohen, *Visions of Social Control*, 116–21.

22. See Gordon, "Review," and Massot, "¿Por qué *Patria* une crítica y público?"

23. Besides those two important prizes, Aramburu's novel was also awarded other national and international prizes such as the Premio Dulce Chacón, Francisco Umbral, Giuseppe Tomasi di Lampedusa, Strega Europeo, and Premio per la Cultura Mediterranea in the two years following its publication.

24. See Martínez Arrizabalaga, "*Patria*," 1–4.

25. It is important to underline that while Erdrich's novel follows more or less a chronological order, at least in what concerns events in the present times (1999), in the case of Aramburu's narrative the story jumps freely from present to past and back to

present time over a period of more than thirty years across 125 different vignettes of particular episodes in the lives of two Basque families.

26. ETA is an acronym for Euskadi Ta Askatasuna (Basque Country and Freedom). ETA was a separatist organization founded in 1959 that initially resisted the Francoist regime and supported Basque culture, but later devolved into a paramilitary group engaged in violent acts such as bombings, assassinations, and kidnappings. It was active from the mid-1960s until 2011, and it killed more than eight hundred people, many of whom were civilians, like Txato Lertxundi.

27. Quoted in Massot, "¿Por qué *Patria* une crítica y público?"

28. Crispin, "*LaRose.*"

29. Erdrich, *LaRose*, 6. The composition of the four families is the following: In *LaRose*, the parents are Landreaux and Emmaline Iron, and Peter and Nola Ravich. Landreaux and Emmaline have four biological children and an adopted one, Hollis Puyat. Peter and Nola only have two, Maggie and Dusty. In *Homeland*, Txato and Bittori Lertxundi have two children, Xabier and Nerea; Joxian and Miren have three, Arantxa, Joxe Mari (the member of the terrorist organization, ETA), and Gorka.

30. Aramburu, *Homeland*, 12.

31. Erdrich, *LaRose*, 14.

32. Ibid., 7.

33. Ibid., 11.

34. Aramburu, *Homeland*, 285.

35. Ibid., 106.

36. Zallo ("Patria asesina versus patria colectiva") and others have found the character of Don Serapio, the local priest, excessively flat and rather unconvincing, taking into account how a majority of the Catholic Church were responding to ETA's violent attacks after the arrival of democracy to Spanish institutions.

37. Erdrich, *LaRose*, 75.

38. See McKee and Feather, "Revenge, Retribution, and Values," 140–42, on the effects of revenge on people.

39. Aramburu, *Homeland*, 22.

40. Erdrich, *LaRose*, 51.

41. Brave Heart, "From Intergenerational Trauma to Intergenerational Healing," 3–5, and Sotero, "A Conceptual Model of Historical Trauma," 97–99.

42. Cf. Washburn, *Tracks on the Page*, 1–14, and Sáez, "La sociedad del silencio," 9–10.

43. Aramburu, *Homeland*, 67. The reason for Txato's ostracism is that graffiti had appeared on many walls around the village, "Txato Txibato" ("Txato the snitch"), after he refuses to pay the "revolutionary tax" that the terrorists are asking for.

44. Gordon, "Review."
45. Erdrich, *LaRose*, 134.
46. Cf. Schacht, "Games of Silence," 63–64.
47. See, for example, vignette number 36 in *Homeland*, "From A to B," 149–52, in which we see Jose Mari's early incursions into the organization.
48. Aramburu, *Homeland*, 53.
49. See Mainer, "Patria Voraz."
50. Aramburu, *Homeland*, 100.
51. Erdrich, *LaRose*, 243.
52. As William Faulkner has his character Gavin Stevens famously say in his novel *Requiem for a Nun*: "The past is never dead. It's not even past."
53. Erdrich, *LaRose*, 132.
54. Aramburu, *Homeland*, 138. Mus is a popular card game often played in the Basque region. Txato and Joxian were often partners in the games.
55. Ibid., 426.
56. McKee and Feather, "Revenge, Retribution, and Values," 139–40.
57. Erdrich, *LaRose*, 64.
58. Ibid., 141.
59. Ibid., 342.
60. Aramburu, *Homeland*, 105.
61. Cf. McCold, "Restorative Justice," 26–30.
62. Hoffman, "Interview."
63. Jacobs, *The Novels of Louise Erdrich*, 108.
64. See Martínez Arrizabalaga, "*Patria*," 1–2.
65. See Johnson, "Review," and Martínez Arrizabalaga, "*Patria*," 8–9.
66. Erdrich, *LaRose*, 11.
67. Charles, "Louise Erdrich's *LaRose*." See also Crispin, "*LaRose*," and Johnson, "Review."
68. Aramburu, *Homeland*, 86.
69. Cf. Ibarrola-Armendariz, "Trauma and Restitution," 58.
70. See Barkan, *The Guilt of Nations*, 309–10, and Gómez-Isa, "Repairing Historical Injustices," 272.
71. Erdrich, *LaRose*, 210.
72. It is interesting to note that Arantxa's own bodily rehabilitation, as she recuperates the ability to walk and to speak, runs in parallel with her family's realization of the need to forgive and repair.
73. Aramburu, *Homeland*, 572–73.
74. Shelton, "The World of Atonement," 308.

75. This is especially conspicuous in the case of the final section of *LaRose*, aptly titled "The Gathering," 347–72, in which the protagonist's incredible powers to bring peace and reconciliation to his community become more than evident. See Ibarrola-Armendariz, "Trauma and Restoration," 59.

76. Aramburu, *Homeland*, 575.

77. See Gordon, "Review," and Sáez, "La sociedad del silencio," 17–18.

78. Erdrich, *LaRose*, 342.

79. For a long list of the arts that LaRose learns from the two families, see Erdrich, LaRose, 208.

80. Aramburu, *Homeland*, 84.

81. See, for example, Charles, "Louise Erdrich's *LaRose*," and Crispin, "*LaRose*." Also Bernal Salgado, "Review," cxx.

82. Aramburu, *Homeland*, 507.

83. Erdrich, *LaRose*, 290.

84. Wan, "Culture Survivance and Religion Healing," 1184.

85. Gone, "A Community-Based Treatment for Native American Historical Trauma," 752. See also Brave Heart, "From Intergenerational Trauma to Intergenerational Healing," 7.

86. Erdrich, *LaRose*, 105–6.

87. Alexander, "Introduction," 12.

88. Erdrich, *LaRose*, 371.

89. Martínez Arrizabalaga, "*Patria*," 3.

90. Esquivias, "La triste y hermosa."

91. Washburn, *Tracks on the Page*, 124, and Martínez Arrizabalaga, "*Patria*," 8–9, refer to this evenhanded treatment of history in their discussions.

92. Erdrich, *LaRose*, 293.

93. Aramburu, *Homeland*, 586.

94. See, for example, Francioni, "Reparation for Indigenous Peoples," 43–45, and Barkan, *The Guilt of Nations*, 311–14.

95. See Stirrup, *Louise Erdrich*, 204–5.

96. Some of these minor steps during the Obama administration were the signing of the American Recovery and Reinvestment Act in 2009 and the Tribal Law and Order Act of 2010, both of which tried to strengthen tribal survival and autonomy. In the Basque Country, the National Victims of Terrorism Memorial Centre opened its doors in Vitoria-Gasteiz in June 2021.

97. Shelton, "The World of Atonement," 291–94, and Ulrich, "The Moral Case for Reparations," 370–73.

BIBLIOGRAPHY

Alexander, Jeffrey C. "Introduction: Toward a Theory of Cultural Trauma." In *Cultural Trauma and Collective Identity*, edited by J. C. Alexander et al., 1–30. Berkeley: University of California Press, 2004.

Aramburu, Fernando. *Homeland*. Translated by Alfred MacAdam. New York: Picador, 2019.

Barkan, Elazar. *The Guilt of Nations: Restitution and Negotiating Historical Injustices*. New York: Norton & Norton, 2000.

Bernal Salgado, José L. "Review of *Patria* by Fernando Aramburu." *Castilla: Estudios de Literatura* 7 (2016): cxviii–cxxii.

Braithwaite, John. *Restorative Justice and Responsive Regulation*. Oxford: Oxford University Press, 2002.

Brave Heart, Maria Y. H. "From Intergenerational Trauma to Intergenerational Healing." *Wellbriety!* 6, no. 6 (May 2005): 2–8.

Cayley, David. *The Expanding Prison: The Crisis in Crime and Punishment and the Search for Alternatives*. Cleveland: Pilgrim Press, 1998.

Charles, Ron. "Louise Erdrich's *LaRose*: A Gun Accident Sets Off a Masterly Tale of Grief and Love." *Washington Post*, May 9, 2016.

Cohen, Stanley. *Visions of Social Control: Crime, Punishment and Classification*. Oxford: Polity Press, 1985.

Crispin, Jessa. "*LaRose* by Louise Erdrich Review—Tragedy and Atonement from One of America's Great Writers." *The Guardian*, May 25, 2016.

Daly, Kathleen. "Restorative Justice: The Real Story." *Punishment and Society* 4 (January 2002): 55–79.

Erdrich, Louise. *LaRose*. New York: HarperCollins, 2016.

Esquivias, Óscar. "La triste y hermosa *Patria* de Aramburu." *20 Minutos*, September 30, 2016. https://www.20minutos.es/opiniones/oscar-esquivias-triste-hermosa-patria-aramburu-2850863/.

Francioni, Francesco. "Reparation for Indigenous Peoples: Is International Law Ready to Ensure Redress for Historical Injustices?" In *Reparations for Indigenous Peoples, International and Comparative Perspectives*, edited by F. Lenzerini, 27–46. Oxford: Oxford University Press, 2008.

Gómez-Isa, Felipe. "'Repairing Historical Injustices: Indigenous Peoples in Post-Conflict Scenarios." In *Rethinking Transitions: Equality and Social Justice in Societies Emerging from Conflict*, edited by G. Oré-Aguilar and F. Gómez-Isa, 265–300. Cambridge: Intersentia, 2011.

Gone, Joseph P. "A Community-Based Treatment for Native American Historical Trauma:

Prospects for Evidence-Based Practice." *Journal of Consulting and Clinical Psychology* 77, no. 4 (2009): 751–62.

Gordon, Mary. "Review of *LaRose* by Louise Erdrich." *New York Times*, May 16, 2016.

Hoffman, Claire. "Interview with Louise Erdrich." *Goodreads*, May 2, 2016. https://www. goodreads.com/interviews/show/1124.Louise_Erdrich.

Ibarrola-Armendariz, Aitor. "Trauma and Restitution in Louise Erdrich's *LaRose*." In *Louise Erdrich's Justice Trilogy: Cultural and Critical Contexts*, edited by Connie A. Jacobs and Nancy J. Peterson, 43–65. East Lansing: Michigan State University Press, 2021.

Jacobs, Connie A. *The Novels of Louise Erdrich: Stories of Her People*. New York: Peter Lang, 2001.

Johnson, Carla K. "Review: In *LaRose*, Erdrich Looks at Atonement." *San Diego Union-Tribune*, May 9, 2016.

Johnstone, Gerry. *Restorative Justice: Ideas, Values, Debates*. Cullompton: Willan Publishing, 2002.

Mainer, José-Carlos. "Patria Voraz" (review of *Patria*, by Fernando Aramburu). *El País*, "Babelia," September 2, 2016. https://elpais.com/cultura/2016/08/29/babelia/1472488716_680855. html.

Martínez Arrizabalaga, María V. "*Patria*: ¿Desde un pasado dividido a un futuro compartido? El relato después de la violencia según Fernando Aramburu." *Olivar* 19, no. 30 (2019): e062. https://doi.org/10.24215/18524478e062.

Martínez de Bringas, Asier. *Exclusión y victimización: Los gritos de los Derechos Humanos en la globalización*. Zarautz: IDH Pedro Arrupe y Alberdania, 2004.

Massot, Josep. "¿Por qué *Patria* une crítica y público?" (review of *Patria*, by Fernando Aramburu). *La Vanguardia*, April 25, 2017. https://www.lavanguardia.com/ cultura/20170425/422025663527/por-que-patria-une-critica-y-publico.html.

McCold, Paul. "Restorative Justice: Variations on a Theme." In *Restorative Justice for Juveniles: Potentialities, Risks and Problems for Research*, edited by L. Walgrave, 19–55. Leuven: Leuven University Press, 1998.

McKee, Ian, and N. T. Feather. "Revenge, Retribution, and Values: Social Attitudes and Punitive Sentencing." *Social Justice Research* 21, no. 2 (June 2008): 138–63.

Sáez, Alicia. "La sociedad del silencio: *Patria* de Fernando Aramburu." Trabajo final de grado, Universitat de Girona, 2018.

Schacht, Miriam. "Games of Silence: Indian Boarding Schools in Louise Erdrich's Novels." *Studies in American Indian Literatures* 27, no. 2 (Summer 2015): 62–79.

Shelton, Dinah. "The World of Atonement: Reparations for Historical Injustices." *Netherlands International Law Review* 50, no. 3 (December 2003): 289–327.

Sotero, Michelle M. "A Conceptual Model of Historical Trauma: Implications for Public Health Practice and Research." *Journal of Health Disparities Research and Practice* 1, no. 1 (Fall 2006): 93–108.

Stirrup, David. *Louise Erdrich.* Contemporary American and Canadian Writers Series. Manchester: Manchester University Press, 2010.

Sullivan, Dennis, and Larry Tifft. "Introduction. The Healing Dimension of Restorative Justice: A One-World Body." In *Handbook of Restorative Justice*, edited by Dennis Sullivan and Larry Tifft, 1–16. New York: Routledge, 2006.

———. *Restorative Justice: Healing the Foundations of Our Everyday Lives.* 2nd edition. Monsey, NY: Willow Tree Press, 2005.

Ulrich, George. "The Moral Case for Reparations: Three Theses about Reparations for Past Wrongs." In *Reparations: Redressing Past Wrong, Human Rights in Development Yearbook 2001*, edited by G. Ulrich and L. K. Boserup, 369–84. Alphen aan den Rijn: Kluwer Law International/Nordic Human Rights Publications, 2003.

Umbreit, Mark S. *Crime and Reconciliation: Creative Options for Victims and Offenders.* Nashville: Abingdon Press, 1985.

———. *Victim Meets Offender: The Impact of Restorative Justice and Mediation.* Monsey, NY: Willow Tree Press, 1994.

Wan, Mei. "Culture Survivance and Religion Healing: On Ojibwe Spirituality in Healing Trauma in *LaRose*." *Journal of Literature and Art Studies* 8, no. 8 (August 2018): 1181–87.

Washburn, Frances. *Tracks on the Page: Louise Erdrich, Her Life and Works.* Women Writers of Color Series. Santa Barbara: Praeger, 2013.

Zallo, Ramón. "Patria asesina versus patria colectiva: Sobre la novela *Patria* de Fernando Aramburu." *SinPermiso*, March 12, 2017. https://www.sinpermiso.info/textos/patria-asesina-versus-patria-colectiva-sobre-la-novela-patria-de-fernando-aramburu.

Zehr, Howard. *Changing Lenses: A New Focus for Crime and Justice.* Scottdale, PA: Herald Press, 1990.

Zernova, Margarita. *Restorative Justice: Ideals and Realities.* Burlington: Ashgate, 2007.

Relational Bodies in Motion

A Trans-Indigenous Reading of Ofelia Zepeda and Irma Pineda's Place-Based Poetry

Anna M. Brígido-Corachán

n *Xilase qui rié di' sicasi rié nisa guiigu' / La nostalgia no se marcha como el agua de los ríos* and *Where Clouds Are Formed*, published only a year apart from each other, Indigenous movements on and with the land become decolonizing actions that challenge settler colonial borders and reinscribe other experiences of place in the Americas. Although their authors, Irma Pineda and Ofelia Zepeda, root their poetic works in very specific Native histories and tribal contexts (those of the Binnizá in southwest Mexico and the Tohono O'odham in the Arizona/Mexico border respectively), they are both driven by a relentless commitment to revitalize Indigenous languages and land-based traditions, drawing attention to social in/justice in their regions. Their poems consider human suffering, racism, migration, environmental awareness, resurgence, and hope through figures in motion that are tied to specific memorial landscapes and communities.[1]

Prominently featured in the titles of Pineda's and Zepeda's books, water in its various shapes (such as rivers, oceans, or rain clouds in movement) grounds their poetic imaginaries. In Mexico's Isthmus of Tehuantepec, the Zapotec call themselves Binnizá, "people of the clouds," and their language, Diidxazá, literally means "cloud language"—diidxa' is used for both "word" and "language" while za stands for "cloud." Zapotec poet Natalia Toledo describes this ontological connection in the following manner:

> Zapotecs say that the diidxazá language descends from the clouds.... I can say that part of my identity comes from the clouds. I like that metaphor because clouds adapt to the soft and warm winds of Tehuantepec, but also morph under the brown winds that shake us in the winter. We are certainly changing beings; clouds go by and other clouds are formed.[2]

The Tohono O'odham also engage rain clouds in their songs and stories, and closely observe their patterns, colors, and direction in the rain-thirsty Sonoran Desert. They use a place-based language of intimacy and respect and seek to pull clouds down, turning them into transformative rain. For the Tohono O'odham the songs and ceremonies that seek to "make rain" have a nurturing purpose, for they aim at "fixing the earth,"[3] reshaping the land to sustain its human and more-than-human dwellers through an act of *grounded normativity* or *place-based solidarity*. First Nations scholars Glen Coulthard and Leanne Betasamosake Simpson define grounded normativity as an ethical framework that draws from Indigenous practices and epistemologies that are relational, reciprocal, and rooted in the land:

> Grounded normativity houses and reproduces the practices and procedures, based on deep reciprocity, that are inherently informed by an intimate relationship to place. [It] teaches us how to live our lives in relation to other people and nonhuman life forms in a profoundly nonauthoritarian, nondominating, nonexploitative manner.... Our relationship to the land itself generates the processes, practices, and knowledges that inform our political systems, and through which *we practice solidarity*.[4]

Ofelia Zepeda's and Irma Pineda's poems engage in such "intimate relationship to place" while stressing movement. For them, the act of walking on the land and with the land becomes a decolonizing strategy to simultaneously vindicate Indigenous mobility rights and more-than-human presence in a borderless North America. Like rivers ceaselessly journeying through the material landscape while connected to a site of origin, Ofelia Zepeda and Irma Pineda present a series of Indigenous figures in transit whose experiences and voices are shaped by their relationship to place. Experiences of wandering motion and migration, at times brutally imposed and at times willfully undertaken, are presented in the poems as a product of historical, social, and natural forces that are often beyond the control of the human and more-than-human figures confronting them. Walking with the land, these moving figures display a deep ethics of care and solidarity in their reciprocal engagement with their home territory and with each other.[5]

In this chapter I examine Pineda's and Zepeda's place-based poetic praxis through a transborder and trans-Indigenous lens. Drawing from Chadwick Allen's trans-Indigenous methodologies, I believe that Native American literatures written across the continent can shed further light over particular experiences of settler domination when they are placed in conversation with one another. When we compare literary works from different cultural regions such as the Zapotec in Mexico and the Tohono O'odham in the United States, land-based strategies to revitalize Indigenous languages and traditional environmental knowledge are shared while anticolonial "alliances of co-resistance and liberation" forged by Indigenous-led political actions and movements in their territories are strengthened.[6]

Zepeda's and Pineda's poetic works narrate the violence and cultural disorientation triggered by contemporary migration processes, the defiant continuity of Native traditions, and the central role of Indigenous traveling figures as grounded agents in relationship with other human and more-than-human communities on the move. These Indigenous trajectories, rooted in tribal understandings of place, challenge (neo)colonial mappings that continue to lock Native bodies within fixed historical compartments and territories. As Mishuana Goeman poignantly argues, the quotidian, material dimension of practiced space must be valued and recuperated as a source of cultural and historical meaning for Indigenous communities,[7] and these poetic works deeply explore such material and symbolic practices, as we will see in the sections that follow. Pineda's and Zepeda's redefinition of home as an expansive and dynamic place creatively interrogates the neo/colonial "cognitive mapping of Native lands and bodies" in settler North America.[8]

Theoretical Framework: Trans-Indigenous Readings and Cognitive Remapping

Native histories have always been transborder, trans-Indigenous, and multilingual, as tribes established historical networks of trade and cultural exchange through the Americas prior to the arrival of the European invaders. When we place Zepeda's and Pineda's poems in conversation with one another, several thematic and cultural affinities emerge—affinities that can be easily explained when we consider the Native Americas as one interconnected territory. Situating Indigenous literatures from Mexico and the United States in dialogue with one another can revitalize these ancient connections and routes, and enhance their contemporary mapping strategies. Moreover, such trans-Indigenous, multilingual comparisons can contribute to the decolonization of knowledge organization in contemporary academia and in the Anglocentric world of literary publishing. For example, why are American Indian literatures often compared to their Canadian or Australian counterparts but rarely to the literary production of their Indigenous Mexican or Mesoamerican neighbors? Is this a purely linguistic issue? In this chapter, I propose that we look at the creative work of these two North American poets through a trans-Indigenous, multilingual framework to amplify Native-based actions and contribute to decolonize Western-based academic disciplines such as American studies or world literature.[9]

Chadwick Allen defines trans-Indigeneity as the act of "reading *across, through,* and *beyond* tribally and nationally specific Indigenous texts and contexts," while respecting tribal specificity.[10] Trans-Indigenous paradigms illuminate and enhance particular readings and may urge readers to question their Anglo-predisposition, opening the text's layered realities through the inscription of other languages such as Tohono O'odham, Diidxazá, or Spanish.

For Allen, the "trans" prefix in trans-Indigenous readings (also manifest in related terms such as *trans*lation, *trans*national, and *trans*formation) draws our attention to these power imbalances and forces us to consider the "risks of unequal encounters borne by the preposition *across.*"[11] In this regard, I have to acknowledge that my understanding of these Indigenous-language texts is via the poets' self-translations into two imperial languages, English and Spanish, which vividly exemplifies the linguistic and cultural mediation shaping academic readings and my own limitations as a non-Diidxazá and non-O'odham speaker. Nonetheless, it should also be noted that these colonial languages, English and Spanish, are frequently appropriated as a lingua franca by the poets themselves (through self-translation) to communicate with other Indigenous writers and with tribal members who may not be (textually) fluent in Diidxazá or O'odham, for their aim is to reach a wide readership at home and beyond. When considered within such a multilingual context, Allen's concept of trans-Indigeneity becomes a useful tool to decolonize the literary field as it "denaturaliz[es] the settler nation-state" as an exclusive and constraining arena wherein Native American languages and literatures should be interpreted.[12] Trans-Indigenous approaches also "acknowledge the mobility and multiple interactions of Native peoples, cultures, histories, and texts,"[13] and therefore interrogate the fixed status of *Indians*, their histories, cultures, and territories, in the dominant imaginaries of many countries, including my own, Spain.

When exploring the poems of Zepeda and Pineda using a trans-Indigenous and dialogical lens, a common human experience that quickly emerges is indeed that of movement and motion as key to adaptation, survival, and artistic creation. Songs and poetry in the Native American and Indigenous traditions of the United States and the Mexican southwest present agents in motion and often appear to be moving themselves, thriving in the dynamic spaces that open up between here and there in an all-encompassing world. Ofelia Zepeda's oft-cited bilingual poem "Cewagĭ," where the "summer clouds sit silently . . . gathering strength" to make thunder, so that the earth and the whole community of beings vibrate with them, is a perfect example.[14] Her poems record the everyday activities and material traces of O'odham spatial practitioners, the sacred itineraries of tribal and individual ceremonies, and the trajectories of human and more-than-human beings intersecting with one another. They also reveal and expose the violent motions and consequences of removal, exile, and economic migration, and the intricate ties that exist between these sociopolitical processes and a colonialist exploitation of the land.

According to Mishuana Goeman, contemporary Indigenous writing can play a part in the reversal of settler spatial policies that have an impact on mobility and land sovereignty.[15] In fact, as Gerald Vizenor has often argued, static Indians frozen in time, inert in colonial and neocolonial narratives, or immobilized by the camera (posing in Edward Curtis's Smithsonian photographs, for example) are not real but mere simulations. These simulations strategically sidestep the absence of real Native persons who were/are erased by hegemonic discourse. Conversely, Vizenor insists that Native motion or *transmotion*, a term he coined to highlight a continuous and active Native presence in North America, is tightly connected to political sovereignty and *survivance*.[16] Such motion is not purely physical or political but also imaginative: "The sovereignty of motion means the ability and the vision to move in imagination and the substantive rights of motion in native communities."[17] For Goeman, Native poetry can question such "dominant spatial norms of fixity of Native people in time and space and allow . . . for a potential restructuring."[18] She further argues that Native women writers such as Diné poet Esther Belin "present . . . space and time as a matter of narrated relationships constructed not only as a critique of colonial orderings but also one embedded in Native epistemologies and narrations that envision the future."[19]

Like Esther Belin, Native poets Irma Pineda and Ofelia Zepeda also present literary counter-maps that draw from dynamic practices and tribal world views as their voices move through and experience the land in a ceremonial but also a deeply material manner. Such cognitive remapping is also grounded in place, and from this homespace they embrace alternative flights of memory and the imagination.

In their introduction to the volume *Home Places*, Ofelia Zepeda and Larry Evers define home as "an earth house, a place to live within ever-widening webs of community that spin out to include not just humans but all the living things of the natural world."[20] Zepeda and Pineda situate their poems in this "earth house" to unveil clashing historical forces and cultural practices that have shaped and that continue to shape the *ever-widening web*.

Movement and Place-Based Relationality in Zapotec Poetry

Irma Pineda is a Zapotec writer, translator, editor, and educator from Juchitán (Oaxaca). She has been president of Mexico's Association of Writers in Indigenous Languages (Escritores en Lenguas Indígenas, AC), has carried out artistic residencies in Chicago (Casa de Arte 1998) and Alberta (Banff Centre 2004), and was recently elected a member of the Permanent Forum on Indigenous Issues of the United Nations (2020–2023). Her work in international institutions and forums as spaces where acknowledgement and respect toward minority languages, literatures, and voices can be found is only a small part of her contribution to Zapotec culture. Most of Pineda's language revitalization work has been carried out as a translator and in elementary schools and bilingual education programs in her hometown, Juchitán. Her books of poetry in Spanish and Diidxazá (the linguistic variant of the Zapotec language that is spoken at the Isthmus of Tehuantepec, in Oaxaca) include *Xilase nisado' / Nostalgias del mar* (2006) and *Guié ni zinebe / La flor que se llevó* (2013). It is worth noting that Pineda's bilingual poems are not mere versions or translations of each other but "parallel poems, mirror poems"[21]—they evince the dual world view that nurtures Pineda's creative process.

Irma Pineda's *Xilase qui rié di' sicasi rié nisa guiigu' / La nostalgia no se marcha como el agua de los ríos* (Nostalgia doesn't flow away like riverwater, 2007) is a dialogical work written in two historically clashing languages, Zapotec and Spanish, facing each other on the page. The poems are told by two interconnected voices and perspectives: an undocumented worker from Juchitán who has migrated to the United States, and the worker's lover, who patiently waits in their village for the migrant's return. About half of the poems are written in the voice of the migrant, while the other half express the great grief, anguish, loneliness, but also the strength and resilience of the person left behind.

The collection contains thirty-six poems and is structured into three parts. The first of these parts is "Chupa ladxidua' / Dos mi corazón" (Two my heart), a grouping of poems that delve into the preparations made by the migrant before departure and in anticipation of the dangers of the road that lay ahead. In the opening poem, "Ni chineu / El equipaje" (The luggage), the migrant's lover becomes the repository of their fears and grief. She willfully takes in the weight of his imminent absence and impels him to travel light, to leave all suffering behind. Through imperative chants such as the verb "leave behind," which is repeated three times, and the emotionally charged placement of the word "gift" in connection with the more-than-human ("Don't forget to take / the gift of the tiger . . . the gift of the eagle"), she exorcises the potential illnesses and weaknesses to come out of him and takes them in herself.[22]

In this and in other poems to follow, the lover identifies key more-than-human beings and cultural Zapotec referents such as the *ombligo* (umbilical cord), the nahual, the tiger, and the eagle as the traveler's most powerful weapons to help him remember, survive, and return. The Binnizá bury the umbilical cord of newborn babies close to the family house to establish a sacred and permanent tie with their place of origin. Grounding him to a particular geographical, cultural, and spiritual site, these sacred beings and elements will protect the traveler in his difficult journey.

Within this first poetic grouping, the poem "Neza / Camino" (Road) vividly delves into the experience of crossing to the other side of the border—a world that is described as a deceiving mirage. Its negative impact can only be confronted through an embodied, place-based memory, that of the village and its people, as expressed in the following stanza:

> Gunna xinga zeu' cherica'
> gudiidxi xquendalu'
>   ni rapa lii ndaani' guendanabani di'
> Buidxigueta lu neza riaana xqui'dxu'
>   ra biaana binnili'dxu'

biiya chahui' xtuuba' ñeelu'
ti gannu pa neza guibiguetu'.

No olvides tu misión por esos caminos
abraza a tu nahual
    el guardian de tu ser en esta vida
Voltea la mirada hacia tu pueblo
    el lugar donde quedó tu gente
mira bien las huellas de tus pies
para recordar el camino por donde debes volver.[23]

Here, the migrant's nahual, an animal/human shapeshifter or guardian spirit in many Indigenous cultures in Mexico, protects him from danger. The nahual thus functions as a cosmological and spatial compass or "homing device," while finding the way back is again placed as an imperative, ceremonial action in the very last line of verse: "the path you *must* retrace" (my emphasis).[24]

The second grouping of poems, "Lu neza / Sobre el camino" (On the road), focuses specifically on the idea of movement as a violent force in the experience of economic migrants. This movement through space leaves material traces on a storied road that has been traveled by many others before. The poem "Neza guete' biaaxha' / Partí del sur" (I left the south) enumerates familiar things left behind in the village (a dried, plowed field, a scrawny ox, an old boat by the sea) while it subtly criticizes the global economic system and its impact on local economies. The family boat is no longer used for fishing as the sea "vomits rusted cans," the local fishermen are forced to leave their home "thrown over the roads of others," and the "deaf sea" turns desert—the desert that must be crossed in order to reach the north.[25]

In "Ca yoo xquidxilu' napaca' lu / Las casas de tu pueblo tienen ojos" (The houses of your village have eyes), the dark, empty houses are rendered as animated beings with eyes, hair, and mouth. They overlook the only "visible artery of [the] village's body," a road through the mountains that leads to the sea. But the streets, like the sea, are empty and deaf; there are no children, no thieves, no birds, no blood left.[26]

The poems in the collection never refer to the north as a specific geographical point although it is made clear that the migrant is moving to a northern city, most likely in the United States.[27] Two poems focus on the geographical coordinate south—"Neza guete' biaaxha' / Partí del sur" (I came from the south) and "Neza guete' bendandaya' / Por el camino del sur he venido" (I came through the southern road). But it is worth noting that the south in traditional Zapotec cosmology—the term guete' or guéete—was not geographical but referred to the direction of the nadir, opposing the celestial north or zenith. According to Zapotec intellectual Wilfrido Cruz, who rooted his historical definition in Fray Juan de Córdoba's *Vocabulario Castellano-Zapoteco* (compiled in the sixteenth century), the traditional Zapotec cardinal points were vertical rather than horizontal coordinates, and thus guete' also means "depth" and is synonymous with the word "below," and with the world below, the world of the dead.[28] Binnizá cardinal points convey the idea of movement: north is *nezaguía* (camino arriba or the upward road) and south is *nezaguete* (camino hacia abajo or the downward road).[29] The Zapotec term *neza* literally means "road" or "path" but can also be used to indicate "way," "course," or "direction." In this respect, it is important to recall that *Neza* was also the title of a foundational literary journal in Juchitán that published texts in Spanish and Zapotec—the word situates Irma Pineda within a very specific literary genealogy.

Continuing with the metaphor of the road as grounded movement, in Pineda's poetry collection we can identify two broad semantic fields that dominate her linguistic expression and set its tenor. The first of these semantic fields is earth-related and includes meaningful agricultural and experiential terms such as root, field, seed, path, prints, stones, sow, plow, or bury. It is a telluric language that evokes the agricultural tasks common in the Isthmus of Tehuantepec, but also its rituals and ceremonies such as the burying of the umbilical cord, or the custom of bringing flowers to the graves of their ancestors. The land of origin is the most powerful and vivid image that is conjured up by the poems—it grounds and entwines the two speaking voices, their movements, memories, and imaginations of each other.

The second semantic field intersects with the first and expresses the poets' nostalgia and sorrow. It encompasses a variety of conflicting nouns such as sadness, pain, thorn, oblivion, separation, tears, sickness, or dark night, although these pessimistic feelings are often mitigated through their opposite pairs: affection, faithfulness, life, remembrance.

If the anguish and pain derived from separation and cultural dislocation are more evident in the first two sections of the volume, the grouping of poems in the third part, "Zedandá ti dxi / Un día llegará" (A day will come), place resilience, relationality, and hope at the center of the migratory experience. The weight of the absence and loneliness that are experienced by both poetic figures on either side of the border seems at times insurmountable, but some energetic, hopeful lines of verse emerge, interspersed in the poems. The traveler carries along the memories of those who will not return, keeping them alive as he walks with the land; the female voice in waiting compares her body to the sea, deep and infinite like her patience and love.[30] "Qui zuuyu naa gate' / No me verás morir" (You will not see me die) conveys a firm refusal to forget their traditions and counteracts the tension and psychological violence of the migratory experience, conjuring memory and hope in an ironic or desperate exorcism against death. The last verse is "see me die," but earlier stanzas emphasize life and continuance in connection with the larger community, which includes the Diidxazá language itself, human and more-than-human persons.

Qui zuuyu naa gate'
qui zanda gusiaandu' naa
Naa nga jñou'
bixhozelu'
diidxa' yooxho' bixhozegolalu'
guirá ni ma bisiaa ca dxi ca lii
nisa ruuna ti guesa ma stale dxi bibani
ti na' yaga ni jmá nabana'
biniti lade bandaga.

No me verás morir
no podrás olvidarme
Soy tu madre
tu padre
la vieja palabra de tu abuelo
la costumbre de los tiempos
la lágrima que brota de un anciano sauce
la más triste de las ramas
perdida entre las hojas.[31]

In the poem's third stanza, the image of a seed, hidden in the bushes by the path, expresses Binnizá futurity and reemergence through the stories, through their children's children, and through interconnected earth movements that will shake the sea.

Structured as a succession of anaphoras and reiterative keywords, this poem again becomes a performative ceremony or prayer that fiercely reimagines a different future for Zapotec communities and for their territory. With its rhythmic repetitions and gripping subject matter, it sets listeners as complicit witnesses, urging them to actively reject this vision of cultural disappearance and replace it with that of the "seed / hidden in the scrub by the path / that must return to this land / and seed the future."[32]

Ofelia Zepeda's poetic movements and place-based strategies, like Pineda's, are also designed as ceremonies that vindicate a Native experience of the land as community. They are grounded on a land-language that seeks to rebuild networks of care between the human and the more-than-human and to reinforce O'odham cultural and linguistic revitalization.

Resignifying the Tohono O'odham Borderlands through Place-Making Motion

Ofelia Zepeda is a Tohono O'odham poet, editor, and linguist. She teaches at the University of Arizona and has also been a coordinator of the American Indian Language Development Institute for many years. A researcher of her people's culture and language, Ofelia Zepeda started writing poems in English and also in Tohono O'odham due to the lack of written materials that she could use in her language classes. Today there are around twenty thousand O'odham in the United States, and the language, from the Uto-Aztecan language family, is related to Yaqui, Hopi, and many of Mexico's Indigenous languages.[33] Despite these numbers, Tohono O'odham is one of the worlds' endangered languages and, in Mexico, it has less than five hundred speakers. Although many O'odham in the United States managed to grow up as "bilingual adults" without experiencing the violent acculturation techniques that were common in other areas of the country, the O'odham written literary tradition is barely twenty-five years old.[34] Zepeda argues that "developing a literature in a Native language, which will then result in a desire for literacy in that language" is mandatory for a purely "pragmatic reason."[35] It is tied to political resurgence and cultural continuance.

Among Zepeda's literary works are her two volumes of poetry, *Ocean Power* (1995) and *Where Clouds Are Formed* (2008), and a Tohono O'odham and Pima poetry anthology that she edited in 1982: *When It Rains / mat hekid o ju*. Zepeda has also penned a variety of scholarly articles—many of which draw attention to the precarious status of endangered Indigenous languages in North America—and also a grammar of the Tohono O'odham language: *A Papago Grammar*.

The O'odham reservation is located in the Sonoran Desert, in a borderland area designated as "wilderness" by the U.S. Congress, as it contains the Saguaro Forest, wildlife refuges, and other sites that are filled with human and more-than-human life. According to Zepeda: "The poems . . . stem from my sense of the environment in which I grew up and in which I live today. The environment includes people, landscape, weather, the traditional stories and songs of the O'odham and how they all interact and offer varying perspectives for me as a participant."[36]

One of the most important elements in this desert environment is water, and the Tohono O'odham have many cloud songs and ceremonies to summon clouds and rain. Also functioning like a ceremony or prayer, the forty poems comprising Zepeda's *Where Clouds Are Formed* map the cultural territory of the Tohono O'odham in a relational and expansive manner, for the O'odham are a transborder community that, like Pineda's, lives straddled across two nations. Zepeda was born within a rural migrant community that worked in cotton farms along the border near Stanfield, Arizona, in the 1950s and 1960s. She reckons that "it is beyond this border where some of [h]er family stories begin," since both her parents came from Mexico, an ancestral place of origin she refers to as "the other side."[37]

Where Clouds Are Formed consists of three sections titled "Lost Prayers," "Other Worlds," and "How to End a Season," and from the very first poem, "The Place Where Clouds Are Formed," language is tightly connected to cloud formation, place, and story. This opening poem functions as an invocation for the clouds to become manifest through the storyteller's voice, which is described as "rich and cool dampness."[38] Clouds, moisture, and mist move and rise in the speaker's memories, as the poet situates herself or imagines other Native characters in movement, inside a train, or in the cab of the father's truck, waiting for the school bus on a rainy day. In the poems that follow, the poet crosses mountains with her "power bundle" and "the pen from the last hotel [she] stayed in"; she also flies over a memorial site in the Tucson Mountains and hikes in Yosemite National Park.[39] Domestic and distant, inner and outer spaces intersect, nurturing the poet's experiences as she walks with the land, always aware of her connection with and responsibility to the particular landscape she is inhabiting at that very moment—a landscape that is also in movement.

In the poem "Lost Prayers" the poet witnesses the experience of migration as a border dweller, noticing the "empty plastic bottles," the "blue flags," marking the way to the water deposits for those crossing the border at night.[40] Unlike the Mexican immigrant in Pineda's poems, the O'odham people can "keep an eye on the horizon, moving . . . They walk knowing the heat and aridity of their namesake place"; they can find water using land-based rather than plastic-made geographical markers.[41]

Part 2, "Other Worlds," opens with a poem titled "Landscape," where a conjunction of ceremonial movements, those of the mother in the house, the clouds being pulled down, the dust rising, or the earth pushed, emphasize the mother's intimate connection to the land and its history:

She didn't lift her feet.
She was in constant contact with the earth.
With each shuffle she pushed the earth along
with each step she dragged time along.
She pushed bits of her past
and bits of her future
in uncertain amounts and
in uncertain directions.[42]

This shuffling movement is reminiscent of Tohono O'odham dancing. In *Ocean Power*, Ofelia Zepeda describes this dancing as a "quiet barefoot skipping and shuffling on dry dirt—movements that cause dust to rise quietly toward the atmosphere, dust that helps to form rain clouds."[43]

In the following bilingual stanzas, the poet communicates with the natural elements, asks the clouds, rain, and dust to move and emerge, like songs. She is "aware of the unevenness of landscape" and of the earth's constant reshaping. She has kept the "memory of glacial movements and carving of landscape" but also notices the man-made signs constantly warning the "pedestrians of earth" to move with caution in the city and on man-made country roads.[44]

The next poem, "The Other World," focuses on cultural perception and on the act of watching. It begins with a female O'odham friend or relative expressing her preference for urban lifestyles, which generates a tension with the poet's more traditional sense of place. This character cannot wait to leave the desert and return to her video store and TV—two spaces where reality is heavily mediated. She first describes this media world as "our world" and then, after the poet's manifest disappointment, as "the other world."[45] For the poet, their world is "this place of sand, rocks, mesquite / rattlesnakes, lizards, and little rain" from which they can watch the Milky Way and, ironically, also interact with technology as they "watch a satellite watching [them]."[46] She acknowledges both worlds as contemporary realities engaged by the Tohono O'odham, aware that the sky offers both cosmic connections and settler surveillance.

Conversely, the next bilingual poem, "Ñeñe'i Ha-ṣa:gid" / "In the Midst of Song," brings together traditional spaces, natural beings, and the people, as it envisions songs moving, "resounding toward the sunset" and toward the sunrise, the north and the south. The song shortens distances and reconfigures the landscape delivering the remote sounds of ocean, wind, and dust storm "near us."[47] Similarly, the next poem, "Music Mountains," places together Tohono O'odham and English terms to name the mountains in the O'odham territory—Cemamagĭ, Tumamoc / Babad Do'ag, Santa Catalina Mountains / Cuk Do'ag, Black Mountains, Tucson Mountains / Cew Do'ag, Rincon Mountains—orally binding the tribal landscape, while the poet explains to the reader how to communicate with it through song:

> To these circling mountains
> we must speak with voices
> in songs, rhythmic speeches, orations, and prayers.
> We must be prepared with repetition,
> a singular, undisturbed beat.
> That is the way of mountains.
> This is what they want to hear.[48]

Using very rich sensorial language and specific details that manifest a lived experience of the land and a familiar connection with it that is not merely symbolic or political but quotidian and intimate, Zepeda maps out and lends her voice to the O'odham territory.[49] This linguistic remapping that is grounded on O'odham cultural histories becomes particularly vivid in the poem titled "Proclamation," which begins with the following stanza:

> Cuk Son is a story.
> Tucson is a linguistic alternative.
> The story is in the many languages

still heard in this place of
Black Mountains.
They are in the echo of lost, forgotten languages
heard here even before the people arrived.

For Zepeda, the O'odham name for Tucson is storied, and these place-based stories have also been conveyed in other Indigenous languages now lost to the speaker:

[the] true story of this place
recalls people walking
deserts all their lives and
continuing today, if only
in their dreams.[50]

History is embodied in their footsteps as they walk with the land, and in place-names like "Wa:k . . . the story of water memories of this desert."[51]

The poem "Blacktop," located in the volume's third section ("How to End a Season"), envisions the open road (an ultimately American symbol) as "animate, a companion, an embodiment of equal, if contradictory desires," as pointed out by Audrey Goodman.[52]

The blacktop carries me in all directions.
    It knows my name.
    I never told it my name.
    It calls me.
    It wants to carry me in all directions.
        It whispers, "You will always see Waw Giwalik
        In your rearview mirror.[53]

Goodman notices that in O'odham, "'Waw Giwalik' means indented rock or peak" and identifies it as Baboquivari Peak, the O'odham's "place of first emergence after the world flood." She explains that "many O'odham visit the mountain as a shrine and leave offerings for good luck. Here Zepeda confirms the *grounding power* of this place of origin while pursuing the open routes of discovery made possible by the blacktop, combining traditional knowledge and modern mobility."[54]

Like a buried umbilical cord in the Zapotec tradition, the blacktop functions as a geographical and spiritual compass for the Tohono O'odham—a relational being that configures their experience of place.

Zepeda's songs resignify local spaces, liberating them from Western meanings, and also transform distant spaces, conforming to an O'odham-centered world view. A case in point is the poem "Aligning Our World," wherein a whole conference hotel room in Dallas is rearranged so that beds can face east, "the origin of the day / the direction you pray." As furniture is moved around and relocated, their world is realigned, the earth's axis clicks "as everything / Falls into its rightful place."[55] Common material objects and the natural spatiality of a hotel room are thus reorganized to make it adhere to Indigenous beliefs and practice.

In the last poem, "Smoke in Our Hair," the poet describes the smell of mesquite, cedar, piñon, and juniper wood burning—a "homing device" that immediately takes her back to her land of origin, even when experienced in distant places like New York, France, and Germany.[56] The connections between outside and inside worlds, local and distant worlds, are poetically entwined via the memorial reverberations produced by a defined tribal smell that can also be experienced outside the reservation. According to Goodman, "Zepeda excavates the sensory language of individual and tribal memory" as she identifies home with the scent.[57] Zepeda is clearly "aware of her people's histories of forced migration," and she "responds with alternate ways of locating identity in and moving through the landscape, often returning to traditional, even outdated modes of travel (walking, wandering), in order to find deeper maps and render cultural comparison in new forms."[58]

Rights of Transmotion and Continuous Sovereignty in the Native Americas

Native American and Indigenous communities have historically engaged in transborder movements, and they continue to expand their place-making practices and stories today. Zepeda's and Pineda's works highlight a continuous breaking of physical, ontological, and political colonial boundaries while key cultural and environmental tenets of their communities are reinserted in the text. They challenge colonial figurations of Native peoples, immobilized and fixed in time and space, and "allow . . . for a potential restructuring."[59] For Mishuana Goeman: "Seeing land as storied and providing stories from time immemorial, rather than as confined place with rigid boundaries, will remind us of the responsibility to each other."[60]

Pineda and Zepeda present these experiences—walking with the land, crossing to the other side, migrating, returning, staying at home—as many ways to express cultural identity today, ways that, needless to say, are not mutually exclusive. Goeman argues that literature written by such women poets as Esther Belin (and I would add Zepeda and Pineda) do not just represent "space as a return to an 'original' past/nation/being" but also as a way to mediate "multiple relationships and, by doing so, navigat[e] ways of being in the world that reflect contemporary Native experiences."[61] In this light, Pineda and Zepeda imagine an Indigenous literary space that is flexible and cross-cultural—one that reinforces territorial, linguistic, and cultural sovereignty for Native communities by interrogating the spatial (physical, political, and literary) confinements that North American Indigenous tribes have been forced to accept since the sixteenth century. For Gerald Vizenor "the presence of natives on this continent is obvious, a natural right of motion, or transmotion, and continuous sovereignty; in other words, natives are neither exiles nor separatists from other nations or territories," but cross-cultural agents that can move through all of these at ease.[62]

Echoing the language of their transborder territories, the emplaced songs of Pineda and Zepeda reveal kindred memories and world views. They recall older, precolonial journeys of Indigenous communities moving across the Northern hemisphere and reinforce trans-Indigenous connections in the twenty-first century. The internal/external movements and rhythms articulating the spatial poetry of Ofelia Zepeda and Irma Pineda arise from such a place-based and yet borderless perspective. Comparative trans-Indigenous readings do not necessarily impose homogenizing categories and views over distinct Native texts but can recognize and honor diversity, tribal specificity, multiple languages, and the "intellectual and artistic sovereignty" of Indigenous cultures.[63] Comparative readings also contribute to the decolonization of academic methodologies and fields when each Indigenous textual tradition is set within a specific tribal context and engaged in an informed and respectful manner.

NOTES

This chapter was written under the auspices of the research projects "Las literaturas (trans) étnicas norteamericanas en un contexto global: Representaciones, transformaciones y resistencias" (GV/2019/114) and "Reconfiguraciones de género, raza y clase social en la literatura étnica norteamericana de la era Obama/Trump" (GV/AICO/2021/249), funded by Valencia's Regional Government.

1. For Leanne Betasamosake Simpson resurgence "maps a way out of colonial thinking by confirming Indigenous lifeways or alternative ways of being in the world." See *As We Have Always Done*, 279.

2. González, *Literatura zapoteca*, 145. For a historical explanation of the term "zá," see also Cruz, *Oaxaca Recóndita*, 145, and De la Cruz, "Estudio Introductorio," 14. Unless otherwise noted, all translations from Spanish are my own.

3. Zepeda, *Ocean Power*, 88.

4. Coulthard and Simpson, "Grounded Normativity / Place-Based Solidarity," 254. See also Coulthard's *Red Skins, White Masks*.

5. Drawing from the work of feminist philosophers Carol Gilligan and Virginia Held, Whyte and Cuomo define "care ethics" as the "approaches to moral life and community that are grounded in virtues, practices, and knowledge associated with appropriate caring and caretaking of self and others." Care ethics emphasizes affectivity, caretaking, attachment, and "the inevitability of dependence and interdependence . . . in the basic fabric of human well-being." In Whyte and Cuomo's environmental ethics, such attachments and interdependencies also extend to the more-than-human world. See Whyte and Cuomo, "Ethics of Caring in Environmental Ethics," 234.

6. Simpson, *As We Have Always Done*, 215. On the connections between Indigenous literatures and political and environmental movements in the Americas, see for example Adamson, American Indian Literature or Monani and Adamson, Ecocriticism and Indigenous Studies.

7. Goeman, "Notes," 169.

8. Ibid., 170.

9. On the decolonizing potential of trans-Indigenous comparisons within the broader field of world literature, see also Brígido-Corachán and Domínguez, "Los mundos subalternos de la literatura mundial," 79–80.

10. Allen, "Decolonizing Comparison," 378.

11. Allen, *Trans-Indigenous*, xiv.

12. Allen, "Decolonizing Comparison," 378. See also Brígido-Corachán and Domínguez, "Los mundos subalternos de la literatura mundial," 79–80.

13. Allen, *Trans-Indigenous*, xiv.

14. Zepeda, *Ocean Power*, 26.

15. Goeman, "Notes," 170.

16. Vizenor, *Fugitive Poses*, 15. Vizenor defines survivance as "more than survival," a combination of survival, resistance, and remembrance that rejects "dominance, tragedy, and victimry," favoring instead such narratives of Native presence that inspire creation, reincarnation, and sovereignty.

17. Ibid., 182.

18. Goeman, "Notes," 171.

19. Ibid., 183.

20. Evers and Zepeda. "Home Places," vii.

21. Call, "Carrying Words across Borders."

22. "Huaxa si qui gusiaandu' chineu / xqenda beedxe' / ti gudxii lulu' ca neza ca / xqenda bisiá" – "Mas no olvides llevar / el don del tigre / para enfrentar los caminos / el don del águila" Pineda, *Xilase*, 8–9.

23. "Do not lose your way on these paths / embrace your nahual / the protector of your being in this life. / Turn your eyes to your village / the place where your people stayed / look closely at the prints left by your feet / to remember the path you *must* retrace." Pineda, *Xilase*, 24–25.

24. The term "homing device" as metaphor to stress movements of return in Native American poetry is mentioned by Allison Hedge Coke in the introduction to the poetic anthology *Sing: Poetry from the Indigenous Americas*. For her, returning home enables the poet to "reveal the witnessings and to revel in the familiar." See Hedge Coke, *Sing*, 1.

25. Pineda, *Xilase*, 41. It is interesting to note that the sea is considered an animate being in traditional Zapotec culture. See Cruz, *Oaxaca Recóndita*, 103.

26. Pineda, *Xilase*, 47.

27. Zapotec migration to the United States began in the early twentieth century and increased particularly in the 1970s and 1980s. Today there are approximately 1.5 million Indigenous immigrants from Mexico in the United States, and close to 20,000 Zapotecs relocated to the Los Angeles and San Diego County areas at the turn of the century. See Mesinas and Pérez, "Cultural Involvement," 482, and Rivera-Salgado, "Welcome to Oaxacalifornia."

28. Wilfrido Cruz discusses the meanings of all four cardinal points at length in *Oaxaca Recóndita*, 62–71. His spelling for south is guéete whereas Pineda uses the standardized guete'. In his web dictionary, Diidxazá speaker Óscar Toledo translates guete' as "sur, al sur, muy al sur, bajo, hondo" (south, to the south, very southern, below, deep); gue'tu means dead. See Toledo Esteva, *Vocabulario*.

29. Cruz, *Oaxaca Recóndita*, 64.

30. For a thorough study of the female body's cosmic connections to the Zapotec territory in Irma Pineda's poetry, see Gloria Chacón's *Indigenous Cosmolectics*, chap. 3.

31. "You will not see me die / you won't forget me / I am your mother / your father / your grandfather's old stories / age-old traditions / the tear welling from an old willow / the saddest branch / lost among the leaves." Translation by Wendy Call, "Carrying Words across Borders."

32. "...xuba' / ga'chi' lade gui'xhi' nuu lu neza / ndaani' guidxi di' zabigueta' / ne laa gusindani guendanabani" – "...semilla / escondida entre los matorrales del camino / que a esta tierra ha de volver / y sembrará el futuro". Ibid.

33. Zepeda, *Ocean Power*, 87.

34. Zepeda "Autobiography," 408.

35. Ibid., 416.

36. Zepeda, "Five Poems."

37. See Zepeda, "Autobiography," 408.

38. Zepeda, *Where Clouds Are Formed*, 3.

39. Ibid., 9, 17, and 38.

40. Ibid., 15.

41. Ibid., 15–16.

42. Ibid., 24.

43. Zepeda, *Ocean Power*, 89.

44. Zepeda, *Where Clouds Are Formed*, 25–26.

45. Ibid., 27.

46. Ibid.

47. Ibid., 29.

48. Ibid., 30.

49. Ibid., 30–31.

50. Ibid., 43.

51. Ibid. Wa:k is an Oʼodham way to refer to natural water sources and is another name for San Xavier del Bac, a Catholic mission located south of Tucson, in the Tohono O'odham reservation. See note in Zepeda, "Proclamation."

52. See Goodman, "The Road West," para. 23.

53. Zepeda, *Where Clouds Are Formed*, 65–66.

54. Goodman, "The Road West," para. 24; my emphasis.

55. Zepeda, *Where Clouds Are Formed*, 71.

56. Hedge Coke's term, *Sing*, 1.

57. Goodman, "The Road West," para. 22.

58. Ibid., para. 26.

59. Goeman, "Notes" 171. On Indian simulations in the official historical archive of the United States, see also Gerald Vizenor's *Fugitive Poses*.

60. Goeman, "From Place to Territories and Back Again," 32.

61. Goeman, "Notes," 183.

62. Vizenor, *Fugitive Poses*, 181.

63. Allen, "Rere Ke," 69.

BIBLIOGRAPHY

Adamson, Joni. *American Indian Literature, Environmental Justice, and Ecocriticism: The Middle Place*. Tucson: University of Arizona Press, 2001.

Allen, Chadwick. "Decolonizing Comparison: Toward a Trans-Indigenous Literary Studies." In *The Oxford Handbook of Indigenous American Literature*, edited by James J. Cox and Daniel Heath Justice, 377–394. Oxford: Oxford University Press, 2014.

———. "Rere Ke / Moving Differently: Indigenizing Methodologies for Comparative Indigenous Literary Studies." *Journal of New Zealand Literature* 24, no. 2 (2007): 44–72.

———. *Trans-Indigenous: Methodologies for Global Native Literary Studies*. Minneapolis: University of Minnesota Press, 2012.

Brígido-Corachán, Anna M., and César Domínguez. "Los mundos subalternos de la literatura mundial: Hacia una comparación de las literaturas indígenas en Abya Yala/las Américas." In *World Literature, Cosmopolitanism, Globality*, edited by Gesine Muller and Mariano Siskin, 76–97. Berlin: De Gruyter, 2019.

Call, Wendy. "Carrying Words across Borders: Zapotec Poetry On/In Migration." *Michigan Quarterly Review* 52, no. 2 (2013).

Chacón, Gloria E. *Indigenous Cosmolectics: Kab'awil and the Making of Maya and Zapotec Literatures*. Chapel Hill: University of North Carolina Press, 2018.

Coulthard, Glen Sean. *Red Skins, White Masks: Rejecting the Colonial Politics of Recognition*. Minneapolis: University of Minnesota Press, 2014.

Coulthard, Glen, and Leanne Betasamosake Simpson. "Grounded Normativity / Place-Based Solidarity." *American Quarterly* 68, no. 2 (2016): 249–255.

Cruz, Wilfrido C. *Oaxaca Recóndita: Razas, Idiomas, Costumbres, Leyendas y Tradiciones del Estado de Oaxaca*. Oaxaca, Mexico: Instituto Estatal de Educación Pública de Oaxaca, (1946) 2002.

De la Cruz, Víctor. "Estudio Introductorio." In *Guie´sti´didxazá: La flor de la palabra*, 7–49. México D.F.: Universidad Nacional Autónoma de México, 2013.

Evers, Larry, and Ofelia Zepeda. "Home Places: An Introduction." In *Home Places: Contemporary Native American Writing from Suntracks*, 405–420. Tucson: University of Arizona Press, 1995.

Gilligan, Carol. *In a Different Voice*. Cambridge, MA: Harvard University Press, 1982.

Goeman, Mishuana. "From Place to Territories and Back Again: Centering Storied Land in the Discussion of Indigenous Nation-Building." *International Journal of Critical Indigenous Studies* 1, no. 1 (2008): 23–34.

———. "Notes toward a Native Feminism's Spatial Practice." *Wicazo Sa Review* 24, no. 2 (Fall 2009): 169–187.

González, Rocío. *Literatura zapoteca ¿resistencia o entropía? A modo de respuesta: Cuatro escritores binnizá*. México D.F.: Universidad Autónoma de la Ciudad de México, 2016.

Goodman, Audrey. "The Road West, Revised Editions." *Miranda* 5 (November 2011). http://journals.openedition.org/miranda/2383.

Hedge Coke, Allison Adelle. *Sing: Poetry from the Indigenous Americas*. Tucson: University of Arizona Press, 2011.

Held, Virginia. *The Ethics of Care: Personal, Political, and Global*. New York: Oxford University Press, 2007.

Mesinas, Melissa, and William Pérez. "Cultural Involvement, Indigenous Identity, and Language: An Exploratory Study of Zapotec Adolescents and Their Parents." *Hispanic Journal of Behavioural Sciences* 38, no. 4 (November 2016): 482–506.

Monani, Salma, and Joni Adamson, eds. *Ecocriticism and Indigenous Studies: Conversations from Earth to Cosmos*. New York: Routledge, 2016.

Pineda, Irma. *Xilase qui rié di' sicasi rié nisa guiigu' / La nostalgia no se marcha como el agua de los ríos*. México D.F.: Escritores en Lenguas Indígenas, A.C., 2007.

Rivera-Salgado, Gaspar. "Welcome to Oaxacalifornia." *Cultural Survival Quarterly Magazine: Indigenous Rights and Self-Determination in Mexico* 23 no. 1 (March 1999). https://www.culturalsurvival.org/publications/cultural-survival-quarterly/welcome-oaxacalifornia.

Simpson, Leanne Betasamosake. *As We Have Always Done: Indigenous Freedom through Radical Resistance*. Minneapolis: University of Minnesota Press, 2017.

Toledo Esteva, Óscar. *Vocabulario del idioma zapoteco istmeño (diidxazá)*. 2019. http://www.biyubi.com/did_vocabulario.html.

Vizenor, Gerald. *Fugitive Poses: Native American Indian Scenes of Absence and Presence*. Lincoln: University of Nebraska Press, 1998.

Whyte, Kyle Powys, and Chris J. Cuomo. "Ethics of Caring in Environmental Ethics: Indigenous and Feminist Philosophies." In *The Oxford Handbook of Environmental Ethics*, edited by Stephen Gardiner and Allen Thomson, 234–247. Oxford: Oxford University Press.

Zepeda, Ofelia. "Autobiography." In *Here First: Autobiographical Essays by Native American Writers*, edited by Arnold Krupat and Brian Swann, 405–420. New York: Modern Library, 2000.

———. *Ocean Power: Poems from the Desert*. Tucson: University of Arizona Press, 1995.

———. "Proclamation." *Poetry Foundation*. https://www.poetryfoundation.org/poems/53448/proclamation.

———. *Where Clouds Are Formed*. Tucson: University of Arizona Press, 2008.

———. "Five Poems." Poetry at Sangam. January 2015. http://poetry.sangamhouse.org/2015/01/five-poems-by-ofelia-zepeda/.

A Prayer from the Galaxy of the Soul

Simon J. Ortiz's Poetry of Continuance

Ewelina Bańka

For centuries, the Americas have been sites of migratory movements triggered by imperial agendas, coupled with environmental destruction and economic and political crises taking place on both local and transnational levels. These conditions have forced thousands of Indigenous people, uprooted from their traditional homelands and pushed to the margins of their societies, to set off on journeys "in search of a better world."[1] Without a doubt, this forced movement is yet another manifestation of the systemic violence and social injustice that Indigenous populations have suffered since colonization. While various state leaders use aggressive tactics to stifle immigration and normalize migrant scaremongering, to many Indigenous people this movement is a signal of a prophesized change, manifested by the rising human masses that must take place to destabilize the colonially grounded systems of power. Suzanne Methot observes: "According to the Anishinabek, we are in the time of the Fifth Fire; according to the Hopi, we are in the Fifth World; according to the Inca, the condor has met the eagle; and according to the Maya, the 13th *baktun* has ended and a new world has begun." Thus, Methot continues, to many people, the change means that "the terror, anger, grief, and loss that has possessed Indigenous communities for the past 500 years is coming to an end."[2]

This prophetic interpretation of reality is grounded in traditional Indigenous systems of knowledge that perceive migration and journey as formative in human

177

growth. As Laguna Pueblo writer Leslie Marmon Silko explains, migration/journey narratives not only created a sense of belonging by referring to geographical locations, but they were also meant to deepen one's self-awareness and the understanding of what it means to be a human community. Such stories were therefore essential in the lives of tribal communities since they described people's "interior" journeys of "awareness and imagination in which they emerged from being within the earth and from everything included in earth to the culture and people they became, differentiating themselves for the first time from all that had surrounded them."[3] If seen from this perspective, the movement of people across the land exposes the roots of the current condition of the human cultural community that has relegated the "undesired" members to the fringes of modern nation-states. Although they are often aggressively stopped on their journeys, the migrating people's resilience and struggle for justice and a dignified life demand acknowledgement and solutions that would force the entities of power to admit their responsibility for the crisis. Thus, movement may lead to political, societal, cultural, and environmental changes that, in turn, contribute to the healing of what Susan Berry Brill de Ramírez acutely calls "the torn fabric of humankind."[4]

Mending the torn fabric of the human community has been the goal of the artistic endeavors, scholarly work, and social activism of Acoma Pueblo poet and storyteller Simon J. Ortiz. In a span of more than fifty years, Ortiz has celebrated Indigenous resilience in song, poetry, and prose, focusing on the revitalization of Indigenous knowledge and cultural practice that center on the importance of land, culture, and community as foundations of Indigenous identity and integrity. Ortiz states that the loss of tribal homelands, traditional languages, and entire systems of knowledge have traumatized Indigenous populations and left people doubtful of their own sense of self:

> In an America, particularly the United States, which is overwhelmingly present every day, in every social, political, cultural, economic, psychological way, it's not hard to feel as if you're confronting a reality that is so powerful that you can't expect it to recognize you. Especially if you are a people who has been historically subjected to the meanest, cruelest treatment by social and economic forces backed up by military power, with the result being a feeling of no self-esteem, insignificance, powerlessness, and of being at the mercy of powers beyond your control.[5]

In order to regain knowledge about themselves and secure their human cultural existence, Indigenous people, says Ortiz, must continue their struggle to control the language of self-expression and to build and protect an environment in which they will be able to practice what is at the core of Indigenous existence, namely responsible care for relationships that they create and maintain with their communities and tribal lands. Much as it is centered on the continuance of the Indigenous world, the poet's writing is undoubtedly universal in scope, always portraying Indigenous populations as part of an interdependent body of creation. The inclusive and outward-oriented view of the world that informs Ortiz's work is based on the principle of interrelatedness, compassionate love, and purposeful living that is found at the heart of Indigenous systems of knowledge. The poet explains that for the Acoma people the importance of mutual care and connectedness is fleshed out though stories that refer to a cultural moment in the history of a people "when meaning was a caring act that formed community. Or when caring by a young lad or lass was a moment of communal meaning. Or cultural meaning arising from a caring act. Perhaps when a child brought a beautiful stone to an elder such as a grandmother or a grandfather or perhaps even to a perfect stranger who was older."[6]

If seen as an act of caring, time, argues Ortiz, sustains meaning and community. Thus, if the passage of time is acknowledged and accepted, then the act of caring (the symbolic gifting and expressing gratitude for the gift) is consciously repeated over generations. In consequence, "culture [is] being sustained by an act of time."[7] The dynamic, reciprocal relationship that is at the heart of the story points not only to the recognition of humanity and dignity of the giver and the receiver of the gift, but also to the land as the primary fabric used to build and nurture the community. In the story, the presence of the stone, which symbolizes the land, allows for the relationship to be formed. As a result, taking care of the land—the provider and sustainer of life—becomes people's moral obligation. What traditional knowledge teaches is therefore that through responsible relationships with the land and others one forms cultural self-consciousness and expresses one's full-fledged humanity. Therefore, argues Ortiz, for Indigenous continuance to be possible, it is fundamental to exercise the knowledge of what it means to be human in a given sociocultural and environmental context. The poet explains in an interview with Sidney I. Dobrin and Christopher J. Keller:

> Native identity has a lot to do with how one is able to maintain oneself as a person with an ethnic background that is Native, or indigenous, and that has to do with the ability and the freedom to be able to be Native. What I mean is that the freedom to be who you are as a Native person has to be in place to truly be able to carry out your responsibility. The story, or knowledge energy that is carried in the story

and maintained through that story, is necessary for that community to function, especially as stewards of the land.[8]

Protected and continued in the form of song, prayer, poetry, and story, traditional knowledge is shared in language understood by Ortiz as a "spiritual energy that is available to all."[9] When reflecting on his father's approach to ceremonial songs and tribal teachings, Ortiz highlights the conversive character of oral tradition that focuses on the intimate connection built by the participants of the ritual singing ceremony or storytelling event.[10] Identifying oral tradition as the foundation of his poetic work, Ortiz stresses that its ritual-centered character becomes crucial in the process of cultural identity formation: "Poetry is prayer . . . it is a celebration of the fact of our existence; when we sing, we sing to bring about our existence, to create ourselves. Song is not just expression, but it really is an enactment, an act of consciousness . . . song is poetry is prayer. Poetry as language is a confirmation of our existence."[11] Thus, for Ortiz, to write poetry and to offer a prayer song is to recognize, experience, and express the connection with everything around you: it is "a way to understand and appreciate our relationship to all things. The song as language is a way of touching."[12]

Being immersed in Acoma tribal knowledge, Ortiz grew into believing that his tribal community was part of "a larger Hanoh (the People) responsible for the earth."[13] Consequently, as he reminisces, being an Acoma person and a writer, he needed to expand his world view from tribal/regional to global/universal. Accepting the responsibility of purposeful living triggered a centrifugal force that would guide him on a journey beyond his tribal grounds and allow him to "become part of a general community."[14] Consequently, Ortiz's work is informed by him envisioning life as a sacred journey made as an offering "for the sake of the land and the people."[15] This concept is first fleshed out in *Going for the Rain* (1977). In the collection, Ortiz braids the stories of his journeys with a narrative of a traditional ceremonial journey undertaken by the Pueblo people to honor the rain-bearing spirits—the Shiwana—so that they can bless people by bringing rain and thus sustaining life in the arid lands of the American Southwest. As Kimberly Blaeser observes, the structure of the collection mirrors the cyclic pattern of the traditional sacred journey performed by the Acoma people that involves four stages: spiritual and physical preparation, leaving, returning, and the experience of rainfall.[16] This ceremonial journey-prayer instills in the travelers a deep sense of communal bonds as they have to protect and rely on each other on their journey. Since the pilgrims' walking is part of their prayer, the pilgrimage becomes also an act of strengthening their kinship bond with the land. At the end of this pilgrimage, Ortiz states, "The man returns to the strength that his selfhood is, his home, people, his language, the knowledge of who he is." Since the traveler's goal is also to "return to himself,"[17] the journey becomes a ceremonial vision quest, and the rainfall can be seen as a blessing that manifests itself as a deeper understanding of one's sense of self that comes with the experience of the journey. This self-realization is also manifested by the communion with the land and by the bond with the community. Thus, the experience allows the travelers to express and understand their humanity that in turn, is fundamental to the continuance of the community they are part of.

The tribally grounded world view of exterior and interior journey as an expression of human cultural existence is explored in *After and Before the Lightning* (1994)—a collection of poetry and prose that documents Ortiz's journey to South Dakota, where he spent a winter season on the Rosebud Sioux Indian Reservation, teaching at Sinte Gleska College. Written in the form of a diary, the book documents a poetic journey toward healing and self-realization that comes from a disciplined, hopeful, and prayer-centered meditation on the cosmic powers that, being so "vividly present and immediate" in Ortiz's life, allow the poet to experience the universe as an interdependent and communitarian body whose structure is compassionate love that holds the human community and all of creation together.[18] The poet writes in the preface to the collection that in South Dakota "I needed a way to deal with the reality of my life and the reality in which I lived. The winter prairie surrounded me totally; it was absolutely present in every moment. I could not put on enough warm clothing nor be prepared enough nor was there a way to avoid it."[19] Described in the poems, the unbearable winter is not only a season but becomes a symbolic representation of "the dreaded reality of despair, death, and loss because of oppressive colonialism"—a burden that the poet carries in his personal experience and history as an Acoma Indian.[20] The poetic story, Ortiz states, becomes therefore a form of addressing the horrors of colonial history that involves confronting the feeling of pain, anger, despair, and fear, born from the fact that Indigenous people "had been made to disappear. We were invisible. We had vanished. Therefore we had no history. And it was almost like we deserved to have no history."[21] Yet, although the history of trauma is crippling and terrifying to deal with, Ortiz emphasizes that not to recognize this reality "would be to deny Existence."[22] He explains with a metaphor: "You can't just give up, you can't always expect that it will pass you by. You can't always be behind the doors closed to the blizzard. You just can't be immune to everything going crazy around you."[23] Thus, acknowledging the purpose of his own life in the cosmic order becomes Ortiz's response to the "blizzard" of colonial history and its genocidal forces. Claiming his place in the "galactic universe," Ortiz composes a prayerful story in which he affirms and celebrates his existence shared with all of creation.[24] In doing so, he refuses the forcefully imposed and omnipresent narrative that operates on the premise that the "civilized" world is essentially a non-Indigenous world. Centered on hope, connection, and growth, the collection is a poetic way of healing that liberates Ortiz from the vision of America as a "burden of steel and mad death" by reconnecting the poet's life "to all Existence with a sense of wonder and awe."[25] It is a testimony to the power of storytelling that seen by Ortiz as a spiritual force that "insists upon the affirmation of life," it becomes a healing practice that sustains, nourishes, and reasserts the continuance of Indigenous people.[26] Ultimately, *After and Before the Lightning* is a journey toward self-awareness and a celebration of Indigenous cultural existence expressed through a prayer song of gratitude and love offered to and sung with "the vast and boundless cosmos of Existence."[27]

The transformative process that focuses on (re)claiming one's sense of self and place is represented already on the structural level of the collection. The narrative is composed with the acknowledgment of specific dates of the poetic and prose entries (from November 18 till March 11) that document change in the lives of the people living on the prairie land as well as in the world of nature. The four parts of the story are placed in between four poem-lightnings: Lightnings I and II open the story while Lightnings III and IV close it. Locating his narrative "after and before the lightning," Ortiz sees his experience as shared and in tune with the rhythm of the natural world, inscribing his story in the life of the universe. In order to comprehend and address the spatial reality of his life shared with creation, he composes a journal-like "map" that abounds in "the abstract images and ideas [that] relate to the immediate and material facts of the winter prairie."[28] The process of map-making alludes to the creation of the haitsee—a traditional hoop with four cardinal directions that the Pueblo people used as a map of "the sky-universe."[29] Making the haitsee, Ortiz claims, is an act of reaffirming one's sense of belonging and, by extension, one's sense of self:

> You make one
> when you prepare to travel.
> So you will always know
> where you are, to where to return.[30]

Ortiz explains that locating himself on the earth as well as in the vast space of the universe, in the past as well as in the present, allowed him to travel on the boundless routes of time, place, and memory. Thus, the poetic journey outward, on the galactic prairie roads, is also an interior journey to the awareness that his life, in all its manifestations, is "the evidence of Existence."[31] Moreover, in the story, the trajectory of Ortiz's journey in time and space is expressed by the use of the subjective personal pronoun "I," the subjective plural/tribal pronoun "we," and the objective plural/universal "we."[32] The poet's constant switching between the pronouns demonstrates that the story of an Acoma Indian man is intertwined with the story of the human community he is part of, which, in turn, is embraced by a larger entity—the universe. The diary therefore manifests the acknowledgement of Acoma cultural knowledge about growing into fully realized personhood that is accomplished by the conscious, intentional, and authentic practice of reciprocal relationships grounded in responsible care and compassionate love.

Ortiz's narrative journey begins with the image of the poet and his fellow travelers facing a winter storm while moving across the prairie. The immediate, dangerous presence of the storm, envisioned by Ortiz as a dragon, confronts him with his own fragility and inevitable dependency on the power of nature that, in a flash, can turn one's body "into molecules, then atoms / fusing apart."[33] His response to the reality of the storm that he faces becomes a message reiterated in the entire collection. Feeling disoriented, the poet refuses to be overwhelmed by a crippling fear and intentionally turns to a hopeful prayer for a safe journey for himself and his fellow travelers. "Lightning II" ends with a prayerful act of loving care extended also to the world of nature. Arriving safely at the destination, Ortiz writes, "This time I pray: Safe passage for you dragon, / sacred mysterious one, and safety for us again." Accepting the presence of the "dragon" in his life and, simultaneously, knowing "the fact that storms don't always last long,"[34] the poet does not succumb to despair but, instead, chooses hope and connection created through a prayer. He declares later in the book, "We know our faith works. With prayer, the human in us must be patient. Always there is more to come, and we will accept what comes."[35] By offering a gift of prayer for the land and the people, Ortiz reenacts the original moment of community building that the Acoma people identify as their cultural origins. Also, the poet's trust in his safe journey home, stressed in both poems, manifests his desire to be defined not by the moment of danger but by his own insistence on living that he reaffirms through the entire collection: "I think we don't survive by instinct much at times. We survive and go beyond by the constructions made by our hope. And history, experience, identity. Memory is our experience at the same time memory is our hope. . . . The future is secured without the construction of certainty. The only way we know Mission is on the horizon we yearn for and finally Okreek is because we want to get there."[36]

If treated metaphorically, the poetic celebration of Ortiz's resilience and gratitude during a winter storm can be also seen as his response to the powerful "dragons" of history that for centuries have tried to obliterate Indigenous presence from the Western world. Refusing to be denied and deprived of his sense of self, the poet focuses on prayer not only for himself and his people, but for all humankind—the ultimate gesture of compassionate love and a manifestation of his humanity.

The prayer-poems offered for the land and the people are reiterated through the entire work, forming a sacred fabric that connects the poet with the whole living cosmos. The process of building connections is exemplified in the prose entry titled "Hot Coffee at Ron's" in which Ortiz describes his friend's house filled with people gathering to warm up and wait out the harsh winter weather. Observing Ron's meditative posture, Ortiz sees him "looking somewhere else, deep inside, or far away as usual. Up there, all around, with the stars, or within. The cosmos."[37] The moment of joy at Ron's house is inscribed by Ortiz in the life of the universe as the host seems to embrace the entire cosmos in his peaceful meditation. The observation of Ron's contemplative journey is followed by an affectionate childhood memory of Ortiz's father telling the young poet a story of singing a prayer song for the Snow Shiwana—the spirits of winter—on a cold winter morning. Through memory, inscribed in the story, Ortiz continues the father's prayer, connecting himself and the people around him with the sacred spirits whose blessing is manifested in the presence of snow on the Lakota prairie land. Thus the bond that Ortiz creates spans not only space but also time as the story of brotherhood at Ron's place, built on trust and solidarity, is stitched together with the memory of the father praying for the blessing of snow.

In integrating the familial memory into the story of a larger human community, Ortiz creates a narrative fabric that becomes part of the history of the universe. The poet's celebration of tribal history as crucial in the continuance of all creation aims at demonstrating that tribal narratives represent "an ongoing living history, a flow of time, event and experience to be lived fully in the 'here and now,' the act of which carries the past into the present, into the future."[38] The story of Ron's house, filled with care, joy, and loving memory of tribal bonds, becomes a tiny atom of sacred energy that continuously multiplied in the form of prayerful poems that compose the collection, becomes the fabric of the ever-evolving, dynamic universe created in the poet's narrative:

> There is no end to things. It is all one. One distance, one dimension. Together in a fabric of winter, sky and land are sewn together, and the rivers and creeks of this prairie are arteries and veins of one body. And we, atoms and cells, move with the sinew of wind, frozen grass, ice-laden trees.... We are graced with a winter certitude we can only acknowledge and cannot deny.[39]

The motif of love and hope as life-giving forces that sustain all creation is explored in the collection via images of humanity envisioned as "the tiniest mirror" of the constellations "locked / in the precious balance of Creation we share / locked to them as cells and atoms are to us."[40] Since the life of the human community is seen as a micro example of all creation, its continuance depends on the practice of meaningful relationships, grounded in love and respect for the land and the people. Building connections rooted in a deep sense of love, worth, and dignity becomes a dynamic force responsible for the balanced existence of the universe. This intimate interrelatedness is envisioned in a two-part poetic piece in which Ortiz describes helping Charley—"an American white man married to a Lakota woman"—build a house.[41] The story becomes a celebration of human solidarity, compassion, and devotion to securing the future of the community. In its message, the story refers to Ortiz's much anthologized poem "A Story of How a Wall Stands," which is a poetic memory of Ortiz's father tending to the cemetery wall at the Acoma Pueblo. As Brill de Ramírez observes, the poem that focuses on the father's devotion to mending the wall becomes a culturally bound symbol of community building. The narrative about the centuries-old wall is "a reflection on the efforts, skill, and care involved in its creation and endurance, and that is a profound metaphor for a people and their ancestors who are supported by the wall."[42] Similarly, in "David Calls Tom a Cynic," Ortiz pays attention to the meticulous work Charley and his fellow workers do together in order to secure the life of the family. Building the house on the Lakota reservation, like mending the cemetery wall at the Acoma Pueblo, becomes an act of caring, thus a reenactment of the original moment of community building, in which one's humanity is expressed by one's capacity for compassionate love for the people and the land.[43] Built with the help of friends, Charley's and his wife's house becomes a "tiny mirror" of a larger body of creation that "will last a long time because it was built to be strong as belief, art, ingenuity, concept, and most of all, prayer and respect, all of that a holy fit."[44] The work done to build the house is also an act of reaffirming one's place in the creation. Watching Charley insert moist sage into the joint that supports the beam on top of the upper wall of the house, Ortiz concludes: "There. It fits now, the people, land, / the sacredness, sky, and walls joined."[45]

The poet's life on the prairie, seen as a continuous reciprocation of love between humanity and creation, is expressed in poems about traveling across space in which the boundary between the prairie and the cosmos is blurred. The farther into the galaxy the poet moves, the deeper the knowledge he gains of "the galaxy that is [his] soul,"[46] ultimately experiencing no separation between the natural world and the human world:

> We are ice and stone,
> fire and air,
>   comets in the galaxy.
> The tail that glistens
> in our wake is our own origin.
> The moment of creation is each day.
>   There is no wonder
> about our curiosity
> of what is in the heavens.
> It is ourselves we try to see.
> The stars, planets, moons, comets
> are our beings, we are the reflection,
> and they are ours, no more, no less.[47]

The travelers' curiosity about the universe may be seen as humanity's desire to grow into full self-understanding that leads to a deeper realization of the role the human community has in creation. The poem also expresses a longing for connection and reaffirmation of the intimate bond that the human community shares with the universe. Reflected in the galaxy of the traveler's soul, the universe becomes a mirror of a true self with which the traveler wants to connect. Understanding that there is no difference between the observer and the observed sensitizes the traveler to the natural world around him. As the poems in the collection show, describing the nature of the universe becomes an act of self-expression. Thus, when meditating on life, the poet very often combines observations of the natural world with reflections on the human community.

In the poem titled "An Insistent Gentle Animal," the prairie, perceived as "an enormous surging animal," becomes a visual manifestation of human nature.[48] Observing the wind sweeping across the hills, the poet sees

> a spirit-creature
> from our other galaxy.
>   The galaxy is within us,
> ferociously powerful and dangerous
> yet so gentle always we trust it
> like we trust a kitten.
>   The wind is gentle
> with the creature, and we have to be gentle too.[49]

Confronting the powers of the prairie, simultaneously dangerous and gentle, the poet acknowledges that the same powers lie within the galaxies of human nature. Therefore, writes Ortiz, on the journey to a full-fledged humanity one must be able to recognize that we are shaped by the "creature" that we choose to align with. He reiterates in the book that in moving toward an authentic expression of personhood, it is necessary to recognize the forces that one chooses to be guided by:

> We are given permission
> by the responsibility we accept
> and carry out. Nothing more,
> nothing less.
>   People are not born.
> They are made when they become
> human beings within ritual,
> tradition, purpose, responsibility.[50]

Without a doubt the poem, like many others in the collection, can also be seen as a reflection on the history of America and the forces that have shaped it. It is also a message that the poet directs to the victims of the destructive forces. As he states, in the face of historical trauma, whose effects still cripple Indigenous populations, it is crucial for the people to continue to reassert the integrity of their humanity by love, trust, and hope. Knowing love, stresses Ortiz, "is what will keep us returning here / from beyond, always returning here," to the true self.[51] He writes in "Field of Scars" that recreating a deep sense of connection with the self and creation enables one to accept the scars that when looked at with compassion, become a source of empowering knowledge about resilience and the value and dignity of human life. Just as the body of the prairie land endures the harshness of winter, human life, an integral part of sacred creation, is able to survive the "blizzards" of violent reality:

> Though we can never be innocent again,
> we have to always hold true
> to the course set by vision
> beyond ours.
> It is the galactic ken
> that is the sacred bond
> that must not break.
> It would be sacrilege,
> so even on the scars we hold
> and build, cherishing the flesh beneath.
> This is the field that is our earth.
> It is from here our seeds grow.[52]

In the book, it is not only the land surrounding the poet but the entire "sparkling, million-eyed universe" that become a source of knowledge about continuance.[53] The immediate knowledge comes in the form of the animals' enduring presence in the face of the harsh winter season, which brings comfort and a reassurance of the purpose of human life.

The celebration of existence, even in its tiny form, is manifested in a poetic meditation on the life of the box elder bugs responding to the first signs of spring. Observing the movement of the insects around the house, Ortiz writes that, although they appear to be "lost and without purpose as they wander . . . they are not lost, they wander here and there, mapping journeys as they make them, as they find them. Perhaps not really sure at moments, but going ahead anyway. . . . Their mystery is mine, since I identify with their wanderings."[54] The tiny creatures, Ortiz adds, are "always fervent with seeking destiny, always urgent to keep on their journey. I thank them, their awareness and endurance."[55] Paying respect to the box elders' passion for life, Ortiz acknowledges that although seemingly invisible in the vast galactic space, every form of life partakes in its balanced existence. Ortiz's prayer honoring the insects is a gift offered in return for the lessons on the insistence on living. It is also an intentional act of self-love that comes from recognizing the poet's true self, manifested in the gesture of the reciprocated love and in the acceptance of his place in the creation.

The resilient struggle for life observed by the poet in the world of nature is mirrored in many poems portraying people's endurance on the prairie land. In "Between South Dakota and There," Ortiz pictures himself with a group of companions on the highway across the prairie, trying to reach home:

> There isn't a single car or truck
> On Highway 18 from Mission to Okreek tonight.
> Except for us.
> > There is nothing but the night sky.
> Stars.
> The moon a huge pendant.
> Stars somewhere
> > between South Dakota
> > and somewhere
> there in the cosmos.
> . . .
> > It is a mirror; we could be the image.
> Travelers on silver roads between galaxies.
>
>
> . . .
> Yet we are hardy, enduring, patient.
> We are anxious to pass through this galaxy to the next.
> Traveling in the night sky,
> > Believing we are its image,
> We know we will reach there.[56]

Just as the space of Ortiz's house becomes galactic in size for the box elders, the vastness of the prairie land becomes a boundless cosmic space in which the travelers can be easily lost on their journey home. Their willingness to stay on the road and continue to journey together, trusting in the "awesome, incomprehensible order of the universe," parallels the box elders' resilient marching outward, responding to the first signals of the new season.[57] The travelers' insistence on seeing themselves as a reflection of the universe expresses their belief that the patience, hope, trust, and gratitude that carry them across the galactic highway are part of the energy that the all-embracing universe is filled with.

The insistence on hope and love, the forces "more vital than anything else,"[58] allows Ortiz to navigate through the "blizzards" that have shaped the experience and history of his community. In "Blind Curse" the snowstorm that the poet travels in may symbolize the (moment of) life filled with anger and despair. Scared for his life, the poet-traveler becomes disoriented, overpowered by "the blind white side / of creation":

> We're there somewhere,
> A tiny struggling cell.
> You just might be significant
> but you might not be anything.
> . . .
> My curse flies out there somewhere,
> and then I send my prayer into the wake
> of the diesel truck headed from Sioux Falls
> one hundred and eighty miles through the storm.[59]

If the traveler's struggle to stay safe in the storm is seen as a metaphor for human struggle against anger, frustration, and fear, the journey is almost impossible to navigate safely. The immediate, palpable presence of the powerful forces makes the traveler painfully aware of the fragility of his life as he becomes disoriented on his journey. How he chooses to respond has a profound effect on the journey. In the poem, the curse, shouted out in anger, is later followed by a blessing with hope to arrive safe at the destination. The blessing manifests the traveler's awareness of the power of words that shape not only the immediate reality but also "the farthest reaches of the galactic universe."[60] Knowing that the way in which the "tiny cells" choose to carry themselves has a crucial role in the life of all creation. The poet, although aware of how dangerous traveling in the storm is, insists on seeing himself and his journey as a blessing. Ortiz declares in "Stellar Tendrils" that self-love leads to the sharing of love with creation and to seeing the natural world not only as coexisting with humanity but as nourishing it, thus reciprocating love:

It's all one yearning.
Births become generations, children
bond us together.
It's all one knowledge.
The unseen tendrils of light
of stars above us,
the unseen tendrils of dark
of roots beneath us,
they are with us,
for us, and we must hold.[61]

Ortiz highlights the belief that knowing that the universe is a source of a sacred love that sustains and nourishes the human community obligates everyone to respond to that gift with a meaningful life filled with respect and love. As the poet reminds the reader/listener: "It's a choice you're given, to be honest and open and aware. Or not to be."[62]

Without a doubt Ortiz's response to the literal and symbolically represented winter is a confrontation of the reality of his life that leads to the poet's turning to the transformative power of love, inclusivity, and meaningful relationships. While Ortiz's poetic journey dominates in the stormy and, therefore, often disorienting "whiteness of creation," the poet's trust in the land and the people guides him toward the blue dawn, where the presence of the buffalo and their sacred spirit awakens the prairie. The prayer song for the buffalo is a gift that honors not only the life of the land, but is also an act of self-love, celebrated in the affirmation of the sacredness of all of creation:

It is this song, this song of light
that I sing for Buffalo right now,
fearfully, lovingly, humbly.
Listen to my song, Buffalo, hear me.

. . .

Thank you, it is beautiful,
you are still alive,
you will always live.
In everything, living.
Everything will live.[63]

A poetic prayer, *After and Before the Lightning* is an expression and experience of love that originated in the sacred homeland of the Acoma people and is carried by Ortiz through South Dakota to the cosmic galaxies of the creation. Seen by the poet as a story interwoven with the history of the Hanoh, his poetic narrative turns into a universal prayer for the continuance of humankind. If treated as an invitation for the readers to join the poet in his prayerful celebration of human existence, Ortiz's work is the gift of an Acoma man, offered to protect and assure the continuance of humankind. Accepting and honoring the story, claims Ortiz, means accepting the existence of the human community and taking responsibility for its cultural continuance. It also means joining Ortiz on the sacred journey of life, the purpose of which is to understand that to be human means "to love, respect, and be responsible to ourselves and others, and to behold with passion and awe the wonders and bounty of creation and the world around us."[64]

NOTES

1. The phrase refers to the title of the book *In Search of a Better World: A Human Rights Odyssey* by Payam Akhavan, which analyzes major struggles to end human rights abuses across the world.
2. Methot, *Legacy*, 25.
3. Silko, "Landscape, History," 505.
4. Brill de Ramírez, "Introduction," 45.
5. Ortiz, *Woven Stone*, 27.
6. Ortiz, "Continuance for All," 28.
7. Ibid.
8. Dobrin and Keller, "Writing the Native American Life," 196–197.
9. Ortiz, "Song, Poetry and Language," 80.
10. According to Susan Berry Brill de Ramírez, the conversive character of storytelling allows individuals to participate "in potentially deep and transforming verbal intercourse where the words and story serve the larger relational ends of interpersonal growth and community building." See Brill de Ramírez, "Writing the Intertwined Global Histories," 177. Analyzing conversive language use, Brill de Ramírez points to its transformative power focused on merging "both senses of conversion and conversation. At the center of conversive storytelling and writing are love and the sacred. . . . The mutual love and affection between the storyteller, the characters in the story, and the storylisteners bring all together in a complete and whole circle of language and life, imagination and

reality, and purpose and meaning." See Brill de Ramírez, "Walking with the Land," 60. Conversively informed Indigenous literatures are, according to the critic, more necessary now than ever, as they give individuals the opportunity to integrate with and form new transborder and transnational communities. See Brill de Ramírez, "Writing the Intertwined Global Histories," 178.

11. Ortiz, Manley, and Rea, "An Interview with Simon Ortiz," 367.
12. Ortiz, "Song, Poetry and Language," 82–83.
13. Zuni Lucero, "Simon J. Ortiz," 155.
14. Ibid., 143.
15. Ortiz, "Introduction," xii.
16. Blaeser, "Sacred Journey, Poetic Journey," 220.
17. Ortiz, *Woven Stone*, 37.
18. Ortiz, *After and Before the Lightning*, xiv.
19. Ibid., xiii.
20. Ibid., xv.
21. Ortiz, *From Sand Creek*, 6.
22. Ortiz, *After and Before the Lightning*, xv.
23. Ibid., 50.
24. Ibid., xiv.
25. Ortiz, *From Sand Creek*, 9, and Ortiz, *After and Before the Lightning*, xiii–xiv, respectively.
26. Dunaway, "Simon J. Ortiz," 99.
27. Ortiz, *After and Before the Lightning*, xiv.
28. Ibid., xv.
29. Ibid., 21.
30. Ibid., 21–22.
31. Ibid., xv.
32. Ibid., xiv.
33. Ibid., 1.
34. Ibid., 2.
35. Ibid., 60.
36. Ibid., 39.
37. Ibid., 3.
38. Zuni Lucero, "Introduction," 14.
39. Ortiz, *After and Before the Lightning*, 5.
40. Ibid., 122.
41. Ibid., 86.

42. Brill de Ramírez, "Introduction," 51.
43. This notion is reinforced by the Acoma tribal story that precedes the narrative piece "David Calls Tom a Cynic." In the tribal story, a young man, Aliyosho, sacrifices the safety of his family to tend to an old horse. The man's compassion and love give the animal strength; in the end, the old horse becomes Caballo Pinto and reciprocates the man's gift of care by helping him secure the future of his family.
44. Ortiz, *After and Before the Lightning*, 86.
45. Ibid., 87.
46. Ibid., 75.
47. Ibid., 37.
48. Ibid., 10.
49. Ibid., 9–10.
50. Ibid., 64–65.
51. Ibid., 18.
52. Ibid., 17–18.
53. Ibid., 46.
54. Ibid., 104–105.
55. Ibid., 105.
56. Ibid., 15–16.
57. Ibid., 25.
58. Ibid., 8.
59. Ibid., 25.
60. Ibid., xiv.
61. Ibid., 97.
62. Ibid., 109.
63. Ibid., 103.
64. Ortiz, *Woven Stone*, 32.

BIBLIOGRAPHY

Akhavan, Payam. *In Search of a Better World: A Human Rights Odyssey*. Toronto, House of Anansi Press, 2017.

Blaeser, Kimberly. "Sacred Journey, Poetic Journey: Ortiz Re-turning and Re-telling from the Colonized Spaces of America." In *Simon J. Ortiz: A Poetic Legacy of Indigenous Continuance*, edited by Susan Berry Brill de Ramírez and Evelina Zuni Lucero, 213–231. Albuquerque: University of New Mexico Press, 2009.

Brill de Ramírez, Susan B. "Introduction, Part II. A Geography of Belonging: Ortiz's Poetic, Lived, and Storied Indigenous Belonging." In *Simon J. Ortiz: A Poetic Legacy of Indigenous Continuance*, edited by Susan Berry Brill de Ramírez and Evelina Zuni Lucero, 25–51. Albuquerque: University of New Mexico Press, 2009.

———. "Walking with the Land: Simon J. Ortiz, Robert J. Conley, and Velma Wallis." *South Dakota Review* 38, no. 1 (Spring 2000): 59–82.

———. "Writing the Intertwined Global Histories of Indigeneity and Diasporization: An Ecocritical Articulation of Place, Relationality, and Storytelling in the Poetry of Simon J. Ortiz." In *Stories through Theories/Theories through Stories: North American Indian Writing, Storytelling, and Critique*, edited by Gordon Henry, Nieves Pascual Sores, and Silvia Martínez-Falquina, 159–190. East Lansing: Michigan State University Press, 2009.

Dobrin, Sidney I., and Christopher J. Keller. "Writing the Native American Life: An Interview with Simon Ortiz." In *Writing Environments*, edited by Sidney I. Dobrin and Christopher J. Keller, 193–205. New York: SUNY Press, 2005.

Dunaway, David. "Simon J. Ortiz: The *Writing the Southwest* Interview." In *Simon J. Ortiz: A Poetic Legacy of Indigenous Continuance*, edited by Susan Berry Brill de Ramírez and Evelina Zuni Lucero, 95–105. Albuquerque: University of New Mexico Press, 2009.

Methot, Suzanne. *Legacy: Trauma, Story, and Indigenous Healing*. Toronto: ECW Press, 2019.

Ortiz, Simon J. *After and Before the Lightning*. Tucson: University of Arizona Press, 1994.

———. "Continuance for All: Land, Culture, Community—An Indigenous American Perspective." In *Americascapes: Americans in/and Their Diverse Sceneries*, edited by Ewelina Bańka, Mateusz Liwiński, and Kamil Rusiłowicz, 27–39. Lublin: Wydawnictwo KUL, 2013.

———. *From Sand Creek*. Tucson: University of Arizona Press, 2000.

———. *Going for the Rain*. Berkley: Turtle Island Foundation, 1977.

———. "Introduction: *Wah nuhtyuh-yuu dyu neetah tyahstih* (Now It Is My Turn to Stand)." In *Speaking for the Generations: Native Writers on Writing*, edited by Simon J. Ortiz, xi–xix. Tucson: University of Arizona Press, 1997.

———. "Song, Poetry and Language." In *Simon J. Ortiz: A Poetic Legacy of Indigenous Continuance*, edited by Susan Berry Brill de Ramírez and Evelina Zuni Lucero, 75–85. Albuquerque: University of New Mexico Press, 2009.

———. *Woven Stone*. Tucson: University of Arizona Press, 1992.

Ortiz, Simon J., Kathleen Manley, and Paul W. Rea. "An Interview with Simon Ortiz." *Journal of the Southwest* 31, no. 3 (Autumn 1989): 362–377.

Silko, Leslie Marmon. "Landscape, History, and the Pueblo Imagination." In *The Woman that I Am*, edited by D. Soyini Madison, 498–511. New York: St. Martin's Press, 1994.

Zuni Lucero, Evelina. "Introduction, Part I. Voice of Experience, Vision of Continuance." In *Simon J. Ortiz: A Poetic Legacy of Indigenous Continuance*, edited by Susan Berry Brill de Ramírez and Evelina Zuni Lucero, 2–24. Albuquerque: University of New Mexico Press, 2009.

———. "Simon J. Ortiz: In His Own Words." In *Simon J. Ortiz: A Poetic Legacy of Indigenous Continuance*, edited by Susan Berry Brill de Ramírez and Evelina Zuni Lucero, 125–169. Albuquerque: University of New Mexico Press, 2009.

Contributors

Ewelina Bańka is assistant professor in the Department of American Literature and Culture at the John Paul II Catholic University of Lublin, Poland. She has written articles on Indigenous literature, border fiction, and art, as well as coedited two volumes: *Americascapes: Americans in/and Their Diverse Sceneries* (2013) and *Borderlands: Art, Literature, Culture* (2016). She is also the author of *View from the Concrete Shore: Visions of Indian Country in the Works of Silko, Vizenor, and Alexie* (2018). Currently she is working on a project that focuses on Indigenous literature as an anti-imperialist challenge to militarization of the U.S.-Mexico border.

Anna M. Brígido-Corachán is associate professor of American studies at the University of Valencia, Spain, where she coordinates the research group LENA (North American Ethnic Minority Literatures in a Global Context). She has published numerous articles and book chapters on contemporary Native American literature and media, critical pedagogy, and ecocriticism and has recently edited the collections *Twenty-First Century American Crises: Reflections, Representations, Transformations* (2017) and *Indigenizing the Classroom: Engaging Native American/First Nations Literature and Culture in Non-Native Settings* (2021). She is currently completing a book about the reconfiguration of history and space in contemporary Indigenous novels from the United States, Mexico, and Guatemala.

Aitor Ibarrola-Armendariz teaches courses in ethnic relations, diversity management, academic writing, and film adaptation in the Modern Languages and Basque Studies Department of the University of Deusto, Bilbao (Spain). He has published articles in international journals such as *Atlantis, International Journal of English Studies, Miscelánea,* and *Revista Chilena de Literatura,* and edited the volumes *Fiction and Ethnicity* (1995), *Entre dos mundos* (2004), *Migrations in a Global Context* (2007), and *On the Move: Glancing Backwards to Build a Future in English Studies* (2016) on minority and immigrant narratives and processes of cultural hybridization. Currently, he is preparing a book on trauma and ethnicity and is also involved in a project on diasporic identities.

A. Robert Lee was professor in the English Department of Nihon University Tokyo (1997–2011) after teaching for nearly three decades at the University of Kent, UK. He has held visiting appointments at Northwestern University, the University of Colorado, the University of California–Berkeley, and the University of New Mexico. His publications include *Postindian Conversations* (with Gerald Vizenor, 1999); *Multicultural American Literature: Comparative Black, Native, Latino/a and Asian American Fictions* (2003), which won the American Book Award of 2003; *Modern American Counter Writing: Beats, Outriders, Ethnics* (2010); *The Native American Renaissance* (edited with Alan R. Velie, 2013); and *Native North American Authorship: Text, Breath, Modernity* (2022).

Silvia Martínez-Falquina is associate professor of U.S. literature at the University of Zaragoza (Spain). A specialist in Native American women's fiction, she has published *Indias y fronteras: El discurso en torno a la mujer étnica* (2004) and coedited *Stories through Theories/Theories through Stories: North American Indian Writing, Storytelling, and Critique* (2009), *On the Turn: The Ethics of Fiction in Contemporary Narrative in English* (2007), and *Beneath the Waves: Feminisms in the Transmodern Era* (2021). Her latest articles and chapters have appeared in *Crossroads: A Journal of English Studies,* Michigan State University Press, *Roczniki Humanistyczne, Lectora: Revista de dones i textualitat, Atlantis, Iperstoria, Humanities,* and Palgrave Macmillan. As part of the "Contemporary Narrative in English" research group, she is currently working on the research project "Literature Of(f) Limits: Pluriversal Cosmologies and Relational Identities in Present-Day Writing in English" (LimLit).

David L. Moore is emeritus professor, retired from the English Department of the University of Montana. He focuses now on writing poetry and music. His major academic publications include a book of literary criticism, titled *That Dream Shall Have a Name: Native Americans Rewriting America* (2013), and an edited collection of essays on author Leslie Marmon Silko (2016). Other publications include an edited volume of *American Indian Quarterly* (1997), as well as dozens of articles and chapters. Across four decades, he taught also at the University of South Dakota, Salish Kootenai College, University of Washington, and Cornell University. At SKC he produced and directed several community theater productions. On Montana Public Radio, he co-hosted "Reflections West," a short weekly literary program, and he has participated in theater productions by the Bearhead Swaney Intertribal Playwrights Project on the Flathead Reservation. He lives with his family in Missoula, Montana.

Kathryn W. Shanley is an enrolled citizen of the Nakoda Nation (Fort Peck Reservation) and holds a PhD in literature and language from the University of Michigan. Shanley has published widely in the field of Native American literature, most notably on the work of Blackfeet/Gros Ventre writer James Welch. Her chapter on Native American women's activism and the right to vote recently appeared in *Culture and Community: Making Citizenship Work* (2022), edited by Rodolfo Rosales. Shanley also coedited *Mapping Indigenous Presence* (2014). As an emeritus professor, Shanley is retired from the University of Montana. Shanley lives in Missoula, Montana, with her husband, literary scholar David L. Moore.

Joanna Ziarkowska is an associate professor at the University of Warsaw, Poland. She is the author of *Indigenous Bodies, Cells, and Genes: Biomedicalization and Embodied Resistance in Native American Literature* (2021) and the coeditor of *In Other Words: Dialogizing Postcoloniality, Race, and Ethnicity* (2012). She has published chapters on Native American literature in *Howling for Justice: New Perspectives on Leslie Marmon Silko's* Almanac of the Dead (edited by Rebecca Tillett, 2014) and in *Indigenous Bodies: Reviewing, Relocating, Reclaiming* (edited by Jacqueline Fear-Segal and Rebecca Tillett, 2013) and articles in *Transmotion* and *Review of International American Studies*.

AMERICAN INDIAN STUDIES SERIES